MICROSOFT CERTIFIED SYSTEMS ENGINEER

TEST YOURSELF MCSE

Designing a Windows® 2000 Network

(Exam 70-221)

Syngress Media, Inc.

Osborne/McGraw-Hill

Berkeley New York St. Louis San Francisco Auckland Bogotá
Hamburg London Madrid Mexico CityMilan Montreal New Delhi
Panama City Paris São Paulo Singapore Sydney Tokyo Toronto

Osborne/**McGraw-Hill**
2600 Tenth Street
Berkeley, California 94710
U.S.A.

For information on translations or book distributors outside the U.S.A., or to arrange bulk purchase discounts for sales promotions, premiums, or fund-raisers, please contact Osborne/**McGraw-Hill** at the above address.

Test Yourself MCSE Designing a Windows 2000 Network (Exam 70-221)

1234567890 AGM AGM 01987654321

ISBN 0-07-212932-8

KEY	SERIAL NUMBER
001	XQXT7IO9DB
002	AW3NU8DTBS
003	ZE7N1G2IO6
004	CYUNCEB6NP
005	A62NO4UBXS

Publisher
Brandon A. Nordin

**Vice President and
Associate Publisher**
Scott Rogers

Editorial Director
Gareth Hancock

Associate Acquisitions Editor
Timothy Green

Editorial Management
Syngress Media, Inc.

Project Editor
Julie Smalley

Project Manager
Laurie Stewart

Acquisitions Coordinator
Jessica Wilson

Technical Editor
Matthew Townley

Copy Editor
Cindy Kogut

Proofreader
Happenstance Type-O-Rama

Computer Designer
Maureen Forys,
Happenstance Type-O-Rama

Illustrator
Jeff Wilson

Series Design
Maureen Forys,
Happenstance Type-O-Rama

Cover Design
Greg Scott

Cover Art
imagebank

This book was composed with QuarkXPress 4.11 on a Macintosh G4.

MICROSOFT CERTIFIED SYSTEMS ENGINEER

TEST YOURSELF MCSE

Designing a Windows 2000 Network

(Exam 70-221)

About Syngress Media

Syngress Media creates books and software for Information Technology professionals seeking skill enhancement and career advancement. Its products are designed to comply with vendor and industry standard course curricula, and are optimized for certification exam preparation. Visit the Syngress Web site at www.syngress.com.

Author

John M. Gunson II (MCSE, MCNE, MCT, and CCNA) is a Senior Consultant for CoreTech Consulting Group, Inc. CoreTech is an e-business Professional Services firm in suburban Philadelphia that excels at helping companies realize the potential of e-business through a mix of Internet technology and traditional business systems, maximizing business benefit while minimizing disruption and risk.

With over 11 years in the Information technology field, John has a very broad background. His experience includes supporting desktop clients, network administration and infrastructure design in both Windows NT/2000 and Netware environments. John's recent engagements have included helping an international corporation design their Windows 2000 architecture and implementing a Windows 2000 Active Directory and Network infrastructure for a wireless communications company.

John graduated from Salisbury State University in Salisbury, Maryland, with a Bachelor of Science degree in Geography.

John lives in Collegeville, PA, with his wife and two children.

Technical Editor

Matthew Townley (MCSE, MCT, and MCP) is a Systems Engineering Manager in the Information Technology Department at Dell Computer Corporation in Austin, Texas. He has played project and technical leadership roles on many large-systems implementations at Dell including the migration from Windows 3.1 to Windows 95, the conversion from NetWare 3.x to Windows NT 4.0, and most recently the desktop deployment of Windows 2000 Professional.

v

Matthew's professional interests include integrating Internet and Web technologies for information interchange, scripting with COM automation, and operations management.

Technical Reviewer

James Truscott (MCSE, MCP+I, and Network+) is an instructor in the MCSE program at Eastfield College and the Dallas County Community College District. He is also Senior Instructor for the Cowell Corporation and is teaching the Windows 2000 track for CLC Corporation in Dallas, Texas. He is also working with DigitalThink of California, developing online training courses for Windows 2000.

He is the Webmaster for Cowell Corporation in Richardson, Texas, and provides consulting services for several Dallas-based businesses. His passion for computers started back in the 1960s when he was a programmer for Bell Telephone. One of his current projects includes developing Web sites for his students.

ACKNOWLEDGMENTS

We would like to thank the following people:

- All the incredibly hard-working folks at Osborne/McGraw-Hill: Brandon Nordin, Scott Rogers, Gareth Hancock, Tim Green, and Jessica Wilson for their help in launching a great series and being solid team players.
- Monica Kilwine at Microsoft Corp., for being patient and diligent in answering all our questions.
- Laurie Stewart and Maureen Forys for their help in fine-tuning the project.

CONTENTS

This book's primary objective is to help you prepare for the MCSE Designing a Microsoft Windows 2000 Network Infrastructure exam under the new Windows 2000 certification track. As the Microsoft program transitions from Windows NT 4.0, it will become increasingly important that current and aspiring IT professionals have multiple resources available to assist them in increasing their knowledge and building their skills.

At the time of publication, all the exam objectives have been posted on the Microsoft Web site and the beta exam process has been completed. Microsoft has announced its commitment to measuring real-world skills. This book is designed with that premise in mind; its authors have practical experience in the field, using the Windows 2000 operating systems in hands-on situations and have followed the development of the product since early beta versions.

In This Book

This book is organized in such a way as to serve as a review for the MCSE Designing a Microsoft Windows 2000 Network Infrastructure exam for both experienced Windows NT professionals and newcomers to Microsoft networking technologies. Each chapter covers a major aspect of the exam, with an emphasis on the "why" as well as the "how to" of working with and supporting Windows 2000 as a network administrator or engineer.

In Every Chapter

We've created a set of chapter components that call your attention to important items, reinforce important points, and provide helpful exam-taking hints. Take a look at what you'll find in every chapter.

Test Yourself Objectives

Every chapter begins with a list of Test Yourself Objectives—what you need to know in order to pass the section on the exam dealing with the chapter topic. Each objective in this list will be discussed in the chapter and can be easily identified by the clear headings that give the name and corresponding number of the objective, so you'll always know an objective when you see it! Objectives are drilled down to the most important details—essentially what you need to know about the objectives and what to expect from the exam in relation to them. Should you find you need further review on any particular objective, you will find that the objective headings correspond to the chapters of Osborne/McGraw-Hill's *MCSE Designing a Windows 2000 Network Study Guide*.

Exam Watch Notes

Exam Watch notes call attention to information about, and potential pitfalls in, the exam. These helpful hints are written by authors who have taken the exams and received their certification; who better to tell you what to worry about? They know what you're about to go through!

Practice Questions and Answers

In each chapter you will find detailed practice questions for the exam, followed by a Quick Answer Key where you can quickly check your answers. The In-Depth Answers section contains full explanations of both the correct and incorrect choices.

The Practice Exam

If you have had your fill of explanations, review questions, and answers, the time has come to test your knowledge. Turn toward the end of this book to the Practice Exam where you'll find a simulation exam. Lock yourself in your office or clear the kitchen table, set a timer, and jump in.

About the Web Site

Syngress Media and Osborne/McGraw-Hill invite you to download one free practice exam for the MCSE Designing a Microsoft Windows 2000 Network Infrastructure exam. Please visit www.syngress.com or www.certificationpress.com for details.

INTRODUCTION

MCSE CERTIFICATION

This book is designed to help you prepare for the MCSE Designing a Microsoft Windows 2000 Network Infrastructure exam. This book was written to give you an opportunity to review all the important topics that are targeted for the exam.

The nature of the Information Technology industry is changing rapidly, and the requirements and specifications for certification can change just as quickly without notice. Table 1 shows you the different certification tracks you can take. Please note that they accurately reflect the requirements at the time of this book's publication. You should regularly visit Microsoft's Web site at http://www.microsoft.com/mcp/certstep/mcse.htm to get the most up to date information on the entire MCSE program.

TABLE I	Core Exams
Windows 2000 Certification Track	**Track 1: Candidates Who Have _Not_ Already Passed Windows NT 4.0 Exams**
	All four of the following core exams are required:
	Exam 70-210: Installing, Configuring, and Administering Microsoft Windows 2000 Professional
	Exam 70-215: Installing, Configuring, and Administering Microsoft Windows 2000 Server
	Exam 70-216: Implementing and Administering a Microsoft Windows 2000 Network Infrastructure
	Exam 70-217: Implementing and Administering a Microsoft Windows 2000 Directory Services Infrastructure

Track 2: Candidates Who Have Passed Three Windows NT 4.0 Exams (Exams 70-067, 70-068, and 70-073)

Instead of the four core exams above, you may take the following:

Exam 70-240: Microsoft Windows 2000 Accelerated Exam for MCPs Certified on Microsoft Windows NT 4.0.

The accelerated exam will be available until December 31, 2001. It covers the core competencies of exams 70-210, 70-215, 70-216, and 70-217.

PLUS—All Candidates

One of the following core exams are required:

***Exam 70-219:** Designing a Microsoft Windows 2000 Directory Services Infrastructure

***Exam 70-220:** Designing Security for a Microsoft Windows 2000 Network

***Exam 70-221:** Designing a Microsoft Windows 2000 Network Infrastructure

Two elective exams are required:

Any current MCSE electives when the Windows 2000 exams listed above are released in their live versions. **Electives scheduled for retirement will not be considered current.** Selected third-party certifications that focus on interoperability will be accepted as an alternative to one elective exam.

***Exam 70-219:** Designing a Microsoft Windows 2000 Directory Services Infrastructure

***Exam 70-220:** Designing Security for a Microsoft Windows 2000 Network

***Exam 70-221:** Designing a Microsoft Windows 2000 Network Infrastructure

Exam 70-222: Upgrading from Microsoft Windows NT 4.0 to Microsoft Windows 2000

* Note that some of the Windows 2000 core exams can be used as elective exams as well. An exam that is used to meet the design requirement cannot also count as an elective. Each exam can only be counted once in the Windows 2000 Certification.

Let's look at two scenarios in Table 1. The first applies to the person who has already taken the Windows NT 4.0 Server (70-067), Windows NT 4.0 Workstation (70-073), and Windows NT 4.0 Server in the Enterprise (70-068) exams. The second scenario covers the situation of the person who has not completed those Windows NT 4.0 exams and would like to concentrate ONLY on Windows 2000.

In the first scenario, you have the option of taking all four Windows 2000 core exams, or you can take the Windows 2000 Accelerated Exam for MCPs if you have already passed exams 70-067, 70-068, and 70-073. (Note that you must have passed those specific exams to qualify for the Accelerated Exam; if you have fulfilled your NT 4.0 MCSE requirements by passing the Windows 95 or Windows 98 exam as your client operating system option, and did not take the NT Workstation Exam, you don't qualify.)

After completing the core requirements, either by passing the four core exams or the one Accelerated exam, you must pass a "design" exam. The design exams include Designing a Microsoft Windows 2000 Directory Services Infrastructure (70-219), Designing Security for Microsoft Windows 2000 Network (70-220), and Designing a Microsoft Windows 2000 Network Infrastructure (70-221). One design exam is REQUIRED.

You also must pass two exams from the list of electives. However, you cannot use the design exam that you took as an elective. Each exam can only count once toward certification. This includes any of the MCSE electives that are current when the Windows 2000 exams are released. In summary, you would take a total of at least two more exams, the upgrade exam and the design exam. Any additional exams would be dependent on which electives the candidate may have already completed.

In the second scenario, if you have not completed, and do not plan to complete the Core Windows NT 4.0 exams, you must pass the four core Windows 2000 exams, one design exam, and two elective exams. Again, no exam can be counted twice. In this case, you must pass a total of seven exams to obtain the Windows 2000 MCSE certification.

HOW TO TAKE A MICROSOFT CERTIFICATION EXAM

If you have taken a Microsoft Certification exam before, we have some good news and some bad news. The good news is that the new testing formats will be a true measure of your ability and knowledge. Microsoft has "raised the bar" for its Windows 2000 certification exams. If you are an expert in the Windows 2000 operating system and can troubleshoot and engineer efficient, cost effective solutions using Windows 2000, you will have no difficulty with the new exams.

The bad news is that if you have used resources such as "brain-dumps," boot camps, or exam-specific practice tests as your only method of test preparation, you will undoubtedly fail your Windows 2000 exams. The new Windows 2000 MCSE exams will test your knowledge and your ability to apply that knowledge in more sophisticated and accurate ways than was expected for the MCSE exams for Windows NT 4.0.

In the Windows 2000 exams, Microsoft will use a variety of testing formats that include product simulations, adaptive testing, drag-and-drop matching, and possibly even "fill-in-the-blank" questions (also called "free response" questions). The test-taking process will measure the examinee's fundamental knowledge of the Windows 2000 operating system rather than the ability to memorize a few facts and then answer a few simple multiple-choice questions.

In addition, the "pool" of questions for each exam will significantly increase. The greater number of questions combined with the adaptive testing techniques will enhance the validity and security of the certification process.

We will begin by looking at the purpose, focus, and structure of Microsoft certification tests and examining the affect that these factors have on the kinds of questions you will face on your certification exams. We will define the structure of exam questions and investigate some common formats. Next, we will present a strategy for answering these questions. Finally, we will give some specific guidelines on what you should do on the day of your test.

Why Vendor Certification?

The Microsoft Certified Professional program, like the certification programs from Cisco, Novell, Oracle, and other software vendors, is maintained for the ultimate purpose of increasing the corporation's profits. A successful vendor certification program accomplishes this goal by helping to create a pool of experts in a company's software and by "branding" these experts so companies using the software can identify them.

We know that vendor certification has become increasingly popular in the last few years because it helps employers find qualified workers and because it helps software vendors like Microsoft sell their products. But why vendor certification rather than a more traditional approach like a college degree in computer science? A college education is a broadening and enriching experience, but a degree in computer science does not prepare students for most jobs in the IT industry.

A common truism in our business states, "If you are out of the IT industry for three years and want to return, you have to start over." The problem, of course, is *timeliness*; if a first-year student learns about a specific computer program, it probably will no longer be in wide use when he or she graduates. Although some colleges are trying to integrate Microsoft certification into their curriculum, the problem is not really a flaw in higher education, but a characteristic of the IT industry. Computer software is changing so rapidly that a four-year college just can't keep up.

A marked characteristic of the Microsoft certification program is an emphasis on performing specific job tasks rather than merely gathering knowledge. It may come as a shock, but most potential employers do not care how much you know about the theory of operating systems, networking, or database design. As one IT manager put it, "I don't really care what my employees know about the theory of our network. We don't need someone to sit at a desk and think about it. We need people who can actually do something to make it work better."

You should not think that this attitude is some kind of anti-intellectual revolt against "book learning." Knowledge is a necessary prerequisite, but it is not enough. More than one company has hired a computer science graduate as a network administrator, only to learn that the new employee has no idea how to add users, assign permissions, or perform the other day-to-day tasks necessary to maintain a network. This brings us to the second major characteristic of Microsoft certification that affects the questions you must be prepared to answer. In addition to timeliness, Microsoft certification is also job-task oriented.

The timeliness of Microsoft's certification program is obvious and is inherent in the fact that you will be tested on current versions of software in wide use today. The job-task orientation of Microsoft certification is almost as obvious, but testing real-world job skills using a computer-based test is not easy.

Computerized Testing

Considering the popularity of Microsoft certification, and the fact that certification candidates are spread around the world, the only practical way to administer tests for the certification program is through Sylvan Prometric or Vue testing centers, which operate internationally. Sylvan Prometric and Vue provide proctor testing services for Microsoft, Oracle, Novell, Lotus, and the A+ computer technician certification. Although the IT industry accounts for much of Sylvan's revenue, the company provides services for a number of other businesses and organizations, such as FAA pre-flight pilot tests. Historically, several hundred questions were developed for a new Microsoft certification exam. The Windows 2000 MCSE exam pool is expected to contain hundreds of new questions. Microsoft is aware that many new MCSE candidates have been able to access information on test questions via the Internet or other resources. The company is very concerned about maintaining the MCSE as a "premium" certification. The significant increase in the number of test questions, together with stronger enforcement of the NDA (Non-disclosure agreement) will ensure that a higher standard for certification is attained.

Microsoft treats the test-building process very seriously. Test questions are first reviewed by a number of subject matter experts for technical accuracy and then are presented in a beta test. Taking the beta test may require several hours, due to the large number of questions. After a few weeks, Microsoft Certification uses the statistical feedback from Sylvan to check the performance of the beta questions. The beta test group for the Windows 2000 certification series included MCTs, MCSEs, and members of Microsoft's rapid deployment partners groups. Because the exams will be normalized based on this population, you can be sure that the passing scores will be difficult to achieve without detailed product knowledge.

Questions are discarded if most test takers get them right (too easy) or wrong (too difficult), and a number of other statistical measures are taken of each question. Although the scope of our discussion precludes a rigorous treatment of question analysis, you should be aware that Microsoft and other vendors spend a great deal of time and effort making sure their exam questions are valid.

The questions that survive statistical analysis form the pool of questions for the final certification exam.

Test Structure

The questions in a Microsoft form test will not be equally weighted. From what we can tell at the present time, different questions are given a value based on the level of difficulty. You will get more credit for getting a difficult question correct than if you got an easy one correct. Because the questions are weighted differently, and because the exams will likely use the adapter method of testing, your score will not bear any relationship to how many questions you answered correctly.

Microsoft has implemented *adaptive* testing. When an adaptive test begins, the candidate is first given a level three question. If it is answered correctly, a question from the next higher level is presented, and an incorrect response results in a question from the next lower level. When 15 to 20 questions have been answered in this manner, the scoring algorithm is able to predict, with a high degree of statistical certainty, whether the candidate would pass or fail if all the questions in the form were answered. When the required degree of certainty is attained, the test ends and the candidate receives a pass/fail grade.

Adaptive testing has some definite advantages for everyone involved in the certification process. Adaptive tests allow Sylvan Prometric or Vue to deliver more tests with the same resources, as certification candidates often are in and out in 30 minutes or less. For candidates, the "fatigue factor" is reduced due to the shortened testing time. For Microsoft, adaptive testing means that fewer test questions are exposed to each candidate, and this can enhance the security, and therefore the overall validity, of certification tests.

One possible problem you may have with adaptive testing is that you are not allowed to mark and revisit questions. Since the adaptive algorithm is interactive, and all questions but the first are selected on the basis of your response to the previous question, it is not possible to skip a particular question or change an answer.

Question Types

Computerized test questions can be presented in a number of ways. Some of the possible formats are used on Microsoft certification exams and some are not.

True/False Questions

We are all familiar with True/False questions, but because of the inherent 50 percent chance of guessing the correct answer, you will not see questions of this type on Microsoft certification exams.

Multiple-Choice Questions

The majority of Microsoft certification questions are in the multiple-choice format, with either a single correct answer or multiple correct answers. One interesting variation on multiple-choice questions with multiple correct answers is whether or not the candidate is told how many answers are correct.

> **EXAMPLE:**
>
> Which two files can be altered to configure the MS-DOS environment? (Choose two.)
>
> or
>
> Which files can be altered to configure the MS-DOS environment? (Choose all that apply.)

You may see both variations on Microsoft certification exams, but the trend seems to be toward the first type, where candidates are told explicitly how many answers are correct. Questions of the "choose all that apply" variety are more difficult and can be merely confusing.

Graphical Questions

One or more graphical elements are sometimes used as exhibits to help present or clarify an exam question. These elements may take the form of a network diagram, pictures of networking components, or screen shots from the software on which you are being tested. It is often easier to present the concepts required for a complex performance-based scenario with a graphic than with words.

Test questions known as *hotspots* actually incorporate graphics as part of the answer. These questions ask the certification candidate to click on a location or graphical element to answer the question. For example, you might be shown the diagram of a network and asked to click on an appropriate location for a router. The answer is correct if the candidate clicks within the *hotspot* that defines the correct location.

Free Response Questions

Another kind of question you sometimes see on Microsoft certification exams requires a *free response* or type-in answer. An example of this type of question might present a TCP/IP network scenario and ask the candidate to calculate and enter the correct subnet mask in dotted decimal notation.

Simulation Questions

Simulation questions provide a method for Microsoft to test how familiar the test taker is with the actual product interface and the candidate's ability to quickly implement a task using the interface. These questions will present an actual Windows 2000 interface that you must work with to solve a problem or implement a solution. If you are familiar with the product, you will be able to answer these questions quickly, and they will be the easiest questions on the exam. However, if you are not accustomed to working with Windows 2000, these questions will be difficult for you to answer. This is why actual hands-on practice with Windows 2000 is so important!

Knowledge-Based and Performance-Based Questions

Microsoft Certification develops a blueprint for each Microsoft certification exam with input from subject matter experts. This blueprint defines the content areas and objectives for each test, and each test question is created to test a specific objective. The basic information from the examination blueprint can be found on Microsoft's Web site in the Exam Prep Guide for each test.

Psychometricians (psychologists who specialize in designing and analyzing tests) categorize test questions as knowledge-based or performance-based. As the names imply, knowledge-based questions are designed to test knowledge, while performance-based questions are designed to test performance.

Some objectives demand a knowledge-based question. For example, objectives that use verbs like *list* and *identify* tend to test only what you know, not what you can do.

EXAMPLE:

Objective: Identify the MS-DOS configuration files.

Which two files can be altered to configure the MS-DOS environment? (Choose two.)

A. COMMAND.COM

B. AUTOEXEC.BAT

C. IO.SYS

D. CONFIG.SYS

Correct answers: B, D

Other objectives use action verbs like *install, configure,* and *troubleshoot* to define job tasks. These objectives can often be tested with either a knowledge-based question or a performance-based question.

EXAMPLE:

Objective: Configure an MS-DOS installation appropriately using the PATH statement in AUTOEXEC.BAT.

Knowledge-based question:

What is the correct syntax to set a path to the D: directory in AUTOEXEC.BAT?

A. SET PATH EQUAL TO D:

B. PATH D:

C. SETPATH D:

D. D:EQUALS PATH

Correct answer: B

Performance-based question:

Your company uses several DOS accounting applications that access a group of common utility programs. What is the best strategy for configuring the computers in the accounting department so that the accounting applications will always be able to access the utility programs?

A. Store all the utilities on a single floppy disk and make a copy of the disk for each computer in the accounting department.

B. Copy all the utilities to a directory on the C drive of each computer in the accounting department and add a PATH statement pointing to this directory in the AUTOEXEC.BAT files.

C. Copy all the utilities to all application directories on each computer in the accounting department.

D. Place all the utilities in the C directory on each computer, because the C directory is automatically included in the PATH statement when AUTOEXEC.BAT is executed.

Correct answer: B

Even in this simple example, the superiority of the performance-based question is obvious. Whereas the knowledge-based question asks for a single fact, the performance-based question presents a real-life situation and requires that you make a decision based on this scenario. Thus, performance-based questions give more bang (validity) for the test author's buck (individual question).

Testing Job Performance

We have said that Microsoft certification focuses on timeliness and the ability to perform job tasks. We have also introduced the concept of performance-based questions, but even performance-based multiple-choice questions do not really measure performance. Another strategy is needed to test job skills.

Given unlimited resources, it is not difficult to test job skills. In an ideal world, Microsoft would fly MCP candidates to Redmond, place them in a controlled environment with a team of experts, and ask them to plan, install, maintain, and troubleshoot a Windows network. In a few days at most, the experts could reach a valid decision as to whether each candidate should or should not be granted MCDBA or MCSE status. Needless to say, this is not likely to happen.

Closer to reality, another way to test performance is by using the actual software and creating a testing program to present tasks and automatically grade a candidate's performance when the tasks are completed. This *cooperative* approach would be practical in some testing situations, but the same test that is presented to MCP candidates in Boston must also be available in Bahrain and Botswana. The most workable solution for measuring performance in today's testing environment is a *simulation* program. When the program is launched during a test, the candidate sees a simulation of the actual software that looks, and behaves, just like the real thing. When the testing software presents a task, the simulation program is launched and the candidate performs the required task. The testing software then grades the candidate's performance on the required task and moves to the next question. Microsoft has introduced simulation questions on the certification exam for Internet Information Server 4.0. Simulation questions provide many advantages over other testing methodologies, and simulations are expected to become increasingly important in the Microsoft certification program. For example, studies have shown that there is a very high correlation between the ability to perform simulated tasks on a computer-based test and the ability to perform the actual job tasks. Thus, simulations enhance the validity of the certification process.

Another truly wonderful benefit of simulations is in the area of test security. It is just not possible to cheat on a simulation question. In fact, you will be told exactly what tasks you are expected to perform on the test. How can a certification candidate cheat? By learning to perform the tasks? What a concept!

Study Strategies

There are appropriate ways to study for the different types of questions you will see on a Microsoft certification exam.

Knowledge-Based Questions

Knowledge-based questions require that you memorize facts. There are hundreds of facts inherent in every content area of every Microsoft certification exam. There are several keys to memorizing facts:

Repetition The more times your brain is exposed to a fact, the more likely you are to remember it.

Association Connecting facts within a logical framework makes them easier to remember.

Motor Association It is often easier to remember something if you write it down or perform some other physical act, like clicking on a practice test answer.

We have said that the emphasis of Microsoft certification is job performance and that there are very few knowledge-based questions on Microsoft certification exams. Why should you waste a lot of time learning filenames, IP address formulas, and other minutiae? Read on.

Performance-Based Questions

Most of the questions you will face on a Microsoft certification exam are performance-based scenario questions. We have discussed the superiority of these questions over simple knowledge-based questions, but you should remember that the job-task orientation of Microsoft certification extends the knowledge you need to pass the exams; it does not replace this knowledge. Therefore, the first step in preparing for scenario questions is to absorb as many facts relating to the exam content areas as you can. In other words, go back to the previous section and follow the steps to prepare for an exam composed of knowledge-based questions.

The second step is to familiarize yourself with the format of the questions you are likely to see on the exam. You can do this by answering the questions in this book, or by using Microsoft assessment tests. The day of your test is not the time to be surprised by the construction of Microsoft exam questions.

At best, performance-based scenario questions really do test certification candidates at a higher cognitive level than knowledge-based questions. At worst, these questions can test your reading comprehension and test-taking ability rather than your ability to use Microsoft products. Be sure to get in the habit of reading the question carefully to determine what is being asked.

The third step in preparing for Microsoft scenario questions is to adopt the following attitude: Multiple-choice questions aren't really performance-based. It is all a cruel lie.

These scenario questions are just knowledge-based questions with a story wrapped around them.

To answer a scenario question, you have to sift through the story to the underlying facts of the situation and apply your knowledge to determine the correct answer. This may sound silly at first, but the process we go through in solving real-life problems is quite similar. The key concept is that every scenario question (and every real-life problem) has a fact at its center, and if we can identify that fact, we can answer the question.

Simulations

Simulation questions really do measure your ability to perform job tasks. You must be able to perform the specified tasks. One of the ways to prepare for simulation questions is to get experience with the actual software. If you have the resources, this is a great way to prepare for simulation questions.

SIGNING UP

Signing up to take a Microsoft certification exam is easy. Sylvan Prometric or Vue operators in each country can schedule tests at any testing center. There are, however, a few things you should know:

- If you call Sylvan Prometric or Vue during a busy time, get a cup of coffee first because you may be in for a long wait. The exam providers do an excellent job, but everyone in the world seems to want to sign up for a test on Monday morning.

- You will need your social security number or some other unique identifier to sign up for a test, so have it at hand.

- Pay for your test by credit card if at all possible. This makes things easier, and you can even schedule tests for the same day you call, if space is available at your local testing center.

- Know the number and title of the test you want to take before you call. This is not essential, and the Sylvan operators will help you if they can. Having this information in advance, however, speeds up and improves the accuracy of the registration process.

TAKING THE TEST

Teachers have always told you not to try to cram for exams because it does no good. If you are faced with a knowledge-based test requiring only that you regurgitate facts, cramming can mean the difference between passing and failing. This is not the case, however, with Microsoft certification exams. If you don't know it the night before, don't bother to stay up and cram.

Instead, create a schedule and stick to it. Plan your study time carefully, and do not schedule your test until you think you are ready to succeed. Follow these guidelines on the day of your exam:

- Get a good night's sleep. The scenario questions you will face on a Microsoft certification exam require a clear head.

- Remember to take two forms of identification—at least one with a picture. A driver's license with your picture and social security or credit card is acceptable.

- Leave home in time to arrive at your testing center a few minutes early. It is not a good idea to feel rushed as you begin your exam.

- Do not spend too much time on any one question. You cannot mark and revisit questions on an adaptive test, so you must do your best on each question as you go.

- If you do not know the answer to a question, try to eliminate the obviously wrong answers and guess from the rest. If you can eliminate two out of four options, you have a 50 percent chance of guessing the correct answer.

- For scenario questions, follow the steps we outlined earlier. Read the question carefully and try to identify the facts at the center of the story.

Finally, we would advise anyone attempting to earn Microsoft MCDBA and MCSE certification to adopt a philosophical attitude. The Windows 2000 MCSE will be the most difficult MCSE ever to be offered. The questions will be at a higher cognitive level than seen on all previous MCSE exams. Therefore, even if you are the kind of person who never fails a test, you are likely to fail at least one Windows 2000 certification test somewhere along the way. Do not get discouraged. Microsoft wants to ensure the value of your certification. Moreover, it will attempt to so by keeping the standard as high as possible. If Microsoft certification were easy to obtain, more people would have it, and it would not be so respected and so valuable to your future in the IT industry.

MICROSOFT CERTIFIED SYSTEMS ENGINEER

1

Analyzing Business Requirements

TEST YOURSELF OBJECTIVES

The analysis of a company's business requirements is an important part of planning a network infrastructure. By understanding the needs of the business, you are better able to create a network that enhances the business and allows it to achieve its goals.

To develop a picture of the business requirements, you must have the ability to examine a given business scenario, taking care to uncover the business and company models, company processes, existing and planned organizational structures, and the company strategy. You will also be required to analyze the structure of the information technology (IT) management to understand its function.

TEST YOURSELF OBJECTIVE 1.01

Understanding Business Requirements Analysis

Business requirements are the needs and issues that must be analyzed and addressed when planning a network. Once determined, these are applied to a plan that outlines the technical specifications of a network infrastructure. Business requirements analysis isn't an exact science, but rather a calculation of trade-offs. Different factors affect the network infrastructure you create. The way a business is organized, its ability to change and accept risks, and other variables will each play a part in how a network is planned and implemented.

You need to know the various types of information that can be gathered from a business in order to conduct your analysis. This information can be gathered in a number of ways: you can interview staff members, conduct a survey, or review existing documentation. Once you have gathered the information, it needs to be organized into meaningful documents that will support the network design you are creating.

During the course of a network infrastructure design, you will create several types of documents. These include administrative documents, deployment documents, functional specifications, communication strategies, training plans, capacity plans, and a risk assessment.

■ Administrative documents identify the scope, goals, and objectives of the project.

■ Deployment documents describe the current network environment (if any), gaps between the current environment and the one envisioned, and how Windows 2000 will be integrated into the environment.

■ Functional specifications outline the required features and the details of what the network infrastructure will be.

■ Communication strategies outline how information about the project will be conveyed and how often.

■ Training plans outline issues dealing with how users and support staff will be educated about the new system.

■ Capacity plans estimate minimum, maximum, and average figures on network usage. This includes such factors as how often users log on to the network and the number of Domain Name System (DNS) queries that occur.

■ Risk assessments assess possible risks that the project may face and how these risks may affect the project.

exam
ⓦatch
The ability to analyze a business's requirements is more of a soft skill than a hard technical requirement. However, when you sit down and begin designing your first Windows 2000 network, the data and information that you collect about the business will be just as important as the data you collect about the network. Be very detail oriented, and understand the various documents and plans that are used to capture this information.

QUESTIONS

1.01: Understanding Business Requirements Analysis

1. **Current Situation:** You are an independent consultant working for the IT director of a small law firm in Philadelphia. The firm specializes in Internet law, and they are planning on experiencing significant growth over the next two years. The firm currently has twenty employees. They are planning on upgrading their

486-based Windows 95 peer-to-peer network to Windows 2000. When the research assistants need to access the Internet, they do so by using one of the three PCs that have dial-up access to a local Internet service provider (ISP).

Required Result: You must upgrade the law firm's network to Windows 2000 and prepare for the expected growth.

Optional Desired Result: Provide access to the Internet for the entire firm, rather than just three select PCs.

Proposed Solution: Purchase a new file server and install Windows 2000 Server. Purchase new Pentium III–based PCs and install Windows 2000 Professional. Configure a single domain for the law firm. Install Proxy Server on the file server, and install and configure a modem for Internet access.

What results are provided from the proposed solution?

A. The proposed solution produces the required result only.

B. The proposed solution produces the required result and the optional result.

C. The proposed solution does not produce the required result.

2. While preparing to perform a Windows 2000 upgrade for one of your clients, you decide to prepare a capacity plan. What types of information will you document in the capacity plan?

A. The goals of the network upgrade project

B. Information about the training levels of the organization's employees

C. Data recorded from your network sniffer detailing DNS requests, DHCP queries, network utilization, and frame errors

D. Budget information for the project

TEST YOURSELF OBJECTIVE 1.02

Analyzing the Existing and Planned Business Models

In determining business requirements, it is important to analyze both the existing and planned business models. If a company is restructuring itself or changing how it does business, it may affect your Windows 2000 implementation. It is important to understand the specifics of an organization if you are to understand how your network infrastructure will function.

Once you have gathered the information pertaining to the business model, you can use visual aids to represent the data. Flowcharts and diagrams can show the structure of the business, how data and communication flow, and other aspects of the business model. Examples of these diagrams are the entity relationship diagram (ERD), and hierarchical diagrams, which include organizational charts.

Another way of comparing the existing and planned business models is to conduct a gap analysis. This analysis involves comparing the current environment with the planned environment, often by examining documents, talking to employees, and watching how employees interact and function.

- Visual aids provide a graphical approach to relaying the information contained in business models.

- A *gap analysis* involves comparing your current environment with your future environment. The gap between these two environments will assist you in determining what is needed to close this gap.

exam
ⓦatch

This objective will test your ability to examine a business model and break it down into its most basic pieces—the business group. Understand what the business model and business group represent, and also understand the various ways you can visually represent this information. Finally, have a good understanding of the gap analysis process. The ability to compare two environments and come away with what's necessary to get from point A to point B is very important.

QUESTIONS

1.02: Analyzing the Existing and Planned Business Models

3. One method of analyzing an existing business model is to diagram the information that you uncover. What type of diagram is shown on the following page?

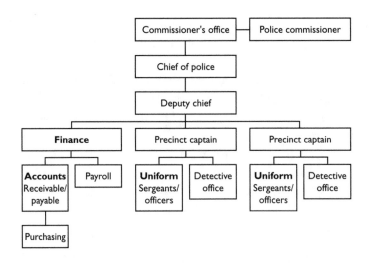

A. Entity relationship diagram (ERD)

B. Network diagram

C. Hierarchical diagram

D. None of the above

4. **Current Situation:** A large manufacturing company has decided to upgrade their network infrastructure. The Chief Information Officer (CIO) has chosen to replace the Novell Netware environment with Windows 2000. Although you are new to the company, he has asked you to lead the project. Your company has 30 servers in a central computing center, with 200 PCs spread throughout a two-story administration building. The building is wired with Category 3 wire.

Required Result: You must conduct a thorough gap analysis to determine what components of your existing network will meet the minimum requirements for your new Windows 2000 network infrastructure.

Optional Desired Results:

1. Document the functional specifications for the new network.

2. Prepare a capacity plan for the existing network.

Proposed Solution: You decide to compare the minimum requirements for Windows 2000 with the network documentation that was completed three years ago by the Server Team. This comparison reveals that your servers do not meet the specifications for Windows 2000. You make note of this in your functional specification for the new network. You also make note of the single DNS server that is running on a spare 486-class computer in the corner of the computing center. After padding out the functional specification with more details of the Windows 2000 requirements, you hand this and the gap analysis to the CIO.

What results are provided from the proposed solution?

A. The proposed solution produces the required result only.

B. The proposed solution produces the required result and one of the optional results.

C. The proposed solution produces the required result and both of the optional results.

D. The proposed solution does not produce the required result.

TEST YOURSELF OBJECTIVE 1.03

Analyzing the Company Model and the Geographic Scope

When conducting your analysis, you must pay attention to the company model and its geographic scope. Types of company models include subsidiaries and branch offices. The manner in which the company business units are dispersed geographically is perhaps the central consideration in network design, because the geographic structure will often reflect the type of network that is required. Companies may have a regional scope, a national scope, or an international scope.

■ Many of the factors that determine how you design your network are determined by the size of the company. As such, analyzing how the company is structured is vital to designing a network infrastructure.

■ In analyzing the company model and geographic scope, you determine how units of the company are separated from one another. You need to investigate whether these units perform the same tasks for their area or if they have unique needs.

exam
Ⓦatch

Understand the various geographic business models and the complexities of designing networks to support each of them. You should know which types of wide area networking circuits are desirable for the national and international structures. You should also be able to choose an appropriate networking technology for branch and subsidiary offices.

QUESTIONS

1.03: Analyzing the Company Model and the Geographic Scope

5. If a LAN is a local area network, which covers a single location, and a WAN is a wide area network, which covers a large area, such as a state or country, what do you call the network spanning a city or small region?

    A. Municipal area network (MAN)

    B. Mega area network (MAN)

    C. Metropolitan area network (MAN)

    D. Mobile area network (MAN)

6. **Current Situation:** You are a consultant working for a Big 5 consulting firm. You have been asked to prepare a network infrastructure proposal for an international pharmaceutical corporation. They currently have local area networks in each office, but do not have a wide area network connecting each office. The organization's headquarters is in Charlotte, and it has offices in New York, a research and development facility in Boston, data centers in Frankfurt and Paris, and manufacturing facilities in London, Tokyo, and Sydney. The company also has two subsidiaries in the United States—one located in Denver and the second in Seattle.

The company sends large amounts of research data between its international locations, plus is investing in videoconference equipment to lower its travel costs between the United States and Europe.

Required Result: You must design a WAN that has sufficient bandwidth to connect the headquarters in Charlotte with the data centers in the two European locations.

Optional Desired Results:

1. Propose an encryption scheme that is acceptable across all corporate locations.

2. Choose a network protocol that will scale to meet the company's needs.

Proposed Solution: You decide to install 256-kilobits-per-second (Kbps) Frame Relay circuits between the Charlotte, Frankfurt, and Paris locations. You also propose to install 128-Kbps ISDN circuits between those locations and the remaining locations.

You decide to use TCP/IP as the standard protocol, and, after doing considerable research, decide on using 56-bit encryption among all of the sites.

What results are provided from the proposed solution?

A. The proposed solution produces the required result only.

B. The proposed solution produces the required result and one of the optional results.

C. The proposed solution produces the required result and both of the optional results.

D. The proposed solution does not produce the required result.

Analyzing Company Processes

A key factor when investigating business requirements is the analysis of the company's business processes. This analysis includes documenting the key business processes and practices, determining service and product life cycles, and identifying the key decision makers in the organization.

Two types of information that you should document and diagram are information flow and communication flow. This information is critical for enabling decision makers to make business decisions.

Identifying the service and product life cycles is important because some are geared toward a particular point in time, such as those services designed for Y2K remediation.

The key decision makers in the organization will have access to greater amounts of information and a higher viewpoint of the organization's processes and practices. They are also the people who are usually responsible for signing off on any large-scale infrastructure projects.

- A *company process* is a function within the business that allows it to deliver its products and services.

- When analyzing company processes, you need to document or diagram workflow, decision-making processes, service and product life cycles, and the flow of communication and information

- *Data flow diagrams* are used to document information flow. A data flow diagram shows business processes in the form of oval shapes, with arrows connecting the various processes. These arrows show the direction information flows, while text above these arrows indicates the name or form of that information.

- A *communication strategy* outlines how information about a project will be conveyed to decision makers, end users, and other stakeholders.

exam
ⓦatch

You will find that the term "key decision maker" is used throughout this book. When you work on a project, the key decision maker can make or break your project because that person usually has the signing authority. Most processes start or end with a key decision maker, and that person should be quickly identified in all of your documentation.

QUESTIONS

1.04: Analyzing Company Processes

7. **Current Situation:** A small company is having difficulty disseminating timely information to its remote sales force. After interviewing the IT staff, you find that the sales team uses laptops connected to the company's network via a remote access server (RAS) connection. You also find that the company uses Microsoft Mail to communicate the sales data on a weekly basis. However, after speaking to a few of the remote users, you learn that these messages sit unopened for a few days.

    Required Result: You must document the communication flow to the remote sales team in this small company.

    Optional Desired Result: You must provide options to help improve the timeliness of the communications.

    Proposed Solution: You take the information that you've gathered and prepare the following data flow diagram of the communication flow:

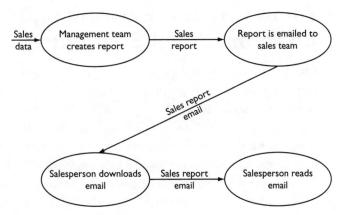

    You recommend that the company upgrade to Microsoft Exchange and Outlook. It is also your recommendation that the company conduct additional sales training, as you feel that part of the problem lies with the users (who are not opening their email).

What results are provided from the proposed solution?

A. The proposed solution produces the required result only.

B. The proposed solution produces the required result and the optional result.

C. The proposed solution does not produce the required result.

8. One of the important steps in the process of analyzing business processes is to look at the product life cycles. Why is it important to consider the life cycle during your planning?

A. You don't want to recommend a product that you know will have an upgrade in a few months.

B. Your client is pushing to have a new upgrade, but doesn't want to be "bleeding edge."

C. Your client wants to continue to use the computers that were purchased five years ago, even though the specifications call for a newer model.

D. All of the above.

TEST YOURSELF OBJECTIVE 1.05

Analyzing the Existing and Planned Organizational Structures

Once you have defined the goals and objectives of a business, it is important to consider what the existing organizational structure is, and how the planned organizational structure will help to achieve those goals.

Components of the structure you must consider are the management model; the company organization; vendor, partner, and customer relationships; and acquisition plans. Not all companies are owned by a single person, or rely on a board of directors answering to stockholders. Some companies are partnerships, where two or more people actually own the company. In such cases, you will need to consider the role the partner plays in the existing and planned organizational structure.

■ The existing organizational structure shows how the company is managed, how it is organized, the partner and customer relationships it has, any acquisition plans, and vendor issues.

- Organizational charts and management models are used to show how the company is structured and the levels of management contained within the business, respectively.

- If a partner is part of the decision-making process, you will need to include the partner in this structure. If the partner is a silent partner and has no say in how the business is run, you won't need to structure your network security, organizational, and management models to include that partner.

- The design of your network infrastructure needs to be flexible to accommodate company acquisitions, divestitures, and reorganization of companies.

exam

ⓦatch

The point of this objective is that your network design needs to remain flexible enough to handle changes in the organizational structure. By conducting a thorough investigation and analysis of the company's organization and future plans, you will have the information required to allow your design to work well into the future.

QUESTIONS

1.05: Analyzing the Existing and Planned Organizational Structures

9. You are the network architect for a midsized accounting firm in New York City. You are beginning to plan your Windows 2000 network design, and you are trying to anticipate any organizational changes that might affect your design. Which of the following might have the greatest impact on your network design?

   A. The release of Windows 2000 Service Pack 1.

   B. The addition of a new office in the Midwest Region.

   C. Your company gets a new Chief Information Officer.

   D. Your company plans to merge with another accounting firm in Philadelphia.

10. As you begin the analysis of your client, you begin to wonder who will be responsible for signing off on the project when it is completed. What is a common way of diagramming the organizational structure of a company?

    A. Entity relationship diagram

    B. Communication flow diagram

    C. Information flow diagram

    D. Organizational chart

TEST YOURSELF OBJECTIVE 1.06

Analyzing Factors That Influence Company Strategies

When starting to design your client's network, it is important to consider their strategic plans and the factors that influence their strategies. First, you need to look at their priorities. These are the issues that take precedence and must be in place before other features of the project. Juggling these priorities will also dictate that trade-offs will be made to achieve the project goals.

Identifying the company's projected growth is crucial, because the addition of new facilities or divisions down the road will affect your network design now. When preparing your network design, you must also take into consideration the laws and regulations of the country where you will be working. Some technologies, such as encryption, are illegal to deploy in some countries.

Finally, you need to conduct a risk assessment to determine ahead of time what could present a problem down the road. There is nothing worse than having a critical piece of hardware fail without having a backup plan. Also, you will need to examine the total cost of ownership (TCO) of the project. Managing the TCO is important to reduce costs and make the project more cost effective.

■ Many factors can influence a company's strategies and have an effect on the success of your project. To deal with these factors, it is important to identify company priorities, the company's projected growth and growth strategies, relevant laws and regulations, and the risk and total cost of operations.

■ In setting priorities, you are dealing with three elements of a project: schedule, resources, and features. Altering one of these elements will affect the other two.

■ To establish priorities in a project and determine what trade-offs will occur, you can use a trade-off matrix. A *trade-off matrix* is a table that is used as a reference tool, allowing your team to decide whether it is more important to stay on schedule, on budget, or to pass off certain features until a later date.

■ It is important to identify the projected growth and review the growth strategy of a company when you analyze business requirements.

■ Failing to identify relevant laws and regulations related to the business can result in criminal and civil prosecution. Protocols, encryption schemes, and other features used on your network may be prohibited, depending on where the company is located.

■ The key to risk management is being proactive.

■ A good risk management plan offers methods of redundancy, which reduce the likelihood that a problem will actually occur.

■ An effective risk management plan involves identifying and analyzing potential risks, quantifying the potential impact of those risks, identifying mission-critical applications, detailing escalation processes, and finding solutions to the risks.

■ The TCO is all costs that are involved in information technology.

■ The TCO model involves three phases: analyze, improve, and manage.

exam
ⓦatch

Risk management. You will need to understand the various components of managing risk in your project. You should learn how to prepare a risk assessment matrix in order to document the risks that you feel are associated with completing the project. By being proactive, you are able to head off any potential problems by showing your foresight and risk-mitigation techniques. Also, most managers like to see that you have thought ahead and attempted to anticipate any problems that might occur down the road.

QUESTIONS

1.06: Analyzing Factors That Influence Company Strategies

11. There are three steps in the TCO model: analysis, improvement, and management. In which step does the analyst recollect data and compare it to the metrics so that one can determine if improvement has occurred?

   A. Analysis

   B. Improvement

   C. Management

Questions 12–13   This scenario should be used to answer questions 12 and 13.

You are the IT Manager for a regional bank, called Mid-Carolina S&L, based out of Georgetown, South Carolina. Mid-Carolina S&L, successfully avoiding large risk, has been in business for over 40 years, and now wishes to acquire another small bank based in Myrtle Beach.

Mid-Carolina S&L has 25 offices scattered throughout central South Carolina. Each of its offices is equipped with Windows 98 PCs connected to a Windows NT 4.0 server. It still uses the workgroup model. The network is 100-megabits-per-second (Mbps) Ethernet in the offices, with 56-Kbps Frame Relay connecting the offices together in a wide area network. They currently use Exchange and Outlook for email communication.

The small bank, Horry County Trust, has ten branches along the coast in Horry County, with two more inland near the old Myrtle Beach Air Force Base. Each of these offices has five to eight Windows 95 PCs connected on a token ring network. Horry County Trust uses a custom loan application based on the AS/400 platform. Each branch is connected with a 56-Kbps dial-up line to exchange data at the end of each day.

12. Which of the following risks presents the greatest threat to Mid-Carolina S&L and should be concentrated on during the due diligence stage of the merger talks?

    A. The AS/400 application unrecoverably crashing

    B. A large hurricane striking Myrtle Beach and destroying the ten branch offices near the shore

    C. The telephone connection between two of the branch offices becoming disabled

    D. The token ring network not being compatible with the Ethernet network in place at Mid-Carolina S&L

13. Once the merger is completed, what should be prepared to keep your team on schedule during the merging of the two IT groups?

    A. Communications flow diagram

    B. Trade-off matrix

    C. Risk assessment

    D. Organizational chart

TEST YOURSELF OBJECTIVE 1.07

Analyzing the Structure of IT Management

Whether you're consulting for a company or working in a company with its own IT staff, there is a need to analyze the structure of IT management. In consulting, you need to determine how IT staff is organized and the functions they currently perform, or the functions they should perform with the new system. If you are part of an IT team in a company, then you will need to determine if current roles should change with the new system, what team roles each person will play, and how IT management will be part of implementing the new infrastructure.

It's important to look at how the network is administered: either centralized or decentralized. You will also need to determine how IT projects are funded. Funding is a risk factor, so it is the role of IT management to handle potential funding problems.

It is also important to determine what part (if any) outsourcing plays in an organization. In some organizations, outsourcing is not an acceptable solution because of security issues, union contracts, or other reasons.

Finally, you will need to uncover the decision-making process for the organization, and the change management process. Since change is an inevitable part of a project, managing change is critical to the success of the project.

■ Analyzing IT management structure includes scrutiny of the type of administration, funding model, decision-making process, change management process, and outsourcing policies.

■ In the decision-making process, each team member has responsibilities for making decisions that will affect the project's success. Ultimately, decision-makers in the business have the final say because they sign off on the project.

exam
ⓦatch
For this objective, you should concentrate on decision-making and change management. Both of these topics are important aspects of IT management. For decision-making, you should understand how the IT management team interacts with the business and the users. Usually they are the intermediary. Change management is also very important, because it can make or break your operation. The first thing that users experience is change, and if you can manage that, the rest of your work will be much easier.

QUESTIONS

1.07: Analyzing the Structure of IT Management

14. You work for a large nationwide insurance company. There are 35 branch offices spread across the country, with the headquarters in Flint, Michigan. The offices are running Windows 3.1, with printers attached to each computer. What kind of administrative model does this indicate?

    A. Centralized

    B. Localized

C. Decentralized

D. Remote

15. You are the CIO for a company that specializes in sporting goods. You are about to embark on an ambitious network upgrade project in order to meet future demand for your soccer equipment. You have a small IT staff and are considering outsourcing the project to a local consulting firm. Which is a valid reason for considering outsourcing this project?

    A. You don't feel that your own staff has the talent to complete the project.

    B. You don't want to hire additional full-time staff for the project.

    C. You cannot take your staff away from their daily administrative tasks to engage them on the upgrade design work.

    D. All of the above.

LAB QUESTION

Objectives 1.01–1.07

Acme Insurance Brokers, a large multistate, multiline insurance brokerage, is experiencing growing pains with their existing network infrastructure. They currently have ten facilities in the northeastern and midwestern United States, with their headquarters in West Chester, Pennsylvania. Each office has between 100 and 200 employees. They plan on adding another office in each of four western states by the beginning of the next calendar year.

Acme is running Windows 95 and 98 on the desktop, with a 10-Mbps Ethernet network. They are using Lotus cc:Mail for messaging. Each office has a Windows NT 4.0 server acting as a file and print server. The company has invested in a mix of Hewlett-Packard network printers as well as a number of directly connected Epson printers throughout the enterprise. For interoffice connectivity, the company has chosen to use 56-Kbps Frame Relay provided by MCI.

The business has just completed its most profitable quarter on record, and the industry buzz is that it's ripe for a takeover by its closest competitor, Jones Insurance Services. JIS is a nationwide insurance broker that specializes in the small to midsized corporate market. The management team at Acme is well seasoned and considered to be above average for the brokerage industry.

Because of the plan for expansion, Acme has hired your consulting firm to plan and implement a network upgrade, to include migrating the entire enterprise to Windows 2000 Server and Professional. Your managing partner has asked that you lead the upgrade team. She wants to have a preliminary report that addresses the business requirements of Acme Insurance Brokers so that she can determine how many more consultants need to be allocated to the project.

The managing partner wants you to answer the following questions in your analysis of the business requirements:

1. A section of your report will address the current network environment. What type of document(s) will you prepare that details the existing state of the network, the types of hardware and software that have been deployed, and provides a baseline of the network utilization?

2. Who are you going to talk with to obtain the current business model?

3. What type of company model does Acme currently employ? How is the company dispersed geographically?

4. Does Acme offer products or services that have a finite life cycle? Do we need to be concerned about recommending upgrade products that might interfere with their line of business offerings?

5. What are the merger and acquisition plans for Acme? Are they planning on expanding in the future? What impact do you think this will have on the current and future network design?

6. Are there any obvious legal requirements associated with this upgrade project? Are there any Windows 2000 technologies that might be prohibited by U.S. law?

7. What type of administration does Acme employ? Will this present any conflicts with the migration to Windows 2000, either technically or culturally?

A QUICK ANSWER KEY

Objective 1.01
1. B
2. C

Objective 1.02
3. C
4. D

Objective 1.03
5. C
6. D

Objective 1.04
7. B
8. D

Objective 1.05
9. D
10. D

Objective 1.06
11. C
12. B
13. B

Objective 1.07
14. C
15. D

IN-DEPTH ANSWERS

1.01: Understanding Business Requirements Analysis

1. ☑ **B.** The proposed solution produces both the required result and the optional result. By looking at the business requirements of the law firm, you identified that the firm had outgrown their peer-to-peer network and needed to upgrade to a client/server network. You also identified that the hardware did not meet the minimum requirements for Windows 2000. Finally, by installing Proxy Server, you were able to provide Internet access for all of the employees over the LAN, rather than from one of the dial-up PCs. By successfully analyzing the business requirements, you were able to meet the current and future needs of the client.

   ☒ **A** and **C** are incorrect because the proposed solution produces both the required result and the optional result.

2. ☑ **C.** Data recorded from your network sniffer detailing DNS requests, DHCP queries, network utilization, and frame errors. The capacity plan is used to estimate minimum, maximum, and average figures on network usage. It should include network utilization data, sniffer captures, and other related data.

   ☒ **A** and **D** are both incorrect because they indicate data and information that would be captured in administrative documents. **B** is incorrect because training information for employees would be captured in the training plan.

1.02: Analyzing the Existing and Planned Business Models

3. ☑ **C.** Hierarchical diagram. A hierarchical diagram is used to show the business objects of a company and the organization of the objects. In this case, the diagram shows the organizational structure of the local police department.

☒   **A** is not correct, as an entity relationship diagram (ERD) is used to show how different entities or business objects relate to each other. You might use an ERD to show how expense reports are handled as they pass from management to finance to payroll. **B** is not correct, as a network diagram would show the objects in a network, such as the servers, hubs, and routers, and then show how they are connected.

4.   ☑   **D.** The proposed solution does not produce the required result. The CIO asked for a thorough gap analysis to be completed. This requires that you do a number of tasks. First, you must look at how the business is currently working with the existing system in place and how it will work with the new system in place. Next, you need to review the documentation of the existing system. This will tell you the details of the system, as well as the history of upgrades and repairs. The documentation will also give you specific details about the hardware and software that has been installed. Finally, you should look at the tasks being performed by the users, and see if your new system will assist or detract from their current workflow. All of this information must be compiled and then analyzed to create the gap analysis. The proposed solution left out much of this work. Neither of the optional results were met, either. Although you began to create a functional specification, many of the details of the new environment were not included, such as the types of hardware needed, network protocol information, and PC upgrade information. The capacity plan was completely neglected.

☒   **A**, **B**, and **C** are incorrect because the proposed solution does not produce the required result.

1.03: Analyzing the Company Model and the Geographic Scope

5.   ☑   **C.** A network that spans a city or small region is called a metropolitan area network (MAN). An example would be a bank with many branch offices in a city.

☒   **A**, **B**, and **D** are all fictitious examples of network acronyms.

6.   ☑   **D.** The proposed solution does not produce the required result. Your decision to use 256-Kbps Frame Relay only provides a fraction of the bandwidth that will be required by this international organization. Since the

corporation is choosing to connect the headquarters in Charlotte and the data centers in Europe as core sites, they should have a minimum of a T1 circuit (1.544 Mbps), if not a T3 circuit (45 Mbps) running between them. Also, their investment in videoconference equipment should send a warning flag up that a large amount of bandwidth will be necessary. It is important to fully understand the bandwidth requirements of an international business model, since it is usually higher than expected, and it is costly to add more bandwidth later rather than to build in a little room from the start.

Their choice of TCP/IP as the standard protocol easily satisfies one of the optional results, and the choice of 56-bit encryption should satisfy as a common encryption scheme. When dealing with international corporations, the laws in the various companies can sometimes play an important role in your network design. In this case, France is very particular about the use of encryption, and only recently relaxed their standards on its use.

☒ **A**, **B**, and **C** are incorrect because the proposed solution does not produce the required result.

1.04: Analyzing Company Processes

7. ☑ **B.** The proposed solution produces the required result and the optional result. The diagram you produced accurately shows the communication flow from the sales team to the remote sales force. Remember, this is a tool that can be used to show management where processes are not working—or, in this case, where they are. Your recommendation to upgrade to Exchange and Outlook is a good start, even though this is a small company. The recommendation for additional training is also on the mark, based on your observations of how users are utilizing the email system.

☒ **A** and **C** are incorrect because the proposed solution produces both the required and optional results.

8. ☑ **D.** All of the above. Believe it or not, all of these answers are good reasons to consider the product life cycle when conducting your analysis. **A** is correct because you don't necessarily want to recommend that Windows NT 4.0 be installed when you know that Windows 2000 is almost on the market. **B** is

correct because although the client really wants the latest and greatest, he or she also realizes the benefits of holding on to a stable release of the current product. Finally, **C** is also correct. Although the specs for the new product call for a newer model of computer, the client wants to extend the life cycle of his or her existing investment. In each of these cases, knowing the life cycle of both the existing and future hardware and software are important to making the best recommendation.

☒ There are no incorrect answers.

1.05: Analyzing the Existing and Planned Organizational Structures

9. ☑ **D.** Your company plans to merge with another accounting firm in Philadelphia. A merger with another company will have the greatest impact on your network design. You will suddenly be forced to become very familiar with the other company's network design, and hope that they spent as much thought on its design as you did on your own. If you take the time to build your network properly, it will make the merger go much smoother.

   ☒ **A** is incorrect because the release of an operating system service pack should not affect your network design. It might, however, affect your implementation— but that's another issue altogether! **B** is incorrect in the company of answer **D**, although it can have an impact on your design. If you don't take the time to plan for a new office, it will cause a few headaches. **C** is also incorrect. A new CIO should not have an impact on your design.

10. ☑ **D.** Organizational chart. The organizational chart is the most common way of diagramming the structure of a company. It quickly locates all of the key players in a top-down relational picture, often highlighting the management structure at the same time.

   ☒ **A** is incorrect because the ERD is used to show relationships between business objects. **B** is incorrect because the communication flow diagram is used to show how communications flow between various related objects. **C** is incorrect because the information flow diagram is used to show the flow of information between various business objects.

1.06: Analyzing Factors That Influence Company Strategies

11. ☑ **C.** Management. You recollect data and make comparisons during the management step.

     ☒ **A** is incorrect because during the analysis phase, you create a baseline to understand where the network is before changes have been implemented. **B** is incorrect because during the improvement phase, you implement changes suggested during the analysis phase.

12. ☑ **B.** A large hurricane striking Myrtle Beach and destroying the ten branch offices near the shore. If you did your homework, you should have created a risk assessment matrix to diagram each risk, its probability, and its impact. The chance of a hurricane coming ashore and destroying branch offices would probably have the highest probability of occurring. What's important is to address this possibility and also devise a mitigation strategy to deal with it, such as investing in strengthening the construction of the branch offices.

     ☒ **A, C,** and **D** are all incorrect. Better said, they are not the *best* answers, because they all could affect the merger between the two banks. It is important to create the risk assessment matrix to show all of the risks, with their probabilities, impacts, and mitigation strategies.

13. ☑ **B.** Trade-off matrix. You should prepare a trade-off matrix so that you can document which tasks are of higher priority than others. This will help you stay on track.

     ☒ **A** is incorrect because the communications flow diagram is used to show the flow of communications between business groups. **C** is incorrect because a risk assessment is used to enumerate risks and assign a probability and impact to each risk. **D** is also incorrect; the organizational chart is used to show the hierarchical relationship between employees in the business.

1.07: Analyzing the Structure of IT Management

14. ☑ **C.** Decentralized. This is a classic example of a decentralized administrative model. Each user basically has control over his or her system.

☒ **A** is incorrect. A centralized administrative model would be characterized by a client/server arrangement, such as a Windows NT 4.0 server in each office with the clients logging on to the domain each morning. **B** and **D** are also incorrect because they represent fictional administrative models.

15. ☑ **D.** All of the above. All of these answers are valid reasons to consider outsourcing a project to a third party. In most cases, the decision is a combination of **A** and **B**—you don't feel that your existing staff has the specialized skills to accomplish the mission and you either don't want to or cannot afford to hire additional trained staff to perform the duties. In some cases, **C** will apply because you are overwhelmed with the current workload and don't want to take your staff away from their duties to work on the new project. In any event, outsourcing is a means of completing the project when your own staff is unable to do so.

☒ There are no incorrect answers.

LAB ANSWER

Objectives 1.01–1.07

Here are the answers to the managing partner's questions:

1. The capacity plan is the document that addresses the current network environment. The capacity plan provides estimates of minimum, maximum, and average utilization, as well as data regarding DNS, DHCP, user login, and other dynamic usage statistics.

2. This question forces you to determine who the key decision-makers are in the organization. There is no "perfect" answer—that will come from interviewing the management team and IT staff to determine who is responsible for signing off on the project. The network administrator may be able to provide the answer, or you may have to speak with the CIO.

3. Acme currently is organized in a regional model, with branch offices. It has a wide area network connecting all of the offices. The future plans will change the model to a national model.

4. The client does have products with a finite life cycle—insurance products are very sensitive to regular changes in policy and law. Based on the information provided, it does not appear that any of the products being recommended will interfere with the client's business products. A thorough interview with the client should uncover any possible problems.

5. The company isn't offering any merger or acquisition plans. Although the lab offered the speculation that Acme is ripe for a takeover by JIS, you cannot assume that the acquisition will occur. The organization does plan to expand its operations to four new locations in the western United Sates. This will have a sizeable impact on your design because this expansion will change the overall complexion of the company (regional to national), as well as introduce hundreds of new users.

6. Unlike international companies, Acme is based solely in the United States. There are no restrictions on the use of encryption within the borders of the United States (unlike using anything greater than 56-bit encryption outside the United States). During your interview process, you may want to determine if Acme does business with any partners oversees, as this may limit their use of restricted technology to intracompany use.

7. Currently, Acme is using the decentralized administrative model. Issues will probably arise when the company migrates to Windows 2000 and the centralized model. These issues will most likely fall into the cultural realm, because users and local administrators will have to report back to a central authority.

MICROSOFT CERTIFIED SYSTEMS ENGINEER

2

Analyzing Technical Requirements

TEST YOURSELF OBJECTIVES

nce you have completed the analysis of the business requirements, you can begin looking at the technical requirements of the corporate environment. This analysis encompasses the overall infrastructure design.

You need to examine the current network environment and compare it with the planned infrastructure changes. At this time, you also examine the company's goals. Another part of this process is to study how the network is utilized by the users and to determine the technical requirements that will provide optimum client access. Finally, you need to review the organization's disaster recovery strategy and techniques to determine their effectiveness in both the current environment and the proposed environment.

TEST YOURSELF OBJECTIVE 2.01

Analyzing Corporate Technical Requirements

In this phase you examine the details of the network and its related components. The purpose of this analysis is to see how well the existing network supports the current business requirements.

This analysis goes much farther than just noting which protocols are being used, or what types of hardware have been deployed in the data center. You should conduct an inventory of all software and hardware that is implemented in the organization, down to service pack levels and IRQ usage; collect information on planned upgrades and additions; prepare diagrams of the logical and physical network; identify all of the line-of-business applications that are being used; and look at what security measures have been put in place, such as firewalls, proxies, and intrusion-detection systems.

As you collect this data, you should be thinking ahead to the future network design and making notes about possible pitfalls that are uncovered.

- A thorough analysis of the technical requirements of the organization, its technical staff, and users should be undertaken before a new infrastructure design is planned and implemented.

- The analytical process can be broken down into phases: information gathering and identification, analysis, design, implementation, and evaluation/assessment (including revision, if necessary).

■ Information needed to begin the analytical process includes hardware and software inventories, network diagrams, documentation of servers, identification of line-of-business applications, and identification of security measures that are in place or planned.

■ Forms, customized to fit the needs of your organization, can be useful in collecting needed information

One type of question on the new Windows 2000 exams presents you with a scenario and asks you to draw conclusions about the material that is presented. Don't be surprised to see a question detailing the current technical environment and asking you to validate your proposed environment against the data.

QUESTIONS

2.01: Analyzing Corporate Technical Requirements

1. You have been asked to diagram the physical network infrastructure for your client. What types of information should be included on this type of diagram? (Choose all that apply.)

    A. Network links, such as WAN connections and ISDN circuits

    B. Trust relationships between domain controllers

    C. Server roles, such as DNS, DHCP, or WINS

    D. Network devices, such as routers, hubs, and switches

2. Which of these steps in the analytical process must be accomplished before you begin to analyze the technical requirements of an organization?

    A. Design

    B. Evaluation

    C. Implementation

    D. Information gathering and identification

3. **Current Situation:** You have been assigned to design a network infrastructure for Acme LiftTruck. This company is a midsized manufacturing firm located in Kansas City. It has numerous sales offices throughout the Midwest, as well as two production facilities—one in St. Louis and the other in Des Moines.

   Required Result: You need to conduct a review of Acme's technical environment.

   Optional Desired Results:

   1. Prepare a detailed inventory of the company's hardware and software.

   2. Prepare a diagram of the physical network.

   Proposed Solution: You begin your analysis by interviewing the key business unit managers to determine the business objectives of Acme LiftTruck. You also talk to the CIO to get an idea of the key business processes that he supports from the Information Services (IS) Department. Once these interviews are complete, you ask the network manager for a listing of the network infrastructure equipment, while deploying a network inventory package.

   What results are provided from the proposed solution?

   A. The proposed solution produces the required result only.

   B. The proposed solution produces the required result and one of the optional results.

   C. The proposed solution produces the required result and both of the optional results.

   D. The proposed solution does not produce the required result.

TEST YOURSELF OBJECTIVE 2.02

Evaluating the Company's Existing and Planned Technical Environments and Goals

Evaluating an organization's existing and future technical environments involves the collection of a diverse set of data. To begin, you look at the size of the company, the number of users, and the number of resources. Next, you document how the users and resources are distributed throughout the organization. You also inspect the network infrastructure within sites and between sites, concentrating on the size of the links, the available network bandwidth, latency, and any problems that the users may be experiencing with the network in general.

Other areas you should examine are the performance and scalability of the network services and the patterns of data and system access on the network. You should also look at how each server is utilized, especially if some are used in multiple roles, such as a PDC (primary domain controller), WINS (Windows Internet Naming Service), and DHCP (Dynamic Host Configuration Protocol). Finally, your analysis should look at the security for the network.

- Network and computer configuration settings for each computer should be documented in the hardware and software inventories.

- Both the physical network and the logical network should be diagrammed.

- The company's size and the geographic distribution of users and network resources are important in determining the best physical and logical infrastructure for the network.

- Your analysis should include information about the WAN links connecting remote sites, including analog phone lines, ISDN, DSL, T-1, satellite, VPN connections, and other long-distance connectivity solutions.

- Bandwidth requirements are dependent on the types of applications in use or planned. High-bandwidth applications include live video, streaming audio, computer-aided design (CAD) and engineering programs, and transfer of very large files.

- Network Monitor and System Monitor (called *Performance Monitor* in NT 4.0) are two administrative tools included in Windows 2000 to assist in gathering data to analyze server and network performance.

- Windows 2000 includes many enhanced and new security features not included in Windows NT, and security requirements should be assessed in light of the new options available.

- By monitoring server performance, you can head off potential issues concerning lack of memory or high processor utilization.

■ Monitor the organization's security measures by using proxy logging, event logging, auditing, and third-party products to obtain a baseline of security-related events.

exam
ⓦatch

Analyzing the technical environment is probably the most important step in the network design for a company. In order to provide suggestions for improvement, you first need to understand what technology is in place. Be prepared on the exam to see a number of case study questions that require you to read through a lot of technical environment detail in order to answer the accompanying sub-questions.

QUESTIONS

2.02: Evaluating the Company's Existing and Planned Technical Environments and Goals

4. One of the areas that you will examine during the analysis of the technical environment is network bandwidth. If a customer has a high-speed, leased line, point-to-point circuit connecting two branch offices, with 1.544 megabits per second (Mbps) of bandwidth, what type of circuit do they have?

   A. Digital subscriber line (DSL)

   B. Integrated Services Digital Network (ISDN)

   C. T3

   D. T1

5. Another portion of your analysis requires that you examine the existing network performance. You have been asked to monitor the network and see what network protocols are in use, paying close attention to users sending

NetBEUI traffic. Which of these Windows 2000 tools allow you to capture packets from the network for analysis?

A. Performance Monitor

B. Event Viewer

C. Network Monitor

D. MMC with the Networking snap-in

6. **Current Situation:** Genny's Supermarkets is a regional supermarket chain in the northeastern United States. They have 20 stores in three states, with their corporate headquarters in the suburbs of Philadelphia. They want to perform a network upgrade, and need your advice. They have a 56-Kbps ISDN connection to the Internet, and want to begin allowing their employees to use Internet Explorer to purchase merchandise cases from a business-to-business (B2B) e-commerce partner. They currently use the connection for light email traffic to a POP3 server at the Internet service provider (ISP).

    Required Result: You must provide an analysis of the security considerations for opening the corporate network to this B2B traffic.

    Optional Desired Result: Make suggestions regarding the current network bandwidth to the Internet in light of the new business model being considered.

    Proposed Solution: After reviewing Genny's Supermarkets' business plans and their network infrastructure, you request that the IS staff provide information regarding their firewall design and security plans and procedures. Based on that information, you can recommend solutions to increase the security for the internal network while allowing the B2B traffic to flow to the Internet. You also review the Internet connection information, and feel that the current method of accessing the Internet should suffice for the new business model.

    What results are provided from the proposed solution?

    A. The proposed solution produces the required result only.

    B. The proposed solution produces both the required result and the optional result.

    C. The proposed solution does not produce the required result.

Analyzing the Impact of Infrastructure Design on the Existing and Planned Technical Environments

Another step in the analysis of the technical requirements is to examine the impact of the infrastructure design on both the existing and planned technical environments. This examination includes the following:

- Assessing the current applications used by the organization
- Analyzing the protocols and hosts being used on the network
- Analyzing the TCP/IP infrastructure
- Evaluating the current hardware
- Evaluating network services, such as DHCP and DNS
- Identifying existing and planned upgrades and rollouts
- Analyzing the technical support structure

Your assessment of the current applications should result in a prioritized list of business applications, a plan for testing application compatibility, a plan for handling application incompatibility, and testing of a tracking and reporting system.

The next step is to examine the network and its hosts to see if any unnecessary protocols or client software have been installed. Once identified, you need to develop a plan to remove the unwanted protocols.

An assessment of the TCP/IP infrastructure is a vital step in developing the deployment plan. If the organization is currently running TCP/IP, you should evaluate the addressing and subnetting schemes to see if they are sufficient to support the planned infrastructure. If the organization is running another protocol, such as IPX/SPX, you will need to develop a comprehensive IP addressing plan. This should include the number of subnets required, the number of addresses per subnet, what type of routing (static or dynamic) you will implement, the use of a public or private address range, the use of DHCP to distribute addresses to clients, and the use of Domain Name System (DNS).

Your assessment of the technical environment must include a plan for upgrading or replacing hardware that does not meet the minimum requirements for Windows 2000.

You should identify which network services will be required in the new environment. These services include DHCP, DNS, WINS, and Routing and Remote Access Service (RRAS), to name a few.

Your examination should uncover the planned or anticipated rollout of new software and hardware upgrades or service packs.

Finally, you should look at how technical support is provided to the organization by the IT department. You should evaluate the training level of the staff, look at the possibility of increasing the staff size to accommodate the rollout of Windows 2000, and evaluate the tracking system for support calls.

- You should develop a prioritized list of network applications and test critical applications in a nonproduction environment prior to the rollout of Windows 2000.

- Identify all network protocols in use, remove unused protocols, and review the binding order to optimize network performance.

- TCP/IP is Microsoft's recommended protocol suite. It is important that you analyze the existing TCP/IP infrastructure and address such issues as subnetting; the placement of routers, domain controllers, and DNS, WINS, and DHCP servers; and IP addressing.

- Evaluate hardware carefully to ensure that it meets minimum requirements for Windows 2000. If it does not, there are several alternatives, including upgrade, replacement, phased deployment, and Terminal Services.

- Identify the network services that are critical to the operation of the network and its important applications, including DHCP, DNS, WINS, proxy services, and RRAS.

- Analyze the technical support structure, and document the impact of changes in the network infrastructure on its personnel. Tech support personnel and users should be trained in the new operating system prior to the rollout.

Know the minimum requirements! This objective of the exam will be the first test of your knowledge of the Windows 2000 minimum requirements. Note that the specs have changed since Beta 3, when some of the Microsoft Press materials were released. Just as Microsoft recommends that you consult the Hardware Compatibility List on their Web site, so too you should refer to the minimum requirements list on the Web site.

QUESTIONS

2.03: Analyzing the Impact of Infrastructure Design on the Existing and Planned Technical Environments

7. You are a network architect consultant for a large insurance company in Massachusetts. You are working on a design for upgrading the network from Novell Netware 3.12 to Windows 2000. You have 500 workstations in a single multistory facility in Boston, plus three branch offices with 25 employees each. The workstations are running Windows 95 with the Novell Client32 software. The major applications that are run on these PCs are Microsoft Word 95 and Excel 95. Based on this information, what is the primary network protocol that is most likely in use at this company?

    A. NetBEUI

    B. TCP/IP

    C. IPX/SPX or NWLink

    D. Frame Relay

8. **Current Situation:** You are a network administrator who has been assigned to the Windows 2000 upgrade team. You must evaluate the company's network hardware in preparation for the upgrade from Windows NT 4.0 to Windows 2000. The illustration on the following page shows the hardware currently in place.

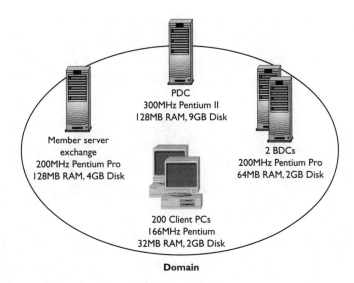

PDC
300MHz Pentium II
128MB RAM, 9GB Disk

Member server
exchange
200MHz Pentium Pro
128MB RAM, 4GB Disk

2 BDCs
200MHz Pentium Pro
64MB RAM, 2GB Disk

200 Client PCs
166MHz Pentium
32MB RAM, 2GB Disk

Domain

Required Result: You must analyze the current hardware and recommend any upgrades required to install Windows 2000 on the primary and backup domain controllers. You should use performance as the main criterion for your recommendations.

Optional Desired Result: You must make a recommendation for upgrading the client PCs to Windows 2000—again, with performance the primary goal.

Proposed Solution: You recommend that the current PDC receive an additional 128MB of RAM for a total of 256MB. You also recommend that the backup domain controllers (BDCs) receive a minimum of 64MB of RAM for a minimum total of 128MB. You state that the client PCs will work fine with their current configurations.

What results are provided from the proposed solution?

A. The proposed solution produces the required result only.

B. The proposed solution produces the required result and the optional result.

C. The proposed solution does not produce the required result.

9. During the design of your TCP/IP network, you consider implementing APIPA (Automatic Private Internet Protocol Addressing) as the default means of assigning addresses to your network clients. What is the most aggravating potential problem with allowing APIPA to give your clients an IP address?

    A. You have no control over what address is assigned to each client.

    B. The IP address and subnet mask that are assigned by APIPA may not match the addresses of your servers and routers.

    C. If APIPA is configured on your PCs, it will assign an address immediately upon startup and not allow DHCP to broadcast for a valid address.

    D. All of the above.

10. The Director of IS has asked that you take a look at her custom applications to see if there will be any issues when you upgrade the network to Windows 2000. She tells you that she has 10 custom Visual Basic applications that are dependent on Windows Sockets, and three that connect to one of your Windows NT 4.0 servers to access a SQL Server 6.5 database using ODBC. How will you analyze her applications to foresee any issues with the upgrade?

    A. Check the application vendors' Web sites to see if they have listed any known incompatibilities with Windows 2000.

    B. Upgrade one of the users to Windows 2000 and monitor that user for a few days to see if the application fails.

    C. Build a test lab, prepare a testing plan, and formally evaluate the custom applications in a clean environment to see if they function properly.

    D. None of the above.

TEST YOURSELF OBJECTIVE 2.04

Analyzing the Network Requirements for Client Computer Access

In this phase you examine the requirements for client access to the network. First, you must determine how the users access the network, and what their business needs are in relation to accessing the network. This can be done by interviewing users, asking them to complete a survey, or simply observing the users during the day. You should perform user trends analysis to uncover periods of peak usage, such as during the morning rush to log on to the network. By combining both of these sets of data, you can get a good idea of client access requirements.

■ The needs of end users, along with their current usage patterns, are assessed carefully in planning the design of the new infrastructure, with anticipated growth taken into account.

exam
Watch

When designing your Windows 2000 network, it is important to be aware of how your normal user traffic will interfere with the Active Directory replication traffic. Be prepared for a question or two regarding the use of sites to keep the replication traffic to a minimum. Using sites also keeps logon traffic on the local subnet—by default, clients will attempt to log on to a domain controller on its own subnet.

QUESTIONS

2.04: Analyzing the Network Requirements for Client Computer Access

11. You are designing your Windows 2000 network, and you need to determine how many domain controllers to deploy to your branch offices. You have a corporate headquarters with 450 users, two offices with over 100 employees each, and a third branch office with 85 employees. Why is it important to know the volume of traffic that is generated during the login process?

A. So that you can let the help desk know when to expect calls about the sluggishness of the network.

B. So that you can accurately size the network links between the branch offices and the main office to accommodate the login traffic.

C. So that you can accurately determine if you need to actually deploy a domain controller to each branch office or if you can let the users log in over the WAN.

D. None of the above.

12. What purpose does interviewing the users about the performance of the network serve during the network design process?

A. It allows them to complain about the performance.

B. It gives the users an opportunity to tell you about things you might not normally hear about, such as constant sluggishness from 8A.M. until 9A.M., or very slow Internet access from 12P.M. to 1P.M., or not being able to access a certain server first thing in the morning.

C. It allows remote users to speak out about nagging features or bugs of the RAS process that you take for granted as a systems engineer.

D. All of the above.

13. After interviewing your end users, you have prepared the following diagram, which shows groups of users, what applications they use, and what resources they access on the network.

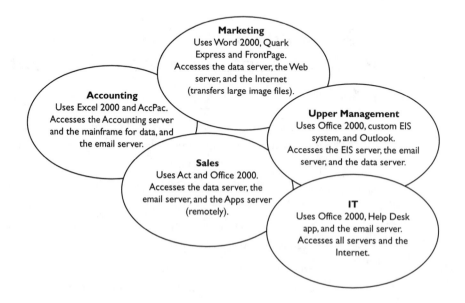

Which of these features would be the most important to add to the network design to support these user requirements?

A. Ensure that the file servers (i.e., Accounting and Data) remain accessible to all user groups via Fast Ethernet connections, such as on a core network subnet connected by switches.

B. Add redundant links to the Internet so that user groups do not lose connectivity.

C. Place one DNS server in close proximity to every group of users so that they can resolve domain names to IP addresses quickly.

D. Build extra capacity in your email server so that users never run out of disk space for their messages.

TEST YOURSELF OBJECTIVE 2.05

Analyzing the Existing Disaster Recovery Strategy

Every production network should have a disaster protection and recovery plan in place. Although the organization may have a number of measures in place, they may not be integrated to ensure the protection of the corporate data. This is the goal of your disaster recovery strategy. This strategy consists of two parts: measures to prevent data loss, and a means of recovering data should a loss occur.

You should be able to explain the disaster recovery features in Windows 2000, including disk fault tolerance, the Recovery console, Windows Backup, and the emergency repair process.

Your analysis of the disaster recovery processes should cover both the client computer and server hardware. You should concentrate your examination on the server hardware, because it is the most vulnerable to data loss.

Finally, you should develop a backup plan, taking into consideration file permissions, backup frequencies, and what data needs to be backed up.

■ A comprehensive disaster recovery plan that includes measures to protect both client computers and servers as well as the integrity of the network itself should be a part of the infrastructure design.

■ Disaster recovery plans consist of two parts: measures to prevent catastrophic data loss, and a means of recovering data quickly and efficiently if catastrophic loss does occur.

■ Windows 2000 disaster protection features include those that address hard-disk failure, damage to operating system or registry files, and complete data loss necessitating reinstallation and restoration.

■ The Windows 2000 Backup utility uses a wizard that guides you through the process of configuring backup options; the utility is started by the NTBACKUP command.

■ Servers are most vulnerable to catastrophic data loss, so protective measures should focus on protecting server hard disks and the data stored there.

exam
ⓦatch

There is sometimes confusion among networking students and even among working network administrators as to the exact meaning of the term fault tolerance. Some will tell you that it refers only to RAID (redundant array of independent disks), a method for providing redundancy of data by mirroring one disk to another or writing data and parity information across disks so that it can be reconstructed if one of the disks should fail. The term actually has a far broader meaning. Fault tolerance is the ability of the computer, operating system, or software to recover from a catastrophic event without loss of data. RAID is a form of disk fault tolerance, and RAID level 1 (mirrored volumes) and level 5 (RAID5 volumes, which were called stripe sets with parity in Windows NT) are supported by Windows 2000 Server operating systems.

QUESTIONS

2.05: Analyzing the Existing Disaster Recovery Strategy

14. When you plan for disaster recovery, you need to prepare for recovering data that has been lost. In most cases, you will use some means of tape backup to

store this data. What should you do with the tapes once they have been used to back up data?

A.   Store them in an organizer in your desk drawer.

B.   Leave them in an organizer next to the server in the data center.

C.   Store the tapes in a fireproof box in your office.

D.   Store the backup tapes at an off-site location or repository.

15. You are preparing the specifications for your new Exchange 2000 server. You are looking at disaster protection, and you want to ensure that if one of the physical hard disks were to fail, none of the data would be lost. Which of these fault-tolerant solutions would protect the Exchange message store in the event of a disk failure with the least disruption to your business?

A.   Installing a RAID5 array on the server, with a minimum of three hard disks

B.   Installing Offline Storage and configuring a fiber channel to the offline storage server

C.   Installing a DAT tape drive and backing up the data nightly

D.   Installing multiple hard disks and putting the message store on one drive, and the transaction log on another disk

Questions 16–18   This scenario should be used to answer questions 16, 17, and 18.

You are working for CareBilling, a large healthcare billing provider, who has decided to abandon its legacy green-screen terminals in favor of a Windows 2000 network. Obviously, this is a large step for the company, and they want to put disaster prevention and recovery at the top of the agenda for designing this new infrastructure.

The company is headquartered in Raleigh, North Carolina. The headquarters is one large office building, consisting of 15 floors. The data center is located on the first floor, adjacent to a cafeteria. There are approximately 700 employees in this facility.

The company has 17 remote locations, which share a building with a sister company. Each location has 30 to 50 employees, all situated on one floor. Each location also has a dedicated server closet for the CareBilling servers and switches.

The current plan is to place two Windows 2000 servers at every remote location. One will be configured as a domain controller, and the second will be a member server providing Exchange 2000. There will be a DHCP server at every location. The headquarters will have nearly 20 new servers, providing everything from Active Directory to Terminal Services. Practically all of these servers will be located in the data center.

16. You start your work by drawing up a disaster protection strategy for the Windows 2000 servers that will be placed in the branch offices. Your first task is to install a tape backup unit in each server and to configure the Windows Backup program to do one Full backup per week and an Incremental backup daily. What purpose does the Incremental backup play in the overall disaster protection strategy?

   A. It allows you to restore the server's data simply by restoring the data on a specific tape.

   B. It allows you to restore a server's data by restoring the last Full backup plus all of the daily Incremental backups since the Full backup.

   C. It provides a means to back up multiple days' worth of data on a single tape, thus saving money.

   D. None of the above.

17. In the days of designing networks for Windows NT 4.0, it was common practice to leave the system volume as FAT, in case you ran into problems and needed to boot the server from a floppy disk. In your design of the CareBilling disaster protection strategy, you decide to complement the NTFS file system on the system volume with the Recovery console. What purpose does the Recovery console play?

   A. It is a utility that you can run to recover the domain administrator's password in case it is lost or forgotten.

   B. It is a utility that can be run from the Windows 2000 setup disks or that can be installed to the hard drive. It allows you to run a number of NTFS utilities against the system drive natively (as opposed to using a third-party tool).

   C. It is a tool that is specifically designed to allow you to recover the Active Directory in case of a disaster.

   D. It is a utility that can be used to rebuild Windows 2000 in case the system volume is destroyed.

18. With well over 1,000 users, you will need to implement some means of disaster protection for the data that is stored on the workstations at CareBilling. Which of these methods will provide the most economical means of disaster protection for the workstations?

    A. Install JAZ removable cartridge drives on all of the computers and configure Windows Backup to perform a daily backup.

    B. Set up a Remote Installation Services (RIS) server to provide the capability to reinstall damaged workstations. Also, configure group policies to redirect folders, such as My Documents, to a network location that is part of a central backup scheme.

    C. Require that users save important data on network drives rather than local hard drives.

    D. Install an additional hard disk drive on each PC and configure a fault-tolerant volume for disaster protection.

LAB QUESTION

Objectives 2.01–2.05

Midwest Telecom is a new communications company that is trying to break into the market. Based in Detroit, they have just contracted to have a new headquarters built, and they want you to provide an analysis of their existing technical environment and then plan a network for the new facility. They are currently a Novell shop, running Netware 5.1 on the back end, with Windows 98 on the client PCs. They desire to migrate their entire operation to Windows 2000 Server and Professional.

Here is an illustration of the current network:

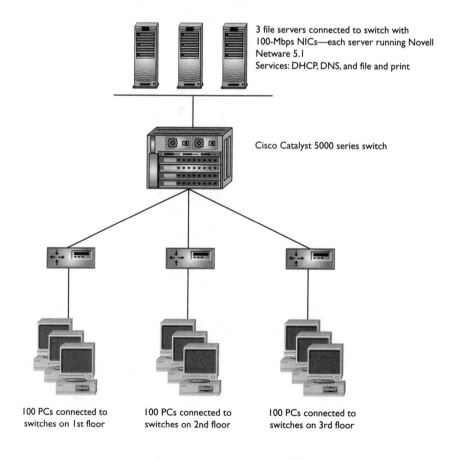

3 file servers connected to switch with 100-Mbps NICs—each server running Novell Netware 5.1
Services: DHCP, DNS, and file and print

Cisco Catalyst 5000 series switch

100 PCs connected to switches on 1st floor

100 PCs connected to switches on 2nd floor

100 PCs connected to switches on 3rd floor

The following chart lists the servers and their specifications. For the most part, the client PCs are all 450MHz Pentium IIs with 128MB of RAM and 6GB of hard disk space.

Server	Processor	Memory	Disk Space	Services
FS1	300MHz Pentium II	256MB	10GB RAID5	File and print, DNS
FS2	300MHz Pentium II	256MB	10GB RAID5	File and print, DHCP
FS3	166MHz Pentium	128MB	9GB mirrored	Groupwise

The company currently employs slightly over 250 people, and it is expecting to grow to nearly 500 employees within a year and a half. These employees are spread evenly across three floors in the current headquarters and will also initially occupy three floors of the new facility. The company plans to expand to a campus arrangement some time after they relocate to the new headquarters.

The following illustration shows the intended building arrangement after the relocation is completed:

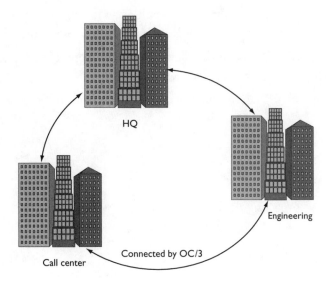

The users are running Microsoft Office 97 and the Groupwise mail client. They also have a customer service application for basic trouble tracking.

Finally, the company would like to implement a disaster recovery policy that can recover a complete failure of all file services within 12 hours.

You have been asked to answer the following questions during your analysis of the technical environment at Midwest Telecom.

1. After reviewing the network diagram, are there any network connectivity issues that might preclude Midwest Telecom from upgrading to Windows 2000?

2. Do the existing servers meet the requirements for Windows 2000? What about the client PCs? Do you anticipate any hardware upgrades being required to make the move?

3. What network protocol is currently being used at Midwest Telecom? Will this protocol work in the new environment? If a network protocol change is required, will anything need to be changed in the routers and switches to allow the configuration to work?

4. Can you run all of the required services for Windows 2000 on the existing three servers, or will the company need to purchase new hardware?

5. How can you determine if the existing network is handling the daily traffic between the clients and servers?

6. Do you foresee any application incompatibilities with the migration to Windows 2000? If so, how can you resolve these issues before the migration?

7. Do you anticipate any technical support issues due to this migration? If so, how can you resolve them?

8. What measures of disaster protection and recovery should Midwest Telecom implement?

A QUICK ANSWER KEY

Objective 2.01

1. A and D
2. D
3. D

Objective 2.02

4. D
5. C
6. A

Objective 2.03

7. C
8. C
9. B
10. C

Objective 2.04

11. C
12. D
13. A

Objective 2.05

14. D
15. A
16. B
17. B
18. C

IN-DEPTH ANSWERS

2.01: Analyzing Corporate Technical Requirements

1. ☑ **A** and **D** are correct. The physical network diagram should include all servers and workstations, LAN and WAN connection links, and connectivity devices, such as switches, hubs, and routers. The following illustration is an example of a physical network diagram:

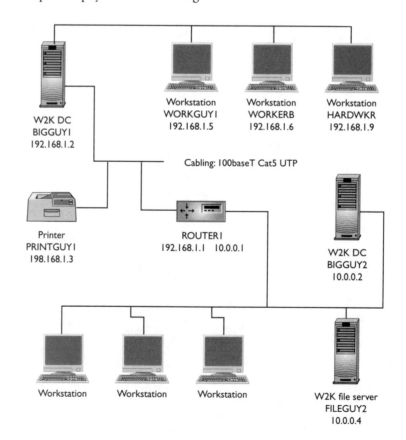

☒ **B** and **C** are incorrect. These represent types of objects that would be found on the logical network diagram. This type of diagram shows the relationships between the network components that make up the domain structure and trust relationships.

2. ☑ **D.** Information gathering and identification. In order to analyze the technical environment, you need to have collected and organized data about the environment.

☒ **A**, **B**, and **C** are incorrect because the correct order of the phases in the analytical process is as follows:

1. Information gathering and identification

2. Analysis

3. Design

4. Implementation

5. Evaluation

3. ☑ **D.** The proposed solution does not produce the required result. A technical environment analysis examines the technical aspects of a company, rather than the business aspects. You began your work by looking at business objectives and processes; these belong in the analysis of business requirements. You should have begun by gathering information related to the network, hardware, and software that had been deployed at Acme, as well as documenting the services on the network servers.

☒ **A**, **B**, and **C** are incorrect because the proposed solution does not produce the required result.

2.02: Evaluating the Company's Existing and Planned Technical Environments and Goals

4. ☑ **D.** The customer has a T1 circuit between the two branch offices. The T1 delivers 1.544 Mbps of bandwidth along a dedicated, digital, point-to-point circuit.

☒ **A** is incorrect. Although many of the features of a T1 are available with DSL—such as being a dedicated, high-speed circuit—it does not come with the

Service Level Agreement associated with a T1. Also, the key to this question is the exact bandwidth of 1.544 Mbps, which is synonymous with a T1 circuit. **B** is incorrect because ISDN is a dial-on-demand circuit, providing channels of 56 and 64 Kbps between locations. **C** is incorrect because a T3 circuit provides almost 45 Mbps of bandwidth. The T1 and T3 share the same characteristics—the T3 is simply a larger circuit.

5. ☑ **C.** Network Monitor. This tool allows you to capture packets that are being transmitted on the network so that they can be examined for errors or for troubleshooting (see illustration).

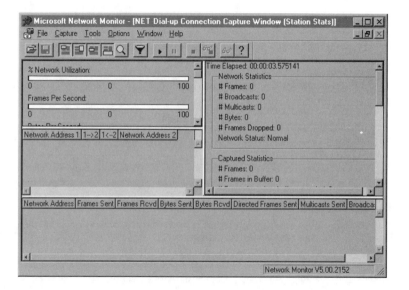

Your network card must be able to operate in promiscuous mode for this tool to work.

☒ **A** is incorrect. The Performance Monitor can provide statistics regarding network traffic and utilization, but it does not allow you to capture packets for analysis. **B** is incorrect because the Event Viewer cannot provide network statistics or a means of capturing network traffic. **D** is incorrect because there is no such thing as a Networking snap-in for the MMC.

6. ☑ **A.** The proposed solution produces the required result. You needed to gather information related to the security of the network infrastructure. By identifying the need for a firewall to secure the business-to-business traffic, you correctly identified the primary security need for Genny's Supermarkets. You

were also able to make recommendations based on the information you received and on your analysis. Your review of the Internet connection was not accurate. The current ISDN connection will not be sufficient or cost effective for this new business activity. By analyzing the company's Internet usage, you should have caught this lack of bandwidth.

☒ **B** and **C** are incorrect because the proposed solution produces the required result.

2.03: Analyzing the Impact of Infrastructure Design on the Existing and Planned Technical Environments

7. ☑ **C.** The network protocol that is most likely in use at the insurance company is IPX/SPX or NWLink. You discovered that the company was using Novell Netware 3.12, and this network operating system uses IPX/SPX as its primary protocol. One step in the analysis of the environment should be the identification of the network protocols that are in use. If TCP/IP is not the primary protocol, you will need to design a TCP/IP infrastructure to support Windows 2000.

☒ **A** is incorrect because NetBEUI is used primarily in a Windows 95/98 environment. This protocol is not routable, and not a good choice for networks that have remote offices that need to communicate with one another. **B** is incorrect because TCP/IP would most likely not be the primary protocol here. You can use TCP/IP with Netware 3.12, but it would not be the logical choice. **D** is incorrect because Frame Relay is not used as a local area network protocol.

8. ☑ **C.** The proposed solution does not produce the required result. The minimum requirements for Windows 2000 Server (posted on the Microsoft Web site) are a 133MHz Pentium , 120MB of RAM, and 2GB of hard disk space. The minimum recommended criteria for Windows 2000 server are a 133MHz Pentium, 128MB of RAM, and a 2GB of hard disk space. The minimum recommended criteria for Windows 2000 Server are a 133MHz Pentium, 256MB of RAM, and a 2GB of hard disk space. The minimum requirements for Windows 2000 Professional are a 133MHz Pentium and 64MB of RAM. Based on these requirements, your recommendation to upgrade the primary domain controller certainly brought it well above the

minimum requirements for Windows 2000 Server. However, upgrading the
BDCs to 128MB of RAM does not meet the published minimums for the OS.
The same goes for the client PCs. By leaving them with 32MB of RAM, they
do not meet the requirements for Windows 2000 Professional.

☒ **A** and **B** are incorrect because the proposed solution does not produce the
required result.

9. ☑ **B.** The IP address and subnet mask that are assigned by APIPA may not
match the addresses of your servers and routers. When APIPA assigns an
address, it is from a pool of addresses in a range from 169.254.0.1 through
169.254.255.254. If your routers, servers, and other statically assigned devices
don't have IP addresses in this range, your clients will not be able to
communicate with the servers or default gateway.

☒ **A** is not correct in the context of this question. Although technically it is
correct—you don't have any control over what address is assigned from the
APIPA range—it is not the cause of the most aggravation. **C** is incorrect
because APIPA only kicks in to assign an address after the client tries and fails
to get an address from DHCP.

10. ☑ **C.** In order to analyze the Director's custom applications, you should build
a test lab, prepare a testing plan, and then test the applications in this clean
environment. Your test lab should represent the common user environment.
Your testing plan should provide detailed steps, including the scope of the tests,
the objectives of the testing, and the methodology—who will test, how they
will test, and so on. The testing should be done in a very controlled manner so
that you can isolate any problems that may surface.

☒ **A** is incorrect because the applications are custom built, not purchased
off the shelf. **B** is incorrect because you should never do compatibility testing in
the production environment.

2.04: Analyzing the Network Requirements for Client Computer Access

11. ☑ **C.** So that you can accurately determine if you need to actually deploy a
domain controller to each branch office or if you can let the users log in over
the WAN. When designing a network to support remote users, you should

always weigh the option of having a domain controller (DC) in every location against having the remote users log in over the WAN. If it comes down to a matter of cost, you may choose the latter, whereas if it's a matter of convenience to the users, you'll probably go with having a DC in every office.

☒ **A** is incorrect because you should never design a network that is purposely sluggish. You should instead go back and review your design to see what can be done to alleviate the sluggishness, without putting the help desk on permanent warning. **B** is incorrect in the context of this question. If you are going into the design knowing that you will have all of the login traffic go across the WAN, then knowing how much traffic there is will allow you to size the links accordingly. In this case, you are still deciding between having DCs everywhere versus logging in across the WAN.

12. ☑ **D.** All of the above. The purpose of interviewing the end user during the technical analysis is to gather the information that your network diagnostic equipment and event logs won't tell you—how the user experiences the network. Many users will find workarounds to processes that don't work just right, or will not call the help desk about network sluggishness. Ask your users to be completely candid because their responses will allow you to design a more efficient network.

☒ There are no incorrect answers; they are all correct.

13. ☑ **A.** Ensure that the file servers (i.e., Accounting and Data) remain accessible to all user groups via Fast Ethernet connections, such as on a core network subnet connected by switches. Making sure that the common file servers, such as the Data server and Accounting server, remain available on fast links would be the most important feature for this design. The one common requirement across all groups is access to resources on the network. In the case of the Marketing Department, they also have a further need of transferring large amounts of data; fast connections would make this process more convenient.

☒ **B** is incorrect because redundant links to the Internet would seem to benefit only one or two groups. It is certainly not the most important feature, considering the number of users involved. **C** is incorrect because most organizations only need one or two DNS servers to support their operations. If this answer had specified multiple DHCP servers, it might have been the correct answer. Answer **D** is incorrect because unlimited disk space on an email server is not a priority, but rather is a policy issue. You should work with your users to limit the amount of space they use instead of continuously adding space.

2.05: Analyzing the Existing Disaster Recovery Strategy

14. ☑ **D.** Store the backup tapes at an off-site location or repository. Although it may present some inconvenience to users who need their data recovered "now," storing tapes off-site provides an additional level of protection for your data. Chances are, if a disaster strikes your data center, it probably will damage your offices as well.

    ☒ **A** is incorrect because you should never leave your backup tapes without protection from fire or theft. **B** is incorrect because your tapes are still exposed to the same threats that might damage your server. **C** is close to being correct, but as mentioned previously, you should store your tapes off-site.

15. ☑ **A.** Installing a RAID5 array is the option that provides fault tolerance with the least disruption to your business. If one of the hard disks were to fail, you could remove it and install a new disk, and the array would repopulate the disk with the data.

    ☒ **B** is incorrect because an Offline Storage server may be able to hold a copy of the Exchange 2000 message store, but you will need to rebuild your server from a backup to utilize the data, which will cause a severe disruption to your service. **C** is incorrect because it too requires that you restore the message store, which will cause a disruption. **D** is incorrect because if the disk with the message store were to fail, you would lose your data.

16. ☑ **B.** It allows you to restore a server's data by restoring the last Full backup plus all of the daily Incremental backups since the Full backup. The Incremental backup allows you to capture the changes made on a daily basis and, combined with a good Full backup, allows you to restore a server to pre-loss conditions. It's usually a good idea to store your backup tapes off-site as another piece of the disaster protection strategy.

    ☒ **A** is incorrect because an Incremental backup only captures the changes made for a specific period of time, as opposed to a Full backup, which captures all of the data. **C** is incorrect because this doesn't describe the Incremental backup's role in the strategy. Although you can store multiple days' worth of data on a single tape, you wouldn't want to do this in production because you would be exposing yourself to risk if the tape were to malfunction.

17. ☑ **B.** It is a utility that can be run from the Windows 2000 setup disks or that can be installed to the hard drive. It allows you to run a number of NTFS utilities against the system drive natively (as opposed to using a third-party tool). The Windows 2000 Recovery console is a tool that can be used to perform a number of tasks against an NTFS-formatted system volume. It will allow you to format disks, start and stop services, and write and delete data from a drive. In the past, you weren't able to do this unless you used a third-party tool.

   ☒ **A** is incorrect because the Recovery console cannot be used to recover the domain administrator's password. **C** is incorrect because this tool cannot recover the Active Directory. The correct utility for this type of work is NTDSUTIL. **D** is incorrect because the Recovery console is not used to recover the operating system from disaster. Windows Backup would be a better choice.

18. ☑ **C.** The most economical choice is to have users save their important data on a network shared folder. This can be done by using a login script to map the drive, and then instructing the users on how to save to a network folder.

   ☒ **A** is incorrect because of the high cost of installing a removable cartridge drive on over 1,000 workstations. **B** is incorrect, primarily because of the effort required to implement the solution relative to answer **C**. However, it might be a good idea to investigate RIS as a disaster recovery mechanism, just in case you do need to rebuild PCs. **D** is incorrect because you cannot create fault-tolerant volumes on Windows 2000 Professional. Also, it is cost prohibitive to install a new hard disk on over 1,000 PCs.

LAB ANSWER

Objectives 2.01–2.05

1. Based on the information provided, there aren't any connectivity issues that will cause a problem with the upgrade to Windows 2000. Each of the servers has a 100-Mbps connection to the core switch, and all of the clients are connected by switches to the core.

2. All of the file servers except for FS3 meet the requirements for Windows 2000. FS3 will need to be upgraded to 256MB of RAM to be compliant. All of the PCs are in compliance.

3. Although it's not explicitly mentioned, this network is running on TCP/IP. Notice that the network diagram shows that DHCP and DNS are running as services on the file servers. This protocol will work, although when upgrading the clients to Windows 2000, you will need to remove the Novell Client32 software and remove the IPX/SPX protocol from the binding. No changes should need to be performed on the routers and switches, although if IPX had been present, you might have wanted to disable routing of IPX on the network.

4. You can easily run the required services on these three servers. Required services are defined as DNS, Active Directory, and DHCP. You might want to leave the 166MHz Pentium as a member server because it has the minimum requirements for Windows 2000. The other two servers should be configured as domain controllers.

5. You can use Network Monitor to capture packets from the network and determine the average bandwidth utilization. You can also analyze the packets for errors, which could be robbing performance from the network.

6. Based on the limited information presented, there might be a problem with the customer service application. By implementing a test lab, you can test this application in a clean Windows 2000 environment and iron out any problems before releasing the application to the production environment. You will

definitely have a problem with Groupwise because it only runs on Netware; you will need to make a recommendation to migrate to Exchange 2000.

7. You should anticipate issues with technical support, based primarily on the lack of Windows 2000 knowledge by the support staff. This can be alleviated by conducting training on the OS prior to rollout, and possibly bringing in temporary help to assist during the migration.

8. Midwest Telecom should implement a backup solution and store the data off-site. The three servers already have a disk fault-tolerant system in place—RAID5 on two servers and mirroring on the third.

MICROSOFT CERTIFIED SYSTEMS ENGINEER

3

Designing a TCP/IP Networking Strategy

TEST YOURSELF OBJECTIVES

N o business can survive without access to the Internet or intranets. This has made Transmission Control Protocol/Internet Protocol (TCP/IP) the de facto standard network protocol on the majority of networks today. Granted, many Novell networks still operate with IPX/SPX, but in order to communicate on the Internet, they must translate into TCP/IP.

You need to have an understanding of the fundamentals of TCP/IP, including comparing it with the Open Systems Interconnection (OSI) model to understand how the protocol stack functions. You must also be able to look at a network design and understand how to assign IP addresses and subnets to allow the network to function properly and efficiently. Once you have designed the IP network, you then need to know how to measure the traffic on it to ensure that your network is working as you had planned. You must demonstrate how to set up software routing on a Windows 2000 server. Finally, you need to be able to describe the various types of WAN circuits.

TEST YOURSELF OBJECTIVE 3.01

Understanding the Fundamentals of Designing TCP/IP Networking Strategies

When designing a TCP/IP network, several things must be taken into consideration. Before you begin the design, you need to understand the main areas of TCP/IP and what components are new to Windows 2000. The underlying theory of the new features is important to designing a fully functional and optimized network.

You need to understand how the Department of Defense (DOD) model compares with the seven-layer OSI model. You should also be familiar with the new features of TCP/IP that have been included in Windows 2000, and be able to describe their implementation.

■ TCP/IP is a stable, routable suite of protocols for multiplatform communications.

■ The core components of TCP/IP have been enhanced with additional security and performance.

■ The implementation of TCP/IP in Windows 2000 adds several new features, such as Automatic Private Internet Protocol Addressing (APIPA), bandwidth control (Bandwidth Allocation Protocol and Quality of Service), and improved security through Layer Two Tunneling Protocol (L2TP), Internet Protocol Security (IPSec), and Encapsulating Authentication Protocol (EAP).

Because Microsoft does not offer an exam specifically for TCP/IP, you will see material about it on a number of the tests, with probably the most detail on this one. If you are familiar with the old Network Essentials exam, you understand the importance that is given to the OSI model. Become very familiar with the seven layers of the OSI model and be able to compare this model with the DOD model.

QUESTIONS

3.01: Understanding the Fundamentals of Designing TCP/IP Networking Strategies

1. You are a remote employee who needs to connect to the corporate network for email. Unfortunately, your office is a long-distance phone call away. Your IT staff does some brainstorming and decides to create a virtual private network (VPN) connection for you. To utilize the VPN, you will dial into a local ISP, and then create a VPN connection to the office's network. What feature of TCP/IP provides for the creation of this communication channel across the Internet?

   A. BAP

   B. PPP

   C. PPTP

   D. SLIP

2. Referring to the illustration below, UserA wants to send a file to UserB. UserA knows that UserB has an IP address of 10.20.4.50.

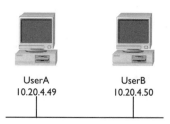

UserA
10.20.4.49

UserB
10.20.4.50

What must the TCP/IP stack do at the Data-Link layer before it can begin to transmit data?

A. Send an ICMP packet to see if UserB's PC responds.

B. Send an ARP request to 10.20.4.50 to get the PC's MAC address.

C. Send an ARP broadcast to 10.20.4.255 to get the PC's MAC address.

D. Send a request to the default gateway to get the MAC address of 10.20.4.50.

TEST YOURSELF OBJECTIVE 3.02

Analyzing IP Subnet Requirements

An IP address is a 32-bit binary number that is converted to dotted decimal notation for ease of use. This address is further divided into the network address and the host address. In analyzing your subnet requirements, you need to know how many hosts will be on each network segment (or subnet), how many network segments you anticipate, and how many wide area network connections your network will have. In many instances, the physical layout of your network will dictate the number of segments you have, just as geography and politics can influence the design.

Another important factor when designing IP subnets is Active Directory replication and DNS zone replication.

- Geography and politics will play a part in your design.
- Active Directory replication can be controlled, but only between sites. Traffic between sites can also be compressed.

■ DNS primary zones can be made part of the Active Directory structure. This provides additional security, as well as multimaster replication of the zone data.

e x a m
ⓦa t c h

Windows 2000 uses the concepts of subnets extensively when referring to sites. A site in Windows 2000 is a collection of highly connected subnets. Highly connected generally means subnets with connections in the Ethernet or Fast Ethernet range. The importance of using sites to segment your Active Directory infrastructure is to the ability to schedule replication traffic bound for remote sites, rather than allowing the default replication schedule to tie up your slow WAN links during the business day.

QUESTIONS

3.02: Analyzing IP Subnet Requirements

3. The AutoGroup Auto Sales Company has multiple locations in the Philadelphia area. The following illustration shows the locations and the connectivity between each site:

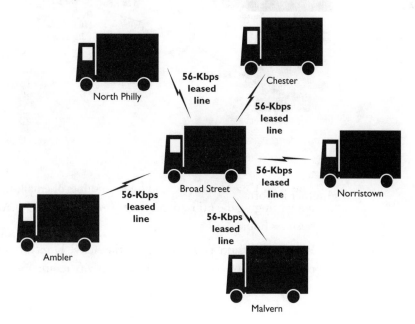

How many subnets are required to support the AutoGroup's IP networking infrastructure, assuming there is one network at each location?

A. 1 subnet

B. 2 subnets

C. 6 subnets

D. 11 subnets

4. **Situation:** You are working on your Active Directory replication model and have reached the site design stage. Your company has offices in Seattle, Portland, Baltimore, Towson (MD), Washington D.C., and New York. The following illustration shows the locations and their WAN links:

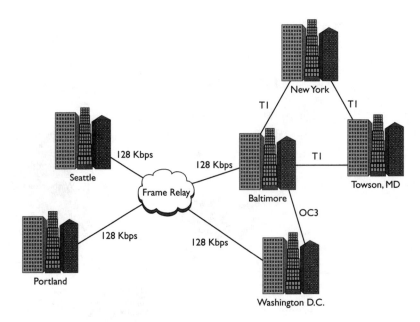

The West Coast locations send huge amounts of email traffic to the WAN, often bringing the utilization of the WAN links to 75 percent or more during business hours.

Required Result: You must define the Active Directory sites for this network, paying attention to the network connectivity requirements.

Optional Desired Results:

1. Identify where Active Directory replication traffic will be compressed.

2. Determine how many IP subnets are being used in this network.

Proposed Solution: You decide to create four sites, as shown in the following illustration:

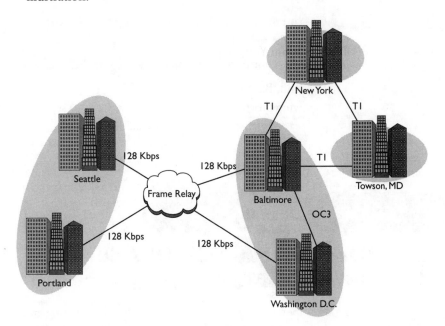

Replication traffic will be compressed between the Seattle and Portland locations, and between the Baltimore and Washington D.C. locations. This network should have at least 14 subnets: one for each location, and one for each wide area network connection.

What results are provided from the proposed solution?

A. The proposed solution produces the required result only.

B. The proposed solution produces the required result and one of the optional desired results.

C. The proposed solution produces the required result and both of the optional desired results.

D. The proposed solution does not produce the required result.

5. You are the network administrator for a telephone call center. Your company has only one location, and only one building at the location. The facility is on one floor, but you have nearly 500 employees at the center. You currently use a Class B IP address with a subnet mask of 255.255.254.0, giving you 510 useable addresses. What technical reason would require you to subnet your network?

   A. You need to divide up the building by teams, and want to keep the teams on the same subnet.

   B. You want to break the network into smaller pieces for manageability and less broadcast traffic.

   C. You want to put a router on the network to separate business units for security reasons.

   D. None of the above.

TEST YOURSELF OBJECTIVE 3.03

Designing a TCP/IP Addressing and Implementation Plan

The most important stage in designing a network is preparing an addressing scheme. When dealing with TCP/IP, you need to choose whether you will use a private addressing scheme, a public addressing scheme, or a combination of the two. You then must divide your network into subnets and assign the appropriate addresses and subnet masks to allow the traffic to flow. Other considerations are the use of Variable-Length Subnet Masking (VLSM) and classless interdomain routing (CIDR) in the design of your network.

■ Use VLSM to subnet your network and to hide the underlying structure of your network from the outside world.

■ Use CIDR to simplify routing calculations, but only use CIDR and VLSM on routers that support them.

■ Watch out for maximum transmission unit (MTU) fragmentation when routing between LANs.

This objective tests your ability to convert from decimal to binary and back again. There are many schools of thought on how you should learn to do binary calculations. Some believe you should just learn it and be able to go back and forth from binary to decimal all day long; others think writing a chart on the scrap paper for the test is the best way. However you choose to do it, one thing's for sure—you have to know decimal-to-binary conversions for this test!

QUESTIONS

3.03: Designing a TCP/IP Addressing and Implementation Plan

6. You have an IP address of 134.10.45.67 and a subnet mask of 255.255.192.0. What is your address class and how many hosts and networks does this subnet mask accommodate?

   A. You have a Class A address with 10 networks and 14,500 hosts.

   B. You have a Class C address with 45 networks and 255 hosts.

   C. You have a Class B address with 2 networks and 8,190 hosts.

   D. You have a Class B address with 2 networks and 16,382 hosts.

7. You have been given an IP address of 38.121.155.33/21. How many subnets will this mask support, and how many hosts can be on each subnet? What is the broadcast address for this subnet?

   A. 30 subnets and 524,286 hosts; the broadcast address is 38.127.255.255

   B. 8,190 subnets and 2,046 hosts; the broadcast address is 38.121.159.255

   C. 2,097,150 subnets and 6 hosts; the broadcast address is 38.121.155.39

   D. 4,094 subnets and 4,094 hosts; the broadcast address is 38.121.159.255

8. **Situation:** You are the network administrator for a midsized company. You have been given a subnetted Class B address of 144.233.32.0/19 for your network. You are thinking about installing a Layer 3 switch in your headquarters in order

to break up the collision domain. You want to create VLANs to segment your network into seven subnets with 300 users apiece.

Required Result: Determine what features need to be enabled on your routers to support this type of addressing.

Optional Desired Results:

1. Determine what subnet mask is required to give the desired number of subnets and hosts.

2. Provide enough room in your design to support the network if it needs to grow to 14 subnets and 450 users.

Proposed Solution: You decide to configure your routers to support CIDR, and come up with the following addressing scheme: you will use a subnet mask of 255.255.254.0, or /23. This will allow you to evenly subnet your network into 14 smaller networks that can support up to 510 users apiece. This will provide adequate room for the future expansion.

What results are provided from the proposed solution?

A. The proposed solution produces the required result only.

B. The proposed solution produces the required result and one of the optional desired results.

C. The proposed solution produces the required result and both of the optional desired results.

D. The proposed solution does not produce the required result.

Questions 9–11 This scenario should be used to answer questions 9, 10, and 11.

You have been working with Johnson Tools to devise a network infrastructure plan. At this point, you are ready to start planning the TCP/IP address scheme for the new network.

Johnson Tools has 14 satellite locations, each having over 75 employees. The main location has one three-story office building, with 345 employees. They have a total of 300 PCs at the main location, plus an additional 30 network-attached printers. The satellite locations have a PC for each employee, plus three network printers.

The main location has three floors in the building. Each floor is connected to a fiber optic backbone and is a separate collision domain.

The satellite locations are connected to the main building via a 512-Kbps Frame Relay circuit. There are no point-to-point connections between the satellite locations. The main location has a T3 circuit connecting it to the Internet through a firewall. The following illustration shows the locations and their details:

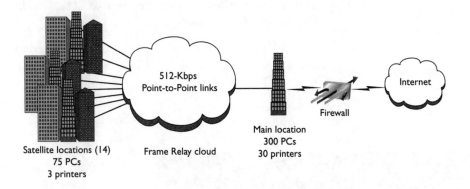

9. Based on the information provided, what is the smallest address class that will support Johnson Tools' requirements?

A. Class A

B. Class B

C. Class C

D. Class D

10. How many subnets are required to support the network that is shown in the diagram?

A. 20 subnets

B. 25 subnets

C. 30 subnets

D. 35 subnets

E. At 40 subnets

11. Your ISP only has two Class C network addresses that they can lease to you. As you know, this will only give you 254 hosts per Class C network address, for a total of 510 addresses, which is obviously too few for your network requirements. What can you do to alleviate this problem without going to another ISP who may be able to better support your needs?

   A. You can use APIPA to provide the needed addresses, and statically assign addresses from the APIPA range for your printers, servers, and routers.

   B. You can use VLSM to sub-subnet the two Class C addresses to provide the number of addresses you need.

   C. You can use a private Class A or Class B network address for your network behind the firewall, and use the public Class C address on the segment from the firewall to the router.

   D. None of the above.

TEST YOURSELF OBJECTIVE 3.04

Measuring and Optimizing a TCP/IP Infrastructure Design

Once you implement your TCP/IP network, you should monitor its performance and then use this data to optimize it.

Monitoring can be accomplished in a number of ways—you can use Network Monitor to capture packets, you can use System Monitor, or you can use a third-party tool, such as a Fluke LANMeter. You should collect a set of data before you make any changes; this is called a *baseline*. You'll use the baseline to verify that any changes you make have in fact worked.

Optimization can take the form of changing the subnet design, or of adding Quality of Service (QoS) to help shape and direct the flow of traffic on your network. It can also take the form of adding redundant links between WAN connections to prevent losses of service.

■ Gather a baseline using performance monitor logs.

■ Design redundant links for your network to ensure constant communications.

■ Use QoS to reserve bandwidth in networks that support QoS.

Quality of Service (QoS) is becoming a hot topic for today's networks. It provides the ability to prioritize certain types of traffic on your network—for example, you can assign a higher value to streaming media as opposed to SMTP traffic. This ensures that your video is smooth while still allowing your email to cross the link, albeit behind the video. This is a new technology for Microsoft, and although it might be covered on the exam, it won't be heavily tested.

QUESTIONS

3.04: Measuring and Optimizing a TCP/IP Infrastructure Design

12. You want to monitor the traffic between your Windows 2000 domain controller and a new PC that's using Remote Installation Services (RIS) to install Windows 2000 Professional. However, you've read that Network Monitor can cause a performance drag on the system that's hosting it, so you decide to install Network Monitor on a stand-alone Windows 2000 server. When you start capturing packets, you cannot see any of the traffic between the domain controller and the client PC. What could be the problem?

   A. Network Monitor cannot be used to monitor client traffic.

   B. Network Monitor must be run on a Windows 2000 server that has Active Directory installed.

   C. The version of Network Monitor that ships with Windows 2000 will only allow you to capture packets that originate from or are destined to the server that has the Monitor installed.

   D. You specified an invalid software key during the installation of the component.

13. You have been monitoring your network for a week or so, and have noticed that the % Network Utilization counter in System Monitor has remained in the high 70 percent range during most of the day. Compared with your

baseline, this represents a large increase in utilization. What might be causing the problem?

A. Lack of memory on your Windows 2000 server

B. A large increase in the amount of daily traffic on your network

C. A default gateway error

D. None of the above

14. **Situation:** You have just designed and built a new Windows 2000 TCP/IP network. You have a number of servers, running Active Directory, DHCP, DNS, and Exchange. You have over 300 client PCs on two subnets separated by a Layer 3 switch. You want to measure the performance of your network so you can tune it for long-term performance.

Required Result: You must choose the appropriate Microsoft tool to conduct your performance testing.

Optional Desired Result: You must provide a means of utilizing the tool with the same settings for your coworkers.

Proposed Solution: You choose to use Microsoft's System Monitor on each of your servers to determine how much traffic is being generated and where it is coming from. In order to recreate the settings, you save the settings as shown in the following illustration:

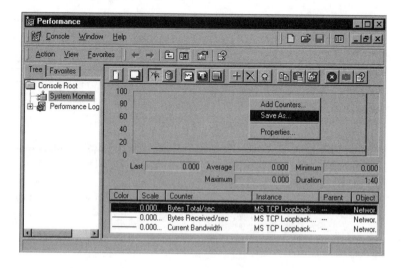

What results are provided from the proposed solution?

A.   The proposed solution produces the required result only.

B.   The proposed solution produces the required result and the optional desired result.

C.   The proposed solution does not produce the required result.

Integrating Software Routing into Existing Networks

Routing and Remote Access Service (RRAS) allows your Windows 2000 server to perform as a software router. This gives you the ability to route traffic from multiple directly connected subnets using one of many routing protocols, including Routing Information Protocol (RIP) version 1, RIP v2, and Open Shortest Path First (OSPF).

RRAS also gives you the ability to perform network address translation (NAT) between two subnets, and adds Layer Two Tunneling Protocol (L2TP) to the VPN feature.

■   RRAS provides inexpensive software-based routing between two or more connected subnets.

■   Use RIP to route traffic in small internetworks where the topology doesn't change frequently and the frequent updates won't affect your normal traffic.

■   Use OSPF when you have a large, frequently changing internetwork, want to reduce traffic, and can spend the time on configuring and maintaining the internetwork.

exam
ⓦatch

An important feature of both OSPF and RIP v2 is the ability to use Variable-Length Subnet Masking (discussed in the previous objective). RIP v1 does not support VLSM. Other routing protocols that support VLSM are Cisco's IGRP and EIGRP. Make sure that your router and routing protocol support VLSM before implementing it in your environment.

QUESTIONS

3.05: Integrating Software Routing into Existing Networks

15. You have a small routed internetwork. The following illustration shows the routers and the speeds of the WAN links between them:

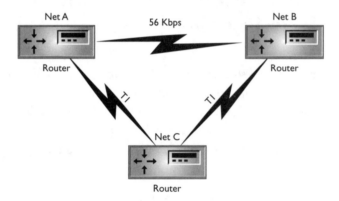

If you are using RIP as your routing protocol, which path will the traffic take to get from router A to router B?

A. The traffic will go from router A to router B because the hop count is less.

B. The traffic will go from router A to router B through router C because the link cost is lower.

C. The traffic will go from router A to router B because the link cost is higher.

D. The traffic will go from router A to router B through router C because the hop count is greater.

16. You currently have a small network connected to the Internet with a 56-Kbps leased line. You have a Windows 2000 server, and you want to segment your network into two subnets using your Windows 2000 server as a router. Once

you add a second network card to the server, you choose to use static routing to allow the traffic on your new subnet to reach the Internet. Referring to the illustration below, what command-line statement will add the correct static route to the Windows 2000 server's routing table to allow the traffic to reach the Internet?

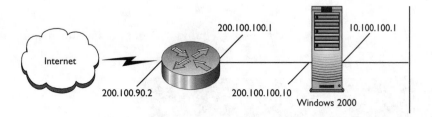

A. ROUTE ADD 200.100.90.0 mask 255.255.255.0 gateway 200.100.100.1

B. ROUTE ADD 200.100.90.0 mask 255.255.255.0 gateway 200.100.90.2

C. ROUTE ADD 200.100.100.0 mask 255.255.255.0 gateway 200.100.100.1

D. None of the above

17. **Situation:** You are designing a network for a multisite company. They want to use software routing based on their Windows 2000 servers rather than invest in additional costly hardware routers. The company wants to use ISDN connections between the offices.

Required Solution: Choose the routing protocol that is best suited for small networks.

Optional Desired Result: Choose the two additional properties that will further reduce network traffic.

Proposed Solution: You choose to implement OSPF for your small company network because this protocol only sends changes to the routing tables when the topology changes. To further reduce network traffic, you first go to the Neighbors tab of the routing protocol's Properties dialog box and select Use Neighbors Instead of Broadcast or Multi-Cast, and then go to the Advanced tab and increase the value of the periodic announcement interval.

What results are provided from the proposed solution?

A. The proposed solution produces the required result only.

B. The proposed solution produces the required result and one of the optional desired results.

C. The proposed solution produces the required result and both of the optional desired results.

D. The proposed solution does not produce the required result.

TEST YOURSELF OBJECTIVE 3.06

Integrating TCP/IP with Existing WAN Connections

Although it may seem easier to create a new network infrastructure, most companies will already have a WAN connection in place. You will need to integrate this existing connection with your planned TCP/IP network.

There are a number of wide area networking technologies that you should be familiar with: T-carriers, ISDN, Frame Relay, and analog dial-on-demand.

- T-1 has high bandwidth (1.544 Mbps) and constant availability.

- ISDN has lower bandwidth, at 64 Kbps to 128 Kbps on Basic Rate Interface (BRI) and up to 1.544 Mbps on Primary Rate Interface (PRI).

- Frame Relay allows you to use more bandwidth if you need it, but only guarantees the specified Committed Information Rate (CIR).

- You should schedule replication to maximize the available bandwidth.

exam
ⓦatch

Although not mentioned in the introduction, there are two additional technologies that are moving up in popularity—DSL and cable. Both offer fast speeds, up to 7 Mbps, but neither offers any guarantee like Frame Relay's CIR. This can be a problem for organizations that require a certain amount of bandwidth to support their operations.

QUESTIONS

3.06: Integrating TCP/IP with Existing WAN Connections

18. You are using a Windows 2000 server to act as a router between your office's network and the headquarters. You have a Frame Relay circuit in place, and you also have an analog dial-up line for redundancy. How would you configure RRAS on the Windows 2000 server to use the Frame Relay connection as the primary link and the analog dial-up connection as a failover?

    A. Configure the server to use the Frame Relay connection. If the link fails, you will reconfigure the server to use the analog connection.

    B. Configure the server to use both the Frame Relay and the analog connections, but give each interface a different metric. Give the Frame Relay interface a metric of 1 and give the analog interface a metric of 20. This will ensure that the analog circuit is only used if the Frame Relay circuit goes down.

    C. Configure the server to use the analog connection. If the link fails, you will reconfigure the server to use the Frame Relay connection.

    D. Configure the server to use both the Frame Relay and the analog connections, but give each interface a different metric. Give the analog dial-up interface a metric of 1 and give the Frame Relay interface a metric of 20. This will ensure that the Frame Relay circuit is only used if the analog circuit goes down.

19. You just contacted your Regional Bell Operating Company (i.e., Verizon, PacBell, etc.) to order a Frame Relay circuit to replace your ISDN connection between your two offices. The customer service representative asked what CIR you would be looking to purchase. What is the CIR?

    A. Calculated Integrity Ratio

    B. Committed Information Rate

    C. Committed Information Ratio

    D. Corporate Information Rate

20. **Situation:** You are the network manager for a midsized financial institution. You currently have green-screen terminals to connect to the company's mainframe. Each office is connected to the data center with a fractional T1 circuit. Twenty of the channels are being used for the telephone switch, while four of the channels are used for data communication. You are about to install a Windows 2000 network using TCP/IP.

    Required Result: You must utilize the existing T1 circuit for connecting to the mainframe using TCP/IP.

    Optional Desired Result: You must be able to perform this operation without spending additional money to lease an IP address from a local ISP.

    Proposed Solution: You cannot use the existing T1 circuit because it is saturated with traffic from the green-screen terminals. You must order an additional circuit from the local telephone company to make the connection. Once that has been done, you choose to use a network address of 193.168.4.0 for your new network hosts because this is a private address range.

    What results are provided from the proposed solution?

    A. The proposed solution produces the required result only.

    B. The proposed solution produces the required result and the optional desired result.

    C. The proposed solution does not produce the required result.

LAB QUESTION

Objectives 3.01–3.06

You are a consultant working for a large book publisher in Minneapolis. This company currently has three locations around the Minneapolis-St. Paul area. Their headquarters building has 4 stories, 325 employees with PCs, and 19 network printers. The second location has 2 stories, 410 employees with PCs, and 35 network printers. The third location has 2 stories, 225 employees with PCs, and 15 network printers.

This company wants to migrate from their existing Netware 4.1 network, which is running on IPX/SPX, to Windows 2000 running on TCP/IP. The company currently does not have a connection to the Internet, but it does have a T3 circuit running between each location, as shown in the following illustration:

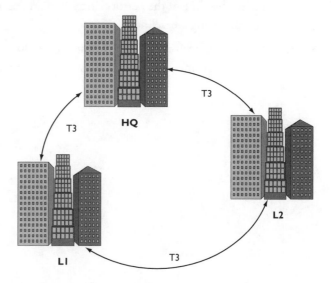

Each of the three buildings has a similar wiring plant: Category 5 cable was run about two years ago to prepare for any future upgrades. The local network managers have reported some issues with performance, but not enough to cause an outage. They seem to think the poor performance is caused by having too many users on each network segment.

Your task is to design a TCP/IP network for this book publisher, using the information provided. Please answer the following questions as they pertain to your work:

1. Since this company is using IPX/SPX, you don't have much to start with. What class of address are you going to need to support this operation? Will your requirements change if you get a private address? What about a public address?

2. Do you need to get a public IP network address?

3. How will you subnet this network to make the most of your IP network address? If you use a Class B network address, can you subnet without using VLSM?

4. Let's assume that you received a public Class B address of 115.34.48.0/20. What is the range of useable IP addresses that you have with this network address?

5. Once you get the TCP/IP network up and running, what tools can you use to obtain a baseline of the performance? Should you make any tuning changes without having a baseline?

6. Do you need to configure your Windows 2000 servers as software routers? If so, which routing protocol would work best for your network?

A QUICK ANSWER KEY

Objective 3.01
1. C
2. C

Objective 3.02
3. D
4. D
5. C

Objective 3.03
6. D
7. B
8. D
9. B
10. C
11. C

Objective 3.04
12. C
13. B
14. B

Objective 3.05
15. A
16. D
17. D

Objective 3.06
18. B
19. B
20. C

IN-DEPTH ANSWERS

3.01: Understanding the Fundamentals of Designing TCP/IP Networking Strategies

1. ☑ **C.** Point-to-Point Tunneling Protocol (PPTP) allows corporations to extend their networks to anyone with access to the Internet. PPTP is an extension of the Point-to-Point Protocol (PPP) that allows someone to "tunnel" through the Internet securely to another private network.

   ☒ **A** is incorrect because Bandwidth Allocation Protocol (BAP) is used to dynamically allocate or de-allocate bandwidth to dial-up users. **B** is incorrect because PPP is a protocol that allows a user to dial directly into a server to create a network connection. **D** is incorrect because Serial Line Internet Protocol (SLIP) is also used to make a direct connection to a server.

2. ☑ **C.** Send an ARP broadcast to 10.20.4.255 to get the PC's MAC address. Before UserA's PC can begin transmitting data to UserB's PC, it must determine the hardware address (Layer 2 address) by using ARP. ARP (Address Resolution Protocol) works by sending a broadcast to the subnet broadcast address (in this case 10.20.4.255) asking all the nodes if they know the Media Access Control (MAC) address for 10.20.4.50. The PC that has a network layer address of 10.20.4.50 will respond with its MAC address in a unicast message back to the sender. Once this has occurred, the data transmission can begin.

   ☒ **A** is incorrect because an ICMP packet is nothing more than a ping. **B** is incorrect because an ARP message is sent to a broadcast address, not a unicast address. **D** is incorrect because the default gateway is not able to respond with the MAC address.

3.02: Analyzing IP Subnet Requirements

3. ☑ **D.** You will need at least eleven subnets to support the network requirements for this company. One subnet will be required at each location, and one subnet will be required for each WAN link.

⊠ **A**, **B**, and **C** are incorrect because you will need at least 11 subnets to support the network requirements for this company.

4. ☑ **D.** The proposed solution does not produce the required result. Sites should contain well-connected subnets. In the proposed solution, the New York, Towson, and Baltimore-Washington D.C. sites fit this requirement. However, the Portland-Seattle site violates this rule because of the connection via a 128-Kbps Frame Relay circuit; the link is also already heavily utilized by email traffic before you even add in replication traffic. Replication traffic will be compressed between sites, not within sites. There are at least 14 subnets in this network: one for each location (not site) and one for each WAN connection.

⊠ **A**, **B**, and **C** are incorrect because the proposed solution does not produce the required result.

5. ☑ **B.** The chief technical benefit to be derived from routing a large network is to create smaller broadcast domains. Having 500 hosts on one subnet will cause a huge overhead in broadcast traffic, effectively crippling your network without even taking data traffic into account.

⊠ **A** is incorrect because it is a political rather than a technical reason for dividing the large network into smaller subnets. **C** is incorrect because just adding a router won't necessarily give you increased security.

3.03: Designing a TCP/IP Addressing and Implementation Plan

6. ☑ **D.** You have a Class B address, and the subnet mask will support two networks and 16,382 hosts per network. By looking at the subnet mask in binary, you will see that it is 11111111.11111111.11000000.00000000. You have 2 bits for the subnet address, and 14 bits for the host address. Using the $2^n - 2$ formula, where n is either the number of subnet bits or host bits, you get $2^2 - 2 = 2$ subnet and $2^{14} - 2 = 16,382$ hosts.

⊠ **A**, **B**, and **C** are all incorrect. Class A addresses range from 1.0.0.0 to 126.255.255.255, Class B addresses range from 128.0.0.0 to 191.255.255.255, and Class C addresses range from 192.0.0.0 to 223.255.255.255.

7. ☑ **B.** This subnet mask will support 8,190 subnets with 2,046 hosts per subnet, and the broadcast address is 38.121.159.255. Using the $2^n - 2$ formula, you will find that 21 bits for the subnet mask will give you $2^{21} - 2 = 8,190$ subnets. You can have a total of 32 bits in an address, so if you subtract 21 from 32, you get 11 bits for the host address, or $2^{11} - 2 = 2,046$ hosts. To find the broadcast address, you need to determine the boundaries of your subnet. The following table shows the subnet information.

Host address	38.121.155.33	00100110.01111001.10011011.00100001
Subnet mask	255.255.248.0	11111111.11111111.11111000.00000000
Subnet address	38.121.152.0	00100110.01111001.10011000.00000000
First subnet address	38.121.152.1	00100110.01111001.10011000.00000001
Last subnet address	38.121.159.254	00100110.01111001.10011111.11111110
Broadcast address	38.121.159.255	00100110.01111001.10011111.11111111

☒ **A, C,** and **D** are incorrect because the subnet mask will support 8,190 subnets with 2,046 hosts per subnet, and the broadcast address is 38.121.159.255.

8. ☑ **D.** The proposed solution does not produce the required result. In order to perform sub-subnetting, you need to enable VLSM, or Variable-Length Subnet Masking, not CIDR, which is classless interdomain routing. The proposed subnet mask of 255.255.254.0 will accommodate the seven subnets that need to be created at this time. An easy way to calculate VLSM subnets is to take the top-level address, which in this case is 144.233.32.0/19, and convert it into binary, which is 10010000.11101001.00100000.00000000. The subnet mask is 19 bits, which leaves 13 bits for host addresses. By using the $2^n - 2$ formula, you can find out how many bits you need to borrow from the host address to make more subnets. In this case, you need at least seven subnets. If you try 3 bits, the formula is $2^3 - 2 = 6$, which is not enough. If you try 4 bits, you get $2^4 - 2 = 14$, which is more than enough. So the subnet mask will grow to /23, which is 255.255.254.0. Since you "took" 4 bits from the host address, that leaves you with 9 bits for the host addresses, which translates into 510 addresses per subnet. Again, this is plenty for your current and future needs.

    ☒   **A, B**, and **C** are incorrect because the proposed solution does not produce the required result.

9.   ☑   **B.** A Class B IP address is the smallest that will accommodate the client's requirements. A Class B address will support over 65,530 host addresses.

    ☒   **A** is incorrect because a Class A address will support over 16,777,200 host addresses—much more than the Class B address. **C** is incorrect because a Class C address will only support 254 hosts. **D** is incorrect because a Class D address is not a valid address to use for networks.

10.   ☑   **D.** This network will require at least 35 subnets. Here's where they are: you will need one subnet for each satellite location (14), one subnet for each Frame Relay point-to-point connection (14), one for each collision domain in the main location (3), and one for the connection from the firewall to the Internet router. This gives you a minimum total of 32 subnets.

    ☒   **A, B**, and **C** are incorrect because the network will require at least 35 subnets.

11.   ☑   **C.** You can use a private Class A network address for your hosts and subnets behind the firewall, and only use one of the public Class C addresses on the public side of the firewall. For example, you could use 10.0.0.0 as your network address. Then, by using VLSM, you can subnet that address and provide up to 16 million addresses for your network.

    ☒   **A** is incorrect because you will not be able to communicate on the Internet with an APIPA address—it's also a private address. **B** is incorrect because you still only have a total of 510 addresses to use with the two Class C network addresses. Your network requires a minimum of 1,000 addresses for the satellite locations alone.

3.04: Measuring and Optimizing a TCP/IP Infrastructure Design

12.   ☑   **C.** The version of Network Monitor that ships with Windows 2000 will only allow you to capture packets that originate from or are destined to the server that has the Monitor installed. You need to use the version of Network Monitor that ships with Systems Management Server to get the full functionality.

    ☒   **A** is incorrect because Network Monitor will monitor traffic originating from any network device. **B** is incorrect because Network Monitor will run on any version of Windows 2000 Server, Advanced Server, or Datacenter Server. **D** is incorrect because you do not need a software key to install Network Monitor.

13. ☑ **B.** A large increase in the amount of daily traffic on your network. A sustained increase in the % Network Utilization counter indicates that the network is experiencing high volume. This might indicate that you need to look at the placement of file servers or application servers to see if they could be grouped together on a high-speed core network that doesn't have any clients.

☒ **A** is incorrect because the % Network Utilization counter does not measure the memory usage. **C** is incorrect because this counter doesn't measure default gateway errors. The Datagrams Outbound No Route counter provides indications of gateway problems.

14. ☑ **B.** The proposed solution produces the required result and the optional desired result. Although you can do this in a number of ways, the System Monitor is more easily implemented on your servers. Once you get the Microsoft Management Console (MMC) configured, you can save your settings by right-clicking in the middle and choosing Save As.

☒ **A** and **C** are incorrect because the proposed solution produces the required result and the optional desired result.

3.05: Integrating Software Routing into Existing Networks

15. ☑ **A.** The traffic will go from router A to router B because the hop count is less. In a network using RIP for a routing protocol, distance between points is a critical determinant when choosing a path. In this case, the distance between router A and B is 1. The distance between A and B through C is 2. Thus, traffic will take the path with the least hops.

☒ **B** is incorrect because it specifies how OSPF works. OSPF takes into account the cost, or speed, of the link in creating its routing tables. **C** is incorrect because traffic never takes the link with the higher cost if other options are available. **D** is incorrect because traffic will always take the route with the smallest hop count.

16. ☑ **D.** None of these statements will correctly route traffic to the Internet—unless, of course, you want to get from the 10.100.100.0 subnet to the 200.100.90.0 subnet. The correct statement should read ROUTE ADD 0.0.0.0 mask 0.0.0.0 gateway 200.100.100.1. This tells the server to send any packets destined for hosts on unknown subnets to this catch-all route. It lets the next router upstream figure out the route.

    ☒ **A**, **B**, and **C** are incorrect because they do not correctly route the traffic to the proper destination.

17. ☑ **D.** The proposed solution does not produce the required result. RIP and RIP v2 are better suited for small networks because of their ease of use and low administrative overhead. Although they send a routing table out every 30 seconds by default, this can be modified through the advanced properties. OSPF is better suited for large networks because of its ability to have more than 16 hops. It takes more administrative time to get it configured properly. If you had chosen RIP v2 for the routing protocol, the settings to further reduce traffic would have been correct. If you configure RIP to only send updates to manually configured neighbors, instead of broadcasting the information, you will cut down on network traffic. By increasing the periodic announcement interval, which is the time between routing table updates, you can also decrease the network traffic. In a small network with practically static topology, you could conceivably increase the interval to minutes or even hours.

    ☒ **A**, **B**, and **C** are incorrect because the proposed solution does not produce the required result.

3.06: Integrating TCP/IP with Existing WAN Connections

18. ☑ **B.** You should configure your server to use both connections, but with widely different metrics—for example, give your Frame Relay circuit a very low metric, like 10, and the analog connection a metric of 150. Lower metrics take priority over higher ones. This will instruct the server to use the Frame Relay circuit as its default connection, until (or unless) it goes down. At that point the server will begin using the analog dial-up connection.

    ☒   **A** is incorrect because you have not configured both connections. **C** is incorrect for the same reason. **D** is incorrect because you have configured the analog connection to be the primary connection, with the Frame Relay circuit as the backup.

19. ☑ **B.** The customer service representative wants to know what Committed Information Rate you would like to purchase. This is the amount of bandwidth that the telephone company will guarantee between your two locations. For example, you might order a Frame Relay circuit with a CIR of 56 Kbps. This means that you will always have at least 56 Kbps of bandwidth available, and you can burst to much higher speeds if the bandwidth in the Frame Relay cloud is available.

    ☒   **A**, **C**, and **D** are incorrect because the CIR is the Committed Information Rate.

20. ☑ **C.** The proposed solution does not produce the required result. The existing fractional T1 circuit will be able to accommodate your TCP/IP traffic, provided the router can handle TCP/IP. There is no need to buy an additional circuit. Also, if you conduct a traffic analysis of your voice circuits, you may find that you can take one or two channels of the T1 away from the phone switch to add capacity to your data network. The address range of 193.168.4.0 will not work because it is a public address. The correct private range is 192.168.x.x.

    ☒   **A** and **B** are incorrect because the proposed solution does not produce the required result.

A LAB ANSWER

Objectives 3.01–3.06

1. You will need all or part of a Class B address to support this network. If you choose to use a private address (i.e., from one of the reserved address ranges, such as 10.x.x.x or 192.168.x.x), your requirements will not change. You will simply have the option to use a larger address class without the ramifications of wasting valuable public addresses. If you choose to go with a public address, you should use the least number of addresses possible without compromising your future growth.

2. You do not need to obtain a public IP address at this point. Your network is not connected to the Internet. You can always use network address translation later to hide your private addresses behind a valid public address.

3. You should subnet your network at a minimum: create one subnet for each office, and create one subnet and use VLSM to sub-subnet it into smaller pieces for the WAN connections. You will need to have at least one subnet for each office.

4. If you received a public Class B network address of 115.34.48.0/20, your useable address range would be 115.34.48.1 to 115.34.63.254.

5. Once you have your network up and running, you can use a number of tools to gather a baseline of network performance. There are two built-in tools in Windows 2000: System Monitor and Network Monitor. In order to use Network Monitor to gather data about the entire network, you will need to use the version that comes with Systems Management Server. The one that ships with Windows 2000 can only see traffic coming into or leaving the Windows 2000 server. You can also use a third-party tool, such as a Fluke LANMeter, or a software package such as Sniffer or CA Unicenter.

6. If you don't already have hardware routers in place, you will need to add a second network interface card to one of your Windows 2000 servers in each location, and then enable RRAS to perform software routing for your T3

circuits between the offices. Given the size of your infrastructure, you could get away with just using static routes between the offices—there is no need to add the complexity or overhead of RIP or OSPF to your network at this point. Because you are using T3s, you may want to seriously consider using hardware routers to route your IP traffic. A T3 can handle up to 45 Mbps of traffic, which could quickly overwhelm your server with routing traffic.

MICROSOFT CERTIFIED SYSTEMS ENGINEER

4

Designing a DHCP Strategy

D ynamic Host Configuration Protocol (DHCP) is an integral part of any TCP/IP network strategy. With Windows 2000, Microsoft has enhanced its implementation of DHCP. To design a DHCP solution for your network, you need to understand how DHCP works and where it makes sense to deploy it.

You need to know how to integrate DHCP into a routed environment, how to integrate DHCP with Windows 2000, and how to use Automatic Private Internet Protocol Addressing (APIPA) with DHCP. You need to understand security issues related to DHCP. You also need to know how to design DHCP to work with remote locations. Finally, you must understand the procedures for measuring and optimizing your DHCP infrastructure.

TEST YOURSELF OBJECTIVE 4.01

Understanding the Windows 2000 DHCP Server

For Windows 2000, Microsoft has taken a good implementation of DHCP and made it better. DHCP is now integrated with Domain Name Sysytem (DNS) to provide Dynamic DNS (DDNS). Enhanced monitoring and statistical reporting have also been made available for DHCP. Other features unique to the Windows 2000 version are vendor-specific and class-ID option support, multicast address allocation, rogue DHCP server detection, Windows clustering support, and an improved DHCP manager.

- DHCP was created from a service called BOOTP, an Internet standard for IP address assignment, and fully supports the functionality of BOOTP, including the existence of a BOOTP table and TFTP server redirection.

- DHCP includes the tailoring of DHCP options based on vendor-specific classes or user-defined classes.

- DHCP includes support for multicast address assignment.

- A *scope* is a logical subnetwork of addresses grouped together for the purpose of assigning DHCP options.

- Reservations allow you to assign IP addresses to machines based on their Media Access Control (MAC) or physical network address.

e x a m
ⓦa t c h

Microsoft's decision to implement Dynamic DNS (DDNS) is geared primarily toward eliminating the dependency on Windows Internet Naming Service (WINS) in a Windows 2000 network infrastructure. DDNS will work with practically any DHCP client, provided you set the proper options for your DHCP server. By default, only Windows 2000 clients will register themselves in DNS. Legacy clients can have DHCP perform the registrations for them.

QUESTIONS

4.01: Understanding the Windows 2000 DHCP Server

1. You are the administrator for a small company that uses DHCP for managing IP addresses. You would like to delegate administrative control of the DHCP console to one of your assistants, but you don't want that person to have administrative rights to anything else on the server or in the domain. How would you accomplish this?

   A. Use the Delegation of Control Wizard and delegate the rights to the DHCP console to your assistant.

   B. Put your assistant in the Domain Administrators group for the domain.

   C. Put your assistant in the DHCP Administrators local group on the server hosting the DHCP service.

   D. You cannot delegate only the rights to the DHCP console.

2. **Situation:** You have a small network consisting of 200 users, 15 network printers, five servers, and one router. You would like to use DHCP to automatically assign IP addresses to your client PCs. You were assigned a Class C address of 210.45.65.0/24 from your ISP.

   Required Result: You must create a new scope on your DHCP server to properly assign addresses to the clients on your network.

   Optional Desired Result: You must configure your DHCP clients with the correct DNS servers and the correct default gateway.

   Proposed Solution: You start the New Scope Wizard on the DHCP server and provide the following information:

   - Scope name: 210.45.65.0 Scope
   - Start IP address: 210.45.65.1
   - End IP address: 210.45.65.254
   - Length: 24
   - Subnet mask: 255.255.255.0
   - No exclusions
   - Lease duration of 8 days

   When asked if you would like to specify DHCP options, you choose Yes. Here, you specify a default gateway address of 210.45.65.1, a DNS name of test.com, and a DNS server address of 210.45.65.2 to be provided with the address lease to the clients.

   What results are provided from the proposed solution?

   A. The proposed solution produces the required result only.

   B. The proposed solution produces the required result and one of the optional desired results.

   C. The proposed solution produces the required result and both of the optional desired results.

   D. The proposed solution does not produce the required result.

TEST YOURSELF OBJECTIVE 4.02

Integrating DHCP into a Routed Environment

Implementing DHCP in a network with multiple segments presents some design challenges that are not found in a simple LAN environment. Because it is the inherent nature of DHCP to rely on broadcasts from client PCs during the lease process, the DHCP process will not work across routed subnets without assistance. This assistance is usually provided by a BOOTP relay agent or a DHCP relay agent. In either case, the relay agent takes the broadcast from the client and forwards it to the DHCP server by means of a unicast packet.

- DHCP is dependent on broadcasts for proper functionality.

- Superscopes allow you to offer more than one defined scope for the same physical segment. This is often referred to as a *multinet*.

- Windows 2000 servers can be configured as relay agents for the DHCP server, that is, designed to relay broadcasts on one network segment to a DHCP server on another network segment.

- BOOTP forwarding is an option contained within most routers that allows them to forward broadcasts on one segment to a predefined DHCP server.

exam
ⓦatch

In Windows NT 4.0, you could configure either an NT server or workstation to be a DHCP relay agent. In Windows 2000, the Professional product cannot be configured as a DHCP relay agent—only the Server, Advanced Server, and Datacenter Server versions will work. If you have a subnet that will not have a DHCP server, you have two choices: build a Windows NT 4.0 workstation and configure it to be a relay agent, or configure your router with an IP helper address (if it supports that feature).

QUESTIONS

4.02: Integrating DHCP into a Routed Environment

3. You have a simple two-segment network, as shown in the illustration below:

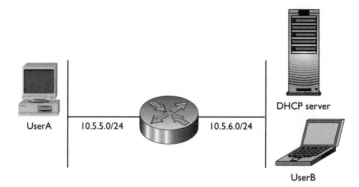

Your DHCP server is configured with two scopes: one for the 10.5.5.0/24 subnet and the second for the 10.5.6.0/24 subnet. What must be done to allow UserA's computer to receive an IP address from the 10.5.5.0/24 scope?

A. You must configure UserB to be a DHCP relay agent pointing to the router interface on the 10.5.5.0 subnet.

B. You must configure UserB to be a DHCP relay agent. Then you must configure the router to have an IP helper address pointing to the DHCP relay agent on the 10.5.6.0 subnet.

C. You must configure the router to have an IP helper address pointing to the DHCP server on the 10.5.6.0 subnet.

D. None of the above.

Questions 4–5   This scenario should be used to answer questions 4 and 5.

You are preparing a DHCP implementation plan for your client, which is a financial services firm with four locations—one headquarters and three branch offices. The headquarters has 300 employees, and each branch office has 30 employees. The branch offices are each connected to the headquarters with a T1 circuit. You plan to use multiple private Class C addresses for each of your network segments.

The following illustration shows the individual subnets and addresses. As you can see, the client is using Variable-Length Subnet Masking (VLSM) on the subnets between the branch offices and the headquarters.

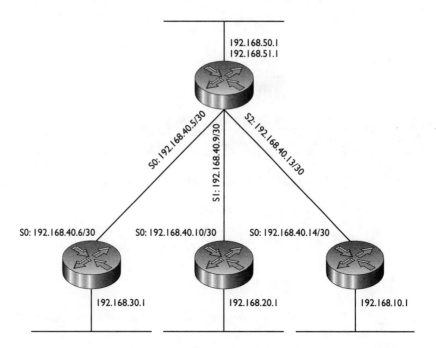

4. The headquarters location has over 300 hosts. If the client is using Class C addresses, it will obviously need more than one Class C address to accommodate the hosts at that location. What feature of Windows 2000

DHCP will allow the server to assign addresses to multiple scopes on the same physical segment?

A. A multicast scope

B. A subscope

C. A superscope

D. A unicast scope

5. If you only have a single DHCP server, how many scopes do you need to configure to support this infrastructure?

A. Four

B. Seven

C. Five

D. Eight

TEST YOURSELF OBJECTIVE 4.03

Integrating DHCP with Windows 2000

The strong point of Microsoft's new implementation of DHCP is its integration with the other Windows 2000 network services. Integration with Routing and Remote Access Service (RRAS), DNS, WINS, and the Active Directory makes DHCP more valuable than the standard DHCP network service and gives the administrator much more flexibility in designing a Windows 2000 network.

- DHCP integrates with RRAS to provide remote-access clients with dynamic IP address assignment.

- DHCP integrates with Dynamic DNS to provide name registration services for clients that do not support DDNS.

- Only Windows 2000 DHCP clients support the fully qualified domain name (FQDN) option that allows them to register their names with Dynamic DNS servers.

- DHCP integrates with WINS by providing WINS server addresses and NetBIOS-over-TCP/IP (NBT) node-type settings to DHCP clients.

■ DHCP integrates with the Active Directory by requiring Active Directory authorization of the DHCP server before allowing it to service clients.

exam
ⓦatch

Dynamic DNS is probably one of the most important networking technologies in Windows 2000. For this test, you should know how it works with DHCP, how to make it work with both Windows 2000 and non–Windows 2000 clients, and how to troubleshoot its operation. DDNS is the replacement for WINS in the Windows 2000 network, and thus you should strive to implement this technology. DHCP is the key to its proper operation.

QUESTIONS

4.03: Integrating DHCP with Windows 2000

6. You have configured your Windows 2000 server as a RAS server. You have configured RAS to use DHCP to assign IP addresses to incoming connections, as shown in the following illustration:

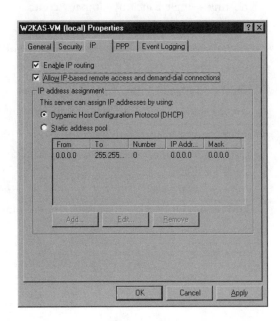

You have a DHCP server on the network, with one scope configured to assign addresses from the Class C address range of 192.168.40.0. You have approximately 100 hosts on your LAN using the same scope. When clients attempt to dial in and use resources on the network, they are unable to do so.

What might be the problem?

A. Your DHCP server has run out of addresses to assign to the RAS clients.

B. Your RAS server cannot connect to the DHCP server to get addresses, and has used APIPA to assign addresses to the RAS clients.

C. Your RAS clients are configured to only use NWLink as a network protocol.

D. The default gateway on your RAS server is incorrectly configured.

7. **Situation:** You are the network administrator for a company that has a Windows NT 4.0 network. You are preparing to fully migrate to Windows 2000, and you would like to use Dynamic DNS to replace your WINS server for name resolution. Before you jump headfirst into your migration, you would like to run a pilot migration at a remote office. The remote office has a mix of Windows NT 4.0 and Windows 95 PCs. You have an existing DNS server running on Windows NT 4.0 with Service Pack 6 at your main location. It is hosting a single zone, mycompany.com.

Required Result: You must configure your network to allow dynamic updates for all of the clients at the branch office (paying attention to the client mix).

Optional Desired Result: You would like to keep all of your DHCP servers at the main location for reasons of manageability and security.

Proposed Solution: You install Windows 2000 Server as a stand-alone server at the remote office and install DNS. You configure DNS to be a secondary zone for mycompany.com. You configure a Windows 2000 server at the main location and install DHCP. You configure it with a scope for the branch office, and set the DNS options as shown in the illustration on the following page.

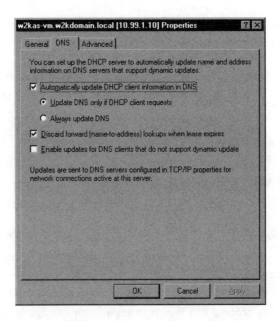

Finally, you add an IP helper address statement on the remote office router pointing to the new DHCP server at the main location.

What results are provided from the proposed solution?

A. The proposed solution produces the required result only.

B. The proposed solution produces the required result and the optional desired result.

C. The proposed solution does not produce the required result.

TEST YOURSELF OBJECTIVE 4.04

Using Automatic Private Internet Protocol Addressing

Automatic Private Internet Protocol Addressing (APIPA) is a feature that allows a Windows 2000 client that has been configured to use DHCP to assign itself an IP address if it cannot get one from DHCP. Once a machine gets an APIPA address, it will continue to try to contact a DHCP server to get a valid IP address.

- APIPA is a feature in Windows 2000 that allows Windows 2000 workstations and servers to self-assign a private IP address when DHCP servers are not available.

- Machines assigned an address by APIPA will attempt to reach a DHCP server on the network every five minutes until successful.

- APIPA can be disabled by editing the registry.

- APIPA cannot be used on a multihomed machine unless both network adapters are connected to the same network segment.

exam

Watch

The most important thing to know about APIPA is that it can cause huge headaches if your clients get addresses in this manner and then need to communicate beyond their subnet. Unless all of your devices have addresses on the same subnet, you will not be able to communicate with them. There are ways around this limitation: you can configure a second IP address from the APIPA range on all of your static devices just in case you encounter problems. Alternatively, you can simply disable APIPA.

QUESTIONS

4.04: Using Automatic Private Internet Protocol Addressing

8. You are assembling a small workgroup of eight Windows 2000 Professional PCs. They will all be on a single physical network segment, and there will be no connectivity outside the segment except for one machine, which has a 56K modem and an ISP account. There are no servers and no network printers. How would you assign IP addresses with the least amount of administrative effort?

   A. When you build each PC, configure a static IP address and subnet mask from the 192.168.x.x network.

   B. When you build each PC, accept the default Network configuration and let DHCP assign an address.

C. When you build each PC, accept the default Network configuration and let the machines get an address from the dial-up connection to the ISP.

D. Accept the default configuration for the Local Area Connection during the PC build, and just place the PC on the network.

9. You have read a lot about APIPA, and you have decided that you absolutely do not want it to exist on your network. Can you force your Windows 2000 PCs to not use APIPA, and if so, how?

A. No, you cannot disable APIPA on the Windows 2000 PCs.

B. Yes, you can disable APIPA. You can do so by going into the Properties page of the Local Area Connection, choosing Advanced Features, and unchecking Use APIPA If DHCP Is Not Available.

C. Yes, you can disable APIPA. You can create a Group Policy Object that will disable the APIPA service on a computer-by-computer basis.

D. Yes, you can disable APIPA. You must edit the registry and add a new value under `HKEY_LOCAL_MACHINE\System\CurrentControlSet\Services\ Tcpip\Parameters\Interfaces\{adapter GUID}`, where `{adapter GUID}` is the globally unique identifier (GUID) for your network adapter.

TEST YOURSELF OBJECTIVE 4.05

Security Issues Related to DHCP

Security is always an issue when discussing networking protocols and services. DHCP is no exception. Although the actual process of assigning IP addresses does not need security—a DHCP server will give an address to any client that asks properly—some of the other processes that DHCP is associated with do need security.

In Windows 2000, two domain local groups have been added to restrict access to the DHCP console. A third group has been added to provide special access to DHCP servers that are configured to register client names in DNS.

Another new feature of Windows 2000 DHCP is the ability to detect rogue DHCP servers and prevent rogue Windows 2000 servers from assigning IP addresses.

■   DHCP is based on the User Datagram Protocol (UDP) and IP protocols, which are inherently insecure.

■ Windows 2000 includes two built-in groups: the DHCP Administrators group and the DHCP Users group. These groups are used to limit access to the DHCP console.

■ The DNSUpdateProxy group is intended to limit the ownership capability of DHCP servers when registering records in DDNS.

■ DHCP servers perform rogue-server detection at startup and during idle times to locate unauthorized DHCP servers.

exam
ⓦatch

The rogue DHCP detection feature in Windows 2000 is a great idea—if your network is a homogenous Windows 2000 network. This feature will not prevent Windows NT 4.0, Novell, or even Linux DHCP servers from assigning IP addresses on your network. If you have a mix of DHCP servers in your enterprise, you will still need to be vigilant when it comes to the presence of rogue servers.

QUESTIONS

4.05: Security Issues Related to DHCP

10. **Situation:** You are implementing a Windows 2000 DHCP solution for a large telemarketing client. They have five offices, with approximately 1,000 users at each location. You are planning on having four DHCP servers, grouped in pairs for redundancy. You currently have Windows 95 clients deployed throughout the enterprise, but you will be upgrading them to Windows 2000 Professional concurrently with the DHCP upgrade.

Required Result: You must ensure that only members of the Enterprise Administrators group have access for changing the scopes on the DHCP servers.

Optional Desired Results:

1. Allow the Windows 95 PCs to get registered in DNS.

2. Ensure that they are still able to do so once you migrate to Windows 2000.

Proposed Solution: To ensure that only the members of the Enterprise Administrators group can have access to change the scopes on the DHCP servers, you put the Enterprise Administrators group in the DHCP Administrators local group on each DHCP server. To enable the Windows 95 PCs to get registered in DNS, you configure the primary DNS zone to allow dynamic updates, and on the Properties page for the DHCP servers, you choose Automatically Update DHCP Client Information in DNS and select Always Update DNS on the DNS tab.

What results are provided from the proposed solution?

A. The proposed solution produces the required result only.

B. The proposed solution produces the required result and one of the optional desired results.

C. The proposed solution produces the required result and both of the optional desired results.

D. The proposed solution does not produce the required result.

11. You are the administrator for two Windows 2000 domains in a publishing company. Each domain has its own set of services (i.e., a separate DNS or DHCP). You want to bring up an additional DHCP server on a Windows 2000 server in stand-alone mode, simply because you want it to work for both of the existing domains. After you build the server and create the scopes on DHCP, you find that it's not assigning addresses to any clients. What is the most likely problem?

A. The scope you created is not appropriate for the physical subnet the server is located on.

B. You neglected to authorize the server in the two domains.

C. You didn't enable the scope on the DHCP server.

D. Your clients aren't configured to use DHCP.

TEST YOURSELF OBJECTIVE 4.06

Designing a DHCP Service for Remote Locations

Implementing DHCP in a large network environment will almost certainly require a solution for remote locations. Often, remote locations are connected to the main network through dial-up networking or other limited-bandwidth connections. To make sure these clients receive the addresses needed to function on the network, you must carefully plan how DHCP will relay addresses to these clients.

■ Lease lengths can be modified to reduce network traffic for remote locations.

■ Relay agents should not be used on network segments that do not have leased-line access to the DHCP server.

■ RRAS clients that access the network from a remote location will be assigned an address when they dial in and do not require a local DHCP server (unless they need to communicate on their local network as well).

exam
ⓦatch

Make sure that you are thoroughly familiar with Routing and Remote Access Service in Windows 2000. An IP address is necessary for connectivity on a network, and RRAS is essentially a connectivity service. A study of Windows 2000 networking is not complete without a good understanding of RRAS.

QUESTIONS

4.06: Designing a DHCP Service for Remote Locations

12. Your company is preparing to open a new office in a small town in Delaware. It will have four employees, each having a Windows 2000 Professional PC. You plan to install a small Ethernet network for workgroup connectivity, and you also plan to connect a laser printer to one of the machines and share it for the rest of the office's use. All of these employees need access to the Internet and the company's network for email and file access. What is the best way to provide these employees with dynamic addressing from your company's Class C address scope?

    A. You can install a modem in each machine and configure RRAS to dial in to a RAS server at the headquarters location. Once this connection is made, you can assign an IP address from the RAS server.

B. You can install a fractional T-1 circuit with 256 Kbps between the remote office and the headquarters, and add an IP helper address on the router to relay DHCP messages to the DHCP server on the corporate LAN.

C. You can put a Windows 2000 server in the office and install DHCP on it to assign addresses from the company's scope. Then you can install an SDSL (symmetric DSL) circuit and use a virtual private network to connect to the corporate network.

D. You can install an ISDN circuit or an SDSL circuit to provide connectivity to the corporate LAN, and configure a DHCP relay agent on the router to pass DHCP requests to the corporate DHCP server.

13. You are designing a remote office DHCP implementation for your new Windows 2000 network. The following illustration shows the network infrastructure:

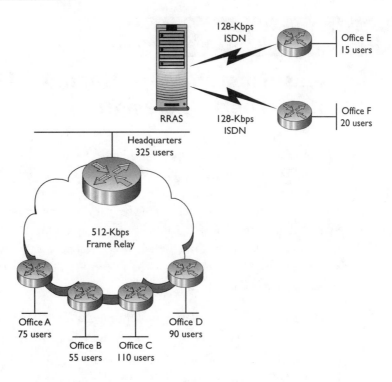

Your headquarters building is connected to four branch offices by a 512-Kbps Frame Relay circuit. There are 325 users at the headquarters, and anywhere from 55 to 110 users at the branch offices in the Frame Relay cloud. You also have two smaller offices, with 15 and 20 users, that are connected to the corporate network via a 128-Kbps ISDN connection to an RRAS server. Where should you place DHCP servers and relay agents for the optimum and most cost-effective DHCP design?

A. Place a DHCP server in every office. Do not use relay agents.

B. Place a DHCP server at the headquarters and the two ISDN-connected offices, and configure DHCP relay agents at the four branch offices.

C. Place a DHCP server at the headquarters, and put DHCP relay agents at all of the branch offices.

D. Place a DHCP server at the headquarters and the four Frame Relay–connected branch offices, and configure DHCP relay agents at the ISDN-connected branch offices.

TEST YOURSELF OBJECTIVE 4.07

Measuring and Optimizing a DHCP Infrastructure Design

Just as it's important to understand how DHCP works and how to configure it for basic operation, so too it's important to understand how to measure the performance of your DHCP implementation, optimize it, and build fault tolerance into the system.

Modifying the default lease times for addresses will affect how much network traffic your clients generate. Also, performing regular maintenance on the DHCP database will allow it to perform more efficiently in a large environment.

Fault tolerance in the DHCP design is critical because if you lose the service of your DHCP server, your clients may not be able to get addresses when they need them or when they try to renew them.

■ The *lease length* is the amount of time that the DHCP server will allow a client in a particular scope to retain an IP address before renewing the address.

■ A *distributed scope* is a method of distributing the load and responsibility of DHCP to two or more servers on your network that reside in the same segment.

- DHCP supports Microsoft Clustering Services.

- DHCP is managed by the DHCP plug-in for the Microsoft Management Console (MMC).

- The Windows 2000 performance monitor can monitor DHCP server performance.

- DHCP logs are written to the %systemroot%\system32\dhcp directory in ASCII format.

- JETPACK.EXE is a command-line utility used for compacting and repairing the DHCP database.

exam

ⓦatch

The rule associated with designing fault tolerance in DHCP is the 80/20 rule: if you have two DHCP servers configured to provide fault tolerance for two scopes, each server should hold 80 percent of the addresses for its scope and 20 percent of the addresses for the other server's scope. This way, if the primary DHCP server goes down, the backup server will still be able to assign up to 20 percent of the addresses from the scope. Remember this rule because you might find it on the test.

QUESTIONS

4.07: Measuring and Optimizing a DHCP Infrastructure Design

14. You are the network manager for a large computer conference. You are expecting to have 4,100 conference attendees, most of whom will be bringing a laptop with them. As part of the conference amenities, you are providing network access for the attendees so they can check their email, stocks, etc. You have a 100-Mbps network, and you have a subnetted Class B address with a 20-bit subnet mask to use for the attendees. How should you configure the lease duration in the DHCP scope for this event?

    A. Leave it at the default—it doesn't make a difference.

    B. Change the lease duration to 2 hours.

    C. Change the lease duration to 8 hours.

    D. Change the lease duration to 14 days.

15. You have a DHCP server running on a Windows NT 4.0 server. It has a number of scopes configured, as well as a number of options set for each scope. You are bringing up a new Windows 2000 server and you want to run DHCP on it. Instead of recreating the DHCP information on the new server, you just want to migrate the existing database to the new server.

What steps are required to successfully move the DHCP database?

    A. Make a backup of the database, copy it to the new server, and start the DHCP service.

    B. Make a backup of the database, export the scope registry entries, copy the database to the new server, import the registry entries, and start the DHCP service.

    C. Connect the two servers and run the Migration Wizard.

    D. None of the above.

LAB QUESTION

Objectives 4.01–4.07

You have been asked to design a DHCP infrastructure for a new client. This particular client has been a Netware IPX/SPX shop for a number of years and has decided to migrate to Windows 2000 and TCP/IP. They will be using the network address of 10.100.0.0/16. You can subnet this address in any manner you see fit. Please describe how you will design this DHCP infrastructure based on the following network information. You must take into account all aspects of a proper DHCP design.

This client has a headquarters, two branch offices connected via 256-Kbps Frame Relay circuits, four branch offices connected with 56-Kbps Frame Relay circuits, and 30 employees who work from their homes and dial in to RAS with 56-Kbps modems. The following illustration shows the network:

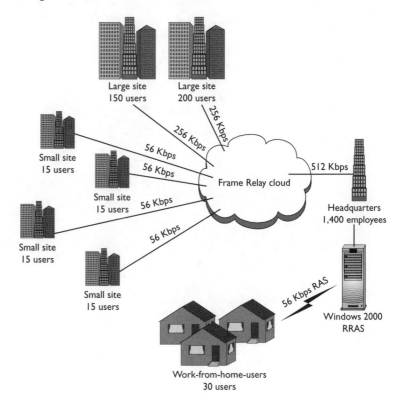

The large sites are connected to the Frame Relay cloud with Cisco 2600 series routers, and the small sites are connected with Cisco 1600 series routers, all running the latest version of the Cisco IOS operating system. The home users will dial in to a Windows 2000 server running RRAS. The server has a multiport serial card that will handle 32 simultaneous connections.

QUICK ANSWER KEY

Objective 4.01
1. C
2. D

Objective 4.02
3. C
4. C
5. C

Objective 4.03
6. B
7. C

Objective 4.04
8. D
9. D

Objective 4.05
10. B
11. B

Objective 4.06
12. D
13. B

Objective 4.07
14. C
15. B

IN-DEPTH ANSWERS

4.01: Understanding the Windows 2000 DHCP Server

1. ☑   **C.** You can put your assistant in the DHCP Administrators local group on the server that is running DHCP (see settings in the following illustration).

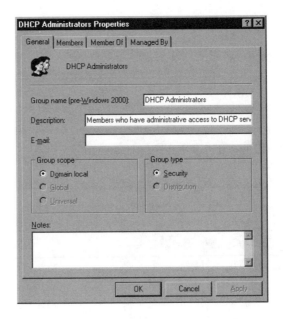

This will give the assistant the ability to fully manage and modify any data at the DHCP server, but without providing unlimited administrative access, such as if the local Administrators group were used instead to provide administrative access to the applicable DHCP server.

☒   **A** is incorrect because you cannot delegate this authority using the Delegation of Control Wizard. **B** is incorrect because it will give the assistant too much access, including the ability to manage user accounts. **D** is incorrect because you can delegate these rights by using the DHCP Administrators local group.

2. ☑ **D.** The proposed solution does not produce the required result. You only have a Class C address for your entire network. That gives you a total of 254 host addresses. Your scope was configured to lease out all 254 addresses to clients. Your scope included the .1 address, which you also configured as the default gateway for your subnet. You will most likely find that your clients cannot access anything outside of the network because the .1 address was assigned to a host PC. You should have configured an exclusion range for your router, servers, and printers so they could have static addresses that won't be given out to a client PC.

☒ **A**, **B**, and **C** are incorrect because the proposed solution does not produce the required result.

4.02: Integrating DHCP into a Routed Environment

3. ☑ **C.** In order for UserA's computer to receive an IP address from the DHCP server on the 10.5.6.0 subnet, the router must be configured with an IP helper address pointing to the DHCP server. This tells the router to intercept any broadcasts for DHCP and relay them via unicast to the DHCP server.

☒ **A** is incorrect because UserB will never hear the broadcast from UserA. The router will not forward any broadcasts. The DHCP relay agent needs to be on a segment that does not have a DHCP server. **B** is also incorrect, because the DHCP relay agent must be on the segment that does not have a DHCP server. Also, you don't configure an IP helper address on a router to point to another relay agent.

4. ☑ **C.** A superscope will allow you to assign addresses to multiple scopes on a single physical subnet. By grouping two or more scopes together into a superscope, you can extend a scope that is running low on addresses to a second or third scope that may have addresses to spare.

☒ **A** is incorrect because a multicast scope is for allocating multicast addresses for use with a Multicast Address Dynamic Client Allocation Protocol (MADCAP) server. **B** and **D** are both meaningless terms.

5. ☑ **C.** You need to configure five scopes to support this network infrastructure. You will need a scope for the following subnets: 192.168.10.0, 192.168.20.0, 192.168.30.0, 192.168.50.0, and 192.168.51.0. You will then need to combine the last two scopes—192.168.50.0 and 192.168.51.0—into a superscope.

   ☒ **A**, **B**, and **D** are incorrect because they specify the incorrect number of subnets. You don't need a scope for any of the WAN subnets.

4.03: Integrating DHCP with Windows 2000

6. ☑ **B.** Your RAS server cannot connect to the DHCP server to get addresses, and has used APIPA to assign addresses to the RAS clients. If your RAS server is configured to use DHCP to assign addresses, it will acquire blocks of ten addresses from the DHCP server to assign to RAS clients. If the RAS server cannot get addresses from the DHCP server, it will use automatic private IP addressing to assign addresses to the RAS clients. When this occurs, the RAS clients will have addresses from the APIPA range, which most likely will not match the subnet of your network.

   ☒ **A** is incorrect because your DHCP scope is configured for a full Class C address and has only assigned 100 addresses to hosts on the LAN. This leaves plenty of addresses for RAS. **C** is incorrect because DHCP cannot assign addresses to NWLink clients. **D** is incorrect because the default gateway on the RAS server has nothing to do with its ability to assign addresses.

7. ☑ **C.** The proposed solution does not produce the required result. The Windows 2000 DNS server is the secondary zone for the domain, and you cannot configure a secondary zone to allow dynamic updates.

   There are a number of things that must be configured for Dynamic DNS to work properly. First, you must have a Windows 2000 DNS server holding the primary zone for the domain. Second, you need clients that can either (a) register themselves in DNS or (b) have a DHCP server register the client's record in DNS for them. Next, you must instruct your DNS primary zone to allow dynamic updates. Once these prerequisites have been met, your Windows 2000 clients will contact the DNS server by default and try to register themselves.

   Since the remote office is purely Windows 2000 (remember, you're doing a migration pilot for this office), the clients do not need DHCP to register anything for them. It doesn't matter that the DHCP server is located across a WAN link.

☒ **A, B**, and **D** are incorrect because the proposed solution does not produce the required result.

4.04: Using Automatic Private IP Addressing

8. ☑ **D.** Accept the default configuration for the Local Area Connection during the PC build, and just place the PC on the network. By choosing the default configuration, you are instructing the PC to use DHCP. By just placing it on the network when the configuration is complete, you are expecting the PC to get an address from DHCP. If it cannot find a DHCP server, it will use APIPA to assign an address. This will work for the remaining seven PCs, and they will all be able to communicate with each other using the APIPA-assigned addresses.

☒ **A** is incorrect because you would now be managing the IP addresses, which, even with eight PCs, is an administrative effort. **B** is incorrect because you don't have a DHCP server on your network. **C** is incorrect because your machines cannot get IP addresses from the ISP by going through a dial-up connection.

9. ☑ **D.** Yes, you can disable APIPA by adding a registry value on each Windows 2000 PC. You must add a value called IPAutoconfigurationenabled, of type REG_DWORD, with a Hex value of 0.

☒ **A** is incorrect because it is possible to disable APIPA. **B** is incorrect because there isn't a setting in the Local Area Connection properties for disabling APIPA. **C** is incorrect because there isn't a GPO for disabling APIPA (although it would be nice!).

4.05: Security Issues Related to DHCP

10. ☑ **B.** The proposed solution produces the required result and one of the optional desired results. By putting the Enterprise Administrators group in the DHCP Administrators local group, you are able to allow them to have change

access to DHCP settings from the console. All of the steps that you performed to allow the Windows 95 PCs to get registered in DNS are correct. However, when you upgrade your clients to Windows 2000, their ability to register themselves in DNS will fail because the DHCP server is the owner of the registration record. You need to place the DHCP server object in the DNSUpdateProxy group so that it will relinquish ownership of the DNS records that it adds for the clients.

☒ **A, C**, and **D** are incorrect because the proposed solution produces the required result and one of the optional desired results.

11. ☑ **B.** The most likely problem is that you failed to authorize your new DHCP server in either of the two Windows 2000 domains. When a Windows 2000 DHCP server starts, it checks with the directory services to see if it is on the authorized servers list. If not, it stops itself and records an error in its event log.

☒ **A** is not correct because even an incorrect scope would give out addresses. **C** is incorrect because the MMC would indicate that the scope had been activated. **D** is incorrect because we already know that the clients are working with the other DHCP servers.

4.06: Designing a DHCP Service for Remote Locations

12. ☑ **D.** The best way to provide addressing is to configure a low-bandwidth connection to the corporate LAN and have a router-based DHCP relay agent pass DHCP messages to the corporate DHCP server.

☒ **A** is incorrect. Although it does succeed in getting an IP address for each machine, you are taking a costly approach to providing access. **B** is incorrect because you are again spending a lot of money to provide basic connectivity to a small number of clients. **C** is incorrect because you are overengineering a simple solution by adding a Windows 2000 server just for DHCP services.

13. ☑ **B.** You should put a DHCP server at the headquarters and have the four Frame Relay–connected branch offices use DHCP relay agents to send the messages to the enterprise DHCP server. This is mainly done because of the large amount of bandwidth you have available across the Frame Relay cloud. You should put a DHCP server at each ISDN-connected office so that you can ensure that addresses are always available regardless of the status of the ISDN

connection. This solution provides the optimum and most cost-effective choice for your DHCP server design.

☒ **A** is incorrect because you are spending a lot of money putting extra Windows 2000 servers in every office. **C** is incorrect, but not improbable. This solution will also work, if you set the lease times to 15 or 20 days to ensure that the network interface cards (NICs) aren't trying to renew their IP addresses every four days. **D** is incorrect, but again only because of cost effectiveness.

4.07: Measuring and Optimizing a DHCP Infrastructure Design

14. ☑ **C.** The best answer would be to change the lease duration to eight hours. The default is eight days, if you recall, which would allow someone who connected on the first day of the conference to hold the same IP address for at least four days. However, you only have 4,094 possible addresses in your scope. If more than 4,094 conference attendees decide to check their mail at the same time, you will have a problem. In this case, it's better to have more network traffic than to have attendees not get addresses. Here you are betting that you won't exhaust all of your addresses before the leases expire.

☒ **A** is incorrect because it allows clients to hold addresses for the duration of the conference; since the number of addresses is tight, this would not be a good idea. **B** is incorrect mainly because of the amount of network broadcast traffic this setting would cause. **D** is incorrect because this setting causes the same problems as the eight-day lease.

15. ☑ **B.** To successfully move the database from a Windows NT 4.0 server to Windows 2000, you must export the registry entries for the scopes to a file, make a backup copy of the database and copy it to the new server, import the Registry entries to the registry of the new server, and start the DHCP service.

☒ **A** is incorrect because it doesn't account for the registry entries. **C** is incorrect because there isn't a Migration Wizard for the DHCP database.

LAB ANSWER

Objectives 4.01–4.07

First, you need to come up with a rough TCP/IP addressing plan. The address you have been given to work with will support up to 65,534 host addresses on one subnet. Since you have multiple sites and WAN connections, you will need to break this address into smaller pieces using VLSM. We'll use a subnet mask of 255.255.240.0 to break our Class B address into 14 subnets of 4,094 addresses.

You should place a DHCP server at each branch office for the following reasons: the two large sites have enough employees that the DHCP traffic across the WAN may cause noticeable congestion. The four small sites have very slow links, and the DHCP traffic will definitely cause noticeable congestion. You should place two DHCP servers at the headquarters location for redundancy and performance—1,400 users can put quite a strain on a single DHCP server. To service the RAS users, configure the RAS server to get addresses from DHCP.

For redundancy, configure each of the headquarters' DHCP servers using the 80/20 rule to allow them to share the load of assigning addresses.

For security, place the users who are to administer the DHCP servers in the DHCP Administrators local group on each server.

5

Designing a DNS Strategy

T he Domain Name System (DNS) is at the heart of Windows 2000. It is so essential to the function of a Windows 2000 network that you cannot install Active Directory (AD) until you have an appropriate DNS Server functioning on the network.

You will need to have a firm understanding of basic DNS concepts and how Windows 2000 implements DNS. You will also need to know how to create a DNS namespace that is functional for both DNS and Active Directory.

You must be familiar with creating DNS designs that are integrated, secure, and highly available. Finally, you must be able to measure the performance of your DNS infrastructure and optimize it.

TEST YOURSELF OBJECTIVE 5.01

Understanding the Windows 2000 Dynamic DNS Server

DNS is a service that resolves domain names to IP addresses. Windows 2000 implements a version of DNS that adds a number of features to the basic DNS implementation.

Windows 2000 DNS uses both primary and secondary servers to hold the zone files. It also allows you to integrate this DNS information into the Active Directory, a feature that gives you the ability to distribute the zone information quickly and securely. Another feature of Windows 2000 DNS is incremental zone transfers, which are transfers of only records that have changed. Finally, Windows 2000 DNS supports dynamic updates to its databases, and the use of service (SRV) records to map IP addresses to services on hosts.

- DNS is a database system that is designed to map fully qualified domain names to IP addresses.

- The four traditional DNS server roles are primary, secondary, master, and caching. In Windows 2000 DNS, Microsoft refers to the first two of these roles as *standard primary* and *standard secondary*.

- Traditional DNS servers require the administrator to add records to the database manually. Microsoft Dynamic DNS (DDNS) allows DHCP (Dynamic Host Configuration Protocol) servers and the client machines to update their records dynamically.

exam
ⓦatch

New features of the Windows 2000 DNS service include Active Directory integration, dynamic and secure dynamic resource record updates, and incremental zone transfers. These features provide the backbone of Windows 2000 DNS and will be hot topics on the test.

QUESTIONS

5.01: Understanding the Windows 2000 Dynamic DNS Server

1. One of the new features in Windows 2000 DNS is incremental zone transfers. How does an incremental zone transfer work?

    A. An incremental zone transfer is a process that divides the zone file into ten equal increments and sends them individually to a secondary DNS server. This is done to save bandwidth.

    B. An incremental zone transfer is a process that occurs when the secondary DNS server pulls the zone file from the primary DNS server incrementally over a period of about an hour.

    C. An incremental zone transfer is a process in which the primary DNS server sends only records that have changed to the secondary DNS server, rather than the entire zone file.

    D. None of the above.

2. You have created a Windows 2000 DNS server, and you intend for your clients to dynamically register themselves in the database. However, after configuring both DHCP and DNS, you find that the clients' records are not appearing in the forward lookup zone. What could have gone wrong?

    A. You didn't configure the forward lookup zone to allow dynamic updates.

    B. You didn't configure DHCP to allow Windows 2000 clients to register themselves in DHCP.

    C. Your Windows 2000 DNS server is not a domain controller.

    D. You configured the zone to be Active Directory integrated, and you cannot do dynamic updates with Active Directory–integrated zones.

Creating a DNS Namespace for the Organization

The DNS namespace for an organization consists of domains and subdomains. A DNS namespace can consist of a single root domain or a hierarchical tree of domains and subdomains. If you are designing an Active Directory infrastructure, these domains will most likely be modeled after your Active Directory design.

Another factor that will influence your design is having two root domains—an internal domain and an external domain, one root domain separated by a firewall, or a public domain outside the firewall and a private domain namespace inside the firewall.

- The generally accepted way of creating a DNS namespace for an organization is to model it on an existing Active Directory design (if the organization does not already have a DNS infrastructure).

- The design element that will affect DNS the most is whether the company will have an external Internet presence or just an internal network.

- DNS is a hierarchical structure. An organization thus has a root domain and subdomains. The subdomains are designed to group computers together in a logical fashion.

exam
Watch

Until recently, Microsoft advocated using a domain name root of .Local for internal, private domain namespaces. The original rationale was that this suffix would be easily recognizable as a nonpublic suffix and would be used only on non–Internet-connected networks. However, Microsoft has changed its mind about using this suffix, and now recommends using an InterNIC-registered domain name for both the internal and external domains.

QUESTIONS

5.02: Creating a DNS Namespace for the Organization

3. You currently have a Windows NT 4.0 DNS infrastructure. The domains and subdomains are configured as shown in the following illustration:

You are preparing to upgrade to Windows 2000 and Active Directory. You are planning to design your AD infrastructure based on your company's geographic organization, which is based on United States regions. There are three regions: Northeast, Southeast, and Midwest. How should you integrate your existing DNS design with the proposed Windows 2000 domain design?

A. Design your AD infrastructure around the existing DNS namespace.

B. Create another DNS root called win2k.syngress.com, and create a geography-based namespace beneath the new root.

C. Add another subdomain to the existing namespace called w2k.syngress.com, and make this a delegated subdomain of the root. Use subdomains or organizational units under w2k.syngress.com to represent the geographical design of AD.

D. None of the above.

4. **Situation:** You are working with BigBrains, a company that wants to implement a Windows 2000 network infrastructure. They currently have a large Novell Directory Services (NDS) infrastructure with a complicated organizational unit structure, and they want to simplify the design as they migrate to Active Directory. This company does not have an Internet presence,

but would like to host their own Web server once this project is complete. Their network architecture will include a firewall with three interfaces: one for the external network, one for the internal network, and one for a demilitarized zone (DMZ) that will hold the Web and mail servers. Their Active Directory infrastructure will have a minimum of three domains (one root domain and two subdomains), which should be based on the company's two business units, manufacturing and consulting.

Required Result: You must propose a DNS namespace that will accommodate name resolution for hosts on the Internet as well as those inside the firewall.

Optional Desired Result: Decide how you will name the Active Directory domains, taking into account the structure of the company.

Proposed Solution: Because of the need for a firewall, you decide to set up two DNS zones, with the inside clients having access to the public resources. The inside zone will be an Active Directory–integrated zone. You choose to use BigBrains.com as the root for the DNS namespace. Inside the firewall, you choose to name the subdomains manufacturing.bigbrains.com and consulting.bigbrains.com. The external DNS zone will contain the records for the Web and mail servers. The two zones will be identical, and named bigbrains.com.

What results are provided from the proposed solution?

A. The proposed solution produces the required result only.

B. The proposed solution produces the required result and the optional desired result.

C. The proposed solution does not produce the required result.

TEST YOURSELF OBJECTIVE 5.03

Creating an Integrated DNS Design

Windows 2000 DNS can be integrated with the Active Directory to provide substantial fault tolerance, performance, and security benefits. By integrating with AD, DNS gains the advantages of multimaster zone replication, secure dynamic updates, and fault tolerance through replication across domain controllers.

Windows 2000 DNS can also be integrated with DHCP to provide dynamic registration and update of host information for both native Windows 2000 and non–Windows 2000 clients, such as Windows NT 4.0 and Windows 95/98 clients.

- Only domain controllers with DNS installed can serve as Active Directory–integrated DNS servers.

- When using Active Directory–integrated DNS servers, only Windows 2000 DNS clients will be able to take advantage of the new features, such as secure dynamic updates, but all clients will receive the level of support and name resolution that they require.

If you decide to use Active Directory–integrated zones (and there's really nothing that should stop you from doing so), you should remember that they can only be created on Active Directory domain controllers. You cannot create AD-integrated zones on a stand-alone server or on a member server in a domain.

QUESTIONS

5.03: Creating an Integrated DNS Design

5. You have set up a Windows 2000 Active Directory infrastructure and are using an Active Directory–integrated DNS server. How can you configure your Windows NT 4.0 clients to dynamically register their records in DNS?

  A. You can configure the Windows NT client to dynamically register its DNS record by choosing Allow Dynamic DNS Registration on the DHCP tab of the TCP/IP Properties page.

  B. Non–Windows 2000 client records cannot be dynamically inserted into DNS.

  C. You can configure the Windows 2000 DNS server to accept client registrations from all clients, not just Windows 2000 clients.

  D. You can configure Windows 2000 DHCP to register client records for all clients, not just those clients who request to be registered.

6. Consider the following illustration. Can the Windows 2000 Active Directory–integrated primary DNS server perform zone transfers to the secondary DNS server? Why or why not?

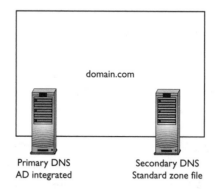

domain.com

Primary DNS
AD integrated

Secondary DNS
Standard zone file

A. No. Active Directory–integrated servers cannot conduct zone transfers to standard secondary zones.

B. Yes. Active Directory–integrated servers can conduct zone transfers to standard secondary zones as long as they are on the same side of a WAN connection.

C. No. The Active Directory–integrated server cannot conduct zone transfers to the standard secondary zone because it doesn't have a secure channel, such as a virtual private network, to communicate through.

D. Yes. An Active Directory–integrated server can conduct zone transfers to a standard secondary zone.

TEST YOURSELF OBJECTIVE 5.04

Creating a Secure DNS Design

There are important security concerns regarding DNS in a standard network environment. Windows 2000 does not use encryption when performing zone transfers. Also, it is very easy for someone to create a secondary DNS server that can receive unauthorized zone transfers from your current DNS servers. Furthermore,

DNS now supports dynamic updates. Given these facts, it is very important that the appropriate security precautions be taken to ensure that only the correct clients update their corresponding host records. Windows 2000 addresses these concerns strongly.

- By default, standard zone transfers take place without using any form of encryption.

- To secure your zone transfers, you should consider using the encryption tools available with Windows 2000. Routing and Remote Access Service (RRAS) in Windows 2000 provides strong support for Internet Protocol Security (IPSec) and highly secure virtual private network (VPN) tunnels.

- When you store zone information in Active Directory, by default the server requires secure updates for dynamically updated resource records.

exam
🐾atch

It is highly recommended that you use secure zone transfers between your primary and secondary DNS servers. For transfers that are to occur on the internal network (LAN, WAN), you should use IPSec to secure the traffic. For zone transfers that occur over the Internet or insecure WANs, you should consider using a VPN.

QUESTIONS

5.04: Creating a Secure DNS Design

7. **Situation:** You have a remote office that connects to the corporate network with a 56-Kbps dial-up connection. The users complain that when they attempt to connect to any intranet or Internet Web sites, domain name queries take an unusually long amount of time. Currently, client computers are configured to use a DNS server at the headquarter locations.

   Required Result: You need to find a way to speed up name resolution for Internet and intranet hosts.

   Optional Desired Result: Recommend changes to make the DNS infrastructure more efficient with regard to resolving names.

Proposed Solution: For this particular office, speeding up name resolution and DNS efficiency go hand in hand. You decide to configure the corporate DNS server to act as a forwarder so that it can reduce the overhead on its operation. You point the forwarder to the DNS server at your ISP. To make the name resolution more efficient at the remote office, you install a stand-alone Windows 2000 DNS server with an Active Directory–integrated secondary zone and reconfigure the clients in the remote office to use the new DNS server for name resolution.

What results are provided from the proposed solution?

A.   The proposed solution produces the required result only.

B.   The proposed solution produces the required result and the optional desired result.

C.   The proposed solution does not produce the required result.

8.   You are designing your DNS infrastructure, and you have a need for very secure transfer of zone information between two DNS servers that lie within the DMZ of your company's firewall. Currently, your DNS servers are running on Windows NT 4.0. What can you do to increase the security of these zone transfers?

A.   Configure the default IPSec security policy to require Kerberos authentication for all communication.

B.   Upgrade your DNS servers to Windows 2000, install Active Directory, and configure your DNS to be AD integrated.

C.   Same as B, except add Kerberos as the authentication mechanism.

D.   None of the above.

TEST YOURSELF OBJECTIVE 5.05

Creating a Highly Available DNS Design

The DNS infrastructure is at the heart of a Windows 2000 network. It is very important that you ensure that clients always have access to the information it contains. The Windows 2000 DNS service continues support for primary and secondary DNS servers. Through integration with Active Directory, even more reliability becomes available because of Active Directory replication. In addition, DNS clustering becomes a viable option for high availability when Windows 2000 Advanced Server or Windows 2000 Datacenter Server is used.

- To enhance reliability in a traditional DNS environment, secondary DNS servers should be employed.

- When you integrate DNS into Active Directory, all zone data is stored in Active Directory and the zone information is replicated using the Active Directory replication process.

- Each Active Directory DNS server hosting a zone is treated as a primary DNS server.

exam
ⓦatch

The most important thing to remember about DNS design is ensuring that you have a secondary server to back up your primary server. Because the Active Directory is dependent on DNS for service, your users will always need access to DNS. By using secondary DNS servers and AD integration, you should never have a problem with reaching an active DNS server.

QUESTIONS

5.05: Creating a Highly Available DNS Design

Questions 9–11   This scenario should be used to answer questions 9, 10, and 11.

You have a Windows 2000 network and domain infrastructure. Your environment consists of a single domain that spans four sites. At headquarters, you have a primary DNS server that is Active Directory integrated. Your network is represented by the illustration on the following page.

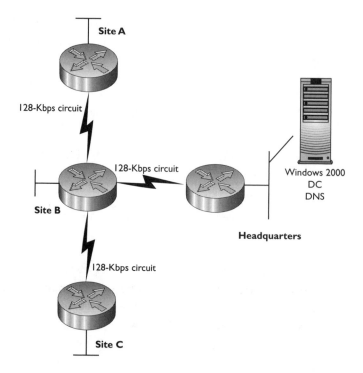

There are between 450 and 600 users at each of the four sites. Each of the four sites is connected via a 128-Kbps circuit. Currently, all of the users throughout the organization resolve domain names using the primary DNS server at the headquarters location.

9. In order to provide better availability for the users at your company, you need to place additional DNS servers in this infrastructure. Where would you place them and what types of servers would you install?

   A. Place one secondary DNS server at site B and point all of the users in sites A and C to resolve against site B's DNS server.

   B. Place an additional primary DNS server at each of sites A, B, and C.

   C. Place an Active Directory–integrated DNS server at site B and configure it to be a secondary DNS server.

   D. Place an AD-integrated DNS server at each of sites A, B, and C, and configure a secondary zone on each of these servers.

10. What benefit will placing forwarders provide if you implement the design specified in the last question?

    A. By configuring a forwarder on the headquarter's DNS server, you can reduce the traffic between clients at the remote sites and the headquarters when clients want to access the Internet.

    B. Forwarders will have no net effect on the name resolution traffic for the design specified above.

    C. By configuring each of the DNS servers in sites A, B, and C to use a forwarder, and then specifying the DNS server at the headquarters as the destination, you can reduce the name resolution traffic across the 128-Kbps WAN links.

    D. None of the above.

11. You would like to create a highly available DNS server. After conducting a lot of research, you decide to place a Windows 2000 DNS server on a Windows 2000 cluster. What is the benefit of clustering your DNS servers?

    A. Clients will always be able to perform name resolution against either a primary or secondary DNS server.

    B. You are practically guaranteeing that your zone transfers will never fail between the clustered DNS servers.

    C. It adds an additional DNS server for clients to send requests to.

    D. It ensures that the clustered DNS server will never be down. If the primary member of the cluster fails, the DNS server on the secondary cluster member will activate within seconds, continuing to service clients.

TEST YOURSELF OBJECTIVE 5.06

Measuring and Optimizing a DNS Infrastructure Design

Once you have developed your DNS design, you must ensure that the implementation of DNS matches your design. This will help prevent problems with name resolution that may trace back to inadequate redundancy, security, or server failures. To prevent these issues from robbing your DNS implementation of performance, you should prepare a monitoring and analysis strategy that will result in a more efficient, optimized DNS infrastructure.

Your monitoring and analysis strategy should take into account the occurrence of certain events, such as unavailability of DNS servers, unresolved DNS queries, and DNS replication failures. The strategy should also encompass the monitoring of logs and data from DNS trace logs, Event Viewer, and System Monitor.

- When enabled, the DNS server service will perform additional trace-level logging of events or messages to assist in troubleshooting and debugging the server.

- The DNS log in Event Viewer contains messages that can warn you of problems that are occurring with the DNS service. DNS client messages are stored in the system log.

- System Monitor allows you to create charts and graphs of server performance in real time by using log files.

exam
Watch

One method of analyzing the performance of your DNS server is through the use of DNS trace logs. These are detailed records of all of the transactions that take place on the DNS server. You must specifically enable this mode, because it is turned off by default. Enabling the DNS trace log puts a huge load on the server because the trace will capture all of the activity that is occurring on the server. You should use this tool sparingly, or it might end up becoming part of the problem.

QUESTIONS

5.06: Measuring and Optimizing a DNS Infrastructure Design

12. You have implemented your DNS design, but you have been getting a number of calls from users who state that their DNS queries aren't being resolved. You

double-check your primary and secondary DNS zones, and verify that your servers are performing zone transfers correctly. You decide to turn on the DNS trace on the primary DNS server in order to find the cause of the problem. The following illustration shows the DNS trace dialog box.

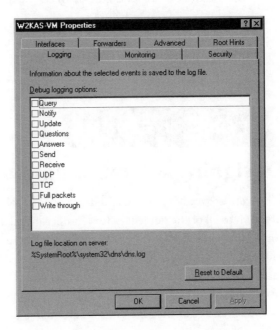

Which options in the DNS trace log should you enable to see the contents of the DNS queries and responses? (Choose all that apply.)

A. Query

B. Questions

C. Answers

D. Send

E. Receive

13. You have designed and implemented a very complex DNS infrastructure. You have utilized Active Directory–integrated zones and secondary servers for redundancy. In both theory and practice, you have done a great job in ensuring

that your users' DNS queries will get answered. Why, then, is it so crucial that you configure alerts for DNS events if your system is so stable?

A. So you can maintain a log of all events that occur on the DNS server.

B. So you can respond quickly to critical alerts, such as a downed server or a DNS replication failure.

C. So you can troubleshoot any problems based on the alert descriptions.

D. None of the above.

TEST YOURSELF OBJECTIVE 5.07

Designing a DNS Deployment Strategy

When you are ready to design and deploy your DNS infrastructure, you must pay attention to all of the guidelines for a proper installation. Your design should address availability and reliability by placing primary and secondary servers close to the users who will be using them for name resolution. Your design should also address security, particularly of the transfer of zone data between DNS servers. Security can be provided by encrypting zone transfers with IPSec or by integrating DNS with Active Directory to take advantage of the inherently secure Active Directory replication.

- Ensure DNS availability by placing secondary DNS servers at remote sites.

- Deploy the primary DNS server first, then implement secondary servers.

- When possible, utilize Active Directory–integrated DNS servers instead of standard primary and secondary DNS servers for increased security and fault tolerance.

exam
ⓌＡｔｃｈ

This objective requires you to pull together all of the pieces of a successful DNS design. During the exam, pay particular attention to all of the details, especially when you are given a lot of information to digest. You will need to weed out the extraneous information and extract just the facts needed to answer the question.

QUESTIONS

5.07: Designing a DNS Deployment Strategy

14. Your client is a large publisher that has five large sites and two small satellite operations. The following table lists the number of employees at each location.

Site	Number of Employees
New York	1,700
Philadelphia	1,100
Pittsburgh	850
Boston	1,375
Baltimore	175
Charlotte	185

The large sites are connected via 1.544-Mbps Frame Relay circuits, while the small sites are connected to the Frame Relay cloud with 256-Kbps circuits. The client wants to implement a DNS solution, and the main requirement is that there cannot be a single point of failure in the DNS infrastructure. They want to use one large DNS zone for the entire company. Which of the following DNS designs will best meet this requirement?

A. Put a primary DNS server at each of the sites.

B. Put a primary DNS server at each of the large sites, and a secondary DNS server at each of the small sites.

C. Put a primary and a secondary DNS server at the New York site, and secondary DNS servers at the remaining six sites.

D. Put a primary DNS server at one of the large sites, and a secondary DNS server at each of the remaining sites.

15. Your company has three sites on the East Coast. You are implementing Windows 2000. As part of your DNS design, you wish to add redundancy to your design, as well as the ability to perform secure dynamic updates. How should you deploy your DNS servers?

    A. Place a primary DNS server at one location, and place secondary DNS servers at the other two locations.

    B. Place Active Directory–integrated DNS servers at all three locations.

    C. Place primary DNS servers at all locations.

    D. None of the above.

LAB QUESTION

Objectives 5.01–5.07

You are a consultant working for a large company that is preparing to migrate to Windows 2000. They have 10,000 users in ten locations across the United States. Their current infrastructure consists of Netware 4.1 servers for file and print access, and Windows 95 clients running the Netware Client. Part of the project is to migrate from Netware to Windows 2000 and from IPX/SPX to TCP/IP. The following illustration shows the network infrastructure:

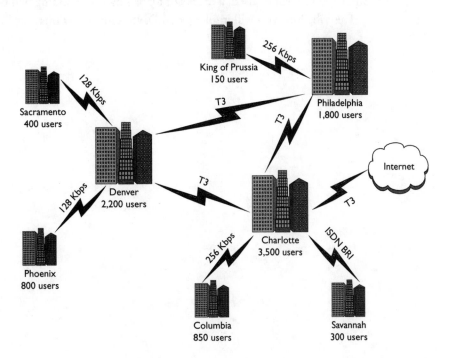

The company owns the publicly registered domain name bigwidgets.com. They would like to use the same domain name throughout the organization, and both inside and outside the firewall. They will have a Web presence after the migration to Windows 2000. They will also have an extensive intranet presence, with Web servers throughout the organization to provide real-time sales and R&D information to a 24-hour workforce. Thus, the DNS servers must be always available to perform name resolution.

The company is currently organized into two divisions: R&D and Sales. Within both divisions, the company is divided by locations. Within the R&D division, you will find the Columbia, Savannah, Charlotte, Philadelphia, and King of Prussia locations. The remaining locations—Denver, Phoenix, and Sacramento—are in the Sales division.

All of the Sales locations have a large number of telemarketers who will be using an IP-based call management package. This package depends on the workstation name to map the user to the telephone station. Once Windows 2000 is in place, the call management package will be configured to use the domain name of the workstation. Since DHCP will be used, a means of managing this mapping will be required.

Describe how you will implement a DNS solution for this company.

A QUICK ANSWER KEY

Objective 5.01	
1.	C
2.	A

Objective 5.02	
3.	C
4.	B

Objective 5.03	
5.	D
6.	D

Objective 5.04	
7.	C
8.	B

Objective 5.05	
9.	D
10.	C
11.	D

Objective 5.06	
12.	A, B, and C
13.	B

Objective 5.07	
14.	C
15.	B

IN-DEPTH ANSWERS

5.01: Understanding the Windows 2000 Dynamic DNS Server

1. ☑ **C.** An incremental zone transfer is the process in which the primary DNS server sends only changes to the zone file to the secondary DNS servers, instead of the full zone file. It makes the zone transfer process much more efficient.

   ☒ **A** is incorrect because the incremental zone transfer process does not divide the file to send it. **B** is also incorrect because the secondary DNS server does not do an "extended" pull of the zone file from the primary server.

2. ☑ **A.** If your clients aren't registering in the forward lookup zone, you need to verify that Allow Dynamic Updates is set to Yes in the properties for the zone, as shown in the following illustration:

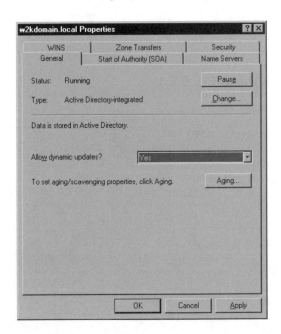

☒ **B** is incorrect because Windows 2000 clients will, by default, attempt to register their own records in DNS. **C** is incorrect because there is no dependency on Active Directory for dynamic updates. **D** is also incorrect because dynamic updates will work with all modes—both database and Active Directory integrated.

5.02: Creating a DNS Namespace for the Organization

3. ☑ **C.** The best way to integrate your new AD domain design into this existing design is to create another subdomain and model your AD domains under this subdomain. This way you can have a geographical domain structure for AD, while keeping the existing DNS namespace intact.

☒ **A** is incorrect because this approach will force you to model your AD namespace around the existing nongeographic DNS namespace. **B** is incorrect because you cannot have two roots with the same domain name.

4. ☑ **B.** The proposed solution produces both the required result and the optional desired result. Your logic is correct in having two identical zones on each side of the firewall. This allows DNS queries from the public side of the firewall to resolve against the public DNS server, and internal queries to resolve against the internal server. Your AD namespace design is functionally correct because it encompasses the wishes of the client. One thing that needs to be pointed out: before implementing a DNS name on the Internet, you need to reserve the name with the InterNIC.

☒ **A** and **C** are not correct because the proposed solution produces both the required result and the optional result.

5.03: Creating an Integrated DNS Design

5. ☑ **D.** To have your non–Windows 2000 clients' records dynamically registered in DNS, you need to have Windows 2000 DHCP perform the registration for them. This can be done by choosing to have Windows 2000 DHCP always update DNS when it automatically updates DHCP client information.

☒ **A** is incorrect because there is not an option in Windows NT 4.0's TCP/IP properties for allowing dynamic registration. **B** is incorrect because it is possible to have non–Windows 2000 clients' records dynamically registered in DNS. **C** is incorrect because only Windows 2000 clients can register themselves in DNS. Non–Windows 2000 clients must have DHCP register the records for them.

6. ☑ **D.** Yes. A primary Active Directory–integrated server can perform zone transfers to secondary DNS servers with standard zones. This ensures compatibility with legacy Windows NT and BIND (Berkeley Internet Name Daemon) DNS servers.

☒ **A** is incorrect because primary Active Directory–integrated DNS servers can perform zone transfers to secondary DNS servers. **B** is incorrect because there is no WAN requirement for zone transfers. **C** is incorrect because zone transfers between AD-integrated and standard zones are not dependent on secure channels.

5.04: Creating a Secure DNS Design

7. ☑ **C.** The proposed solution does not produce the required result. The initial configuration has clients at the remote site sending DNS queries across the 56-Kbps link to the DNS server, which then makes recursive queries from its location to the root servers. By enabling a forwarder on the corporate DNS server, you are not really making any changes that will affect the speed of the remote office queries. You will still have a lot of traffic going across the slow link. The proper design would be to put a DNS server at the remote location and then configure it with a forwarder pointing to the DNS server at the corporate office. When clients make queries, the local server will attempt to resolve against its own database and cache, and then forward the request to a server on the forwarders list. This way, you only have one or two exchanges across the 56-Kbps link, and most of the traffic is between the corporate DNS server and the outside world.

As for the DNS server you installed, you cannot create an AD-integrated DNS server on a stand-alone Windows 2000 server. It must be created on a domain controller.

☒ **A** and **B** are incorrect because the proposed solution does not produce the required result.

8. ☑ **B.** By upgrading your DNS servers to Windows 2000 and then putting Active Directory on them, you can implement AD-integrated zones. Once this has been done, the transfer of zone information between the DNS servers takes place during the AD replication process, which by default is encrypted.

   ☒ **A** is incorrect because you cannot implement Kerberos and IPSec security policy on Windows NT servers. **C** is also incorrect, because you get Kerberos by default when you upgrade to Windows 2000 and Active Directory.

5.05: Creating a Highly Available DNS Design

9. ☑ **D.** To provide better availability, you should put an AD-integrated DNS server at sites A, B, and C. Configure these servers to be secondary to the zone held at the headquarters. By implementing this design, you also place additional domain controllers at the remote sites, which will help with authentication traffic.

   ☒ **A** is incorrect because although you have added a secondary DNS server for redundancy, you still may be leaving a number of users without a DNS server. **B** is incorrect because you can only have one primary DNS server for a domain. **C** is incorrect because you should have a DNS server at all sites connected by slow links.

10. ☑ **C.** Configuring the remote sites' DNS servers to forward DNS queries to the DNS server at the headquarters will reduce name resolution traffic across the WAN links. The DNS server at the headquarters will then be responsible for resolving queries and passing the results back to the DNS server at the site.

    ☒ **A** is incorrect because you are not changing the behavior of the DNS servers at the site locations. They will still do all of the work in the name resolution process. **B** is incorrect because forwarders will have an effect on the traffic across the WAN links.

11. ☑ **D.** Using clustering with your DNS servers ensures that a single DNS server will never be unavailable (except in extreme circumstances). When you cluster two or more servers together, one is designated as a primary, and the others are secondary or failover members. The DNS service is configured on

each of the members of the cluster. If the primary cluster server fails, the next cluster member activates and picks up exactly where the primary server left off.

☒ **A** is incorrect because a clustered DNS server acts and responds like a single server—in fact, only one instance of DNS is running at any one time. You can still have secondary DNS servers, but they are not members of the cluster. **B** is incorrect because clustered DNS servers share the same DNS zone information database. There are no zone transfers between cluster members. **C** is incorrect because although you may have four servers operating in your cluster, only one instance of DNS is running among them.

5.06: Measuring and Optimizing a DNS Infrastructure Design

12. ☑ **A**, **B**, and **C** are all correct answers. The Query option logs all queries received from clients. The Questions option logs the contents of the question section for each DNS query message processed, and the Answers option logs the contents of the answer section for each DNS query message received. Remember that enabling the trace log will result in an intensive use of server resources. Use it sparingly.

☒ **D** and **E** are both incorrect. The Send and Receive options only log the number of DNS query messages sent and received by the DNS server. They will not show any detailed information about the queries.

13. ☑ **B.** Even though you have a stable DNS infrastructure, it's crucial to continuously monitor its performance and react to any problems that may occur. In a highly available, redundant environment, you might not even know that one of your DNS servers has gone down until its backup fails. You will want to know, via alerts, that such an event has occurred so that you can repair the problem before it becomes a bigger problem.

☒ **A** is incorrect because you can use a number of other means of logging the activity, such as traces and the Event Viewer. **C** is incorrect because the alert description is meant to bring a problem to your attention, not to provide enough information to allow troubleshooting.

5.07: Designing a DNS Deployment Strategy

14. ☑ **C.** The best choice for this company would be to place the primary DNS server at the New York site, which is the largest, place a secondary DNS server in New York as well, and then place secondary DNS servers at each of the remaining sites. This ensures that users at any of the sites will be able to resolve names should the WAN connection go down.

    ☒ **A** is incorrect because you cannot have more than one primary DNS server per zone. **B** is also incorrect, for the same reasons as **A**—you cannot have multiple primary DNS servers in a single DNS zone. **D** is incorrect because it doesn't provide for the same level of redundancy that **C** does.

15. ☑ **B.** In order to have secure dynamic updates, you need to have Active Directory–integrated zones. By implementing your DNS servers in this manner, you also build in redundancy, since AD-integrated zones perform zone transfers through multimaster replication.

    ☒ **A** is incorrect because you cannot have secure dynamic updates without Active Directory–integrated zones. **C** is incorrect for the same reason. Both **A** and **C** provide very good redundancy, but you aren't meeting the dynamic update requirement.

LAB ANSWER

Objectives 5.01–5.07

You decide to start with defining the DNS namespace. Based on the company organization, you choose to break the root domain into two subdomains—rd.bigwidgets.com and sales.bigwidgets.com.

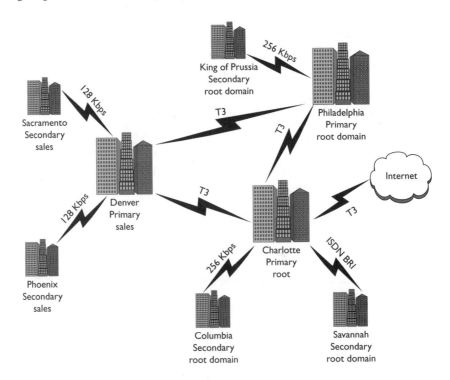

Next, you decide where to place the primary DNS servers for the domains and subdomains. You choose to place a primary DNS server for bigwidgets.com in the DMZ to service name requests for the Web and mail servers from outside the network. You also place another primary DNS server for the bigwidgets.com domain at the Charlotte location inside the firewall. These two primary DNS servers will maintain independent copies of the zone file. (It's important to note that there are two independent zones for bigwidgets.com: one outside the firewall and one inside the firewall.) You decide to put a primary DNS server for the rd.bigwidgets.com subdomain in Philadelphia, and a primary DNS server for the sales.bigwidgets.com subdomain in Denver. For redundancy, you place secondary DNS servers for the rd.bigwidgets.com subdomain in King of Prussia, Columbia, and Savannah, and place secondary DNS servers for the sales.bigwidgets.com subdomain in Sacramento and Phoenix. Finally, for redundancy of the root domain, you place a secondary DNS server in Charlotte. You do the same for the DNS server in the DMZ.

To accommodate the workstations and the need for domain-name-to-user mapping, you configure dynamic updates for the domain. Just to be safe, you choose to convert all of your DNS servers to Active Directory–integrated zones, for redundancy and multimaster replication. This will also give you secure dynamic updates.

MICROSOFT CERTIFIED SYSTEMS ENGINEER

6

Designing a WINS Strategy

W indows Internet Naming Service (WINS) is a NetBIOS name server that has been widely implemented in Microsoft networking. A NetBIOS name server maps NetBIOS names to IP addresses. Prior to Windows 2000, WINS was a critical element of a successful network design because many of the services in Windows NT relied on NetBIOS name resolution.

In Windows 2000, WINS is no longer a required element for Active Directory operations. However, many legacy applications still rely on NetBIOS naming for proper operation. For this reason, you need to understand how to design an WINS infrastructure in Windows 2000.

You need to understand how to design a basic WINS infrastructure, as well as how to implement security and redundancy in your design. Finally, you need to know how to maintain and tune your WINS infrastructure for long-term operation.

TEST YOURSELF OBJECTIVE 6.01

Understanding NetBIOS Name Resolution

NetBIOS, which stands for Network Basic Input Output System, is a network protocol that was designed as a transport protocol for simple, one-segment LANs. NetBIOS is a broadcast-based protocol and can generate enough traffic by itself to cripple a network. NetBIOS is not routable.

Microsoft uses an implementation of NetBIOS called NetBT (NetBIOS over TCP/IP). This allows NetBIOS names to be matched with an IP address, which ultimately allows NetBIOS traffic to travel over routed networks.

■ NetBIOS is a Session layer interface that allows NetBIOS applications to communicate over a TCP/IP network.

■ NetBIOS broadcast messages do not typically cross router interfaces.

■ Microsoft network clients can resolve NetBIOS names to IP addresses by using a number of different methods. The method and the order of execution are determined by the NetBIOS client's node type.

exam
ⓦatch

The most important thing to remember about NetBIOS is that it's not routable. Unlike IPX or TCP/IP, NetBIOS broadcasts will not cross routers without assistance, much like DHCP. Thus, you cannot depend on NetBIOS as your primary network protocol because you would never be able to move traffic from one segment to another via a router.

QUESTIONS

6.01: Understanding NetBIOS Name Resolution

1. There are many ways a computer can resolve the NetBIOS name to an IP address. Which of the following methods is used first when attempting to communicate with another PC?

   A. A NetBIOS broadcast

   B. Checking the LMHOSTS file for a match

   C. Checking the NetBIOS Remote Name Cache for a match

   D. Querying a DNS server

   E. Querying a WINS server

2. **Situation:** You are working for a small company that has 300 PCs spread across three physically divided subnets. The illustration on the following page shows your network design.

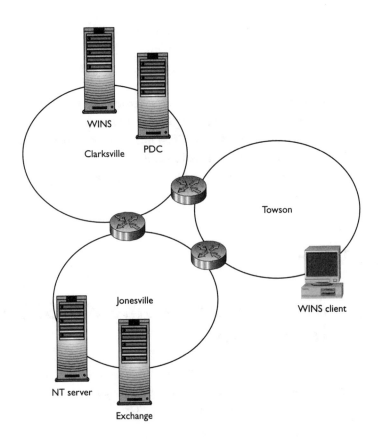

You have a WINS server at the Clarksville site to provide name resolution for your WINS clients. You also have a variety of NT servers in both Clarksville and Jonesville.

Required Result: Your WINS clients must be able to reach the NetBIOS resources at all times, even if the WINS server is unavailable.

Optional Desired Result: Provide a means of using NetBIOS broadcasts as a last resort for finding the NetBIOS resources.

Proposed Solution: You propose to add a HOSTS file to each computer that lists the NetBIOS name and IP address for each server on the network. This way, if WINS were to fail, the PCs could reference the HOSTS file to find the correct path to the servers. To provide the last-resort means for broadcasts, you configure your routers to allow broadcast traffic from UDP ports 137 and 138 to pass across the network links.

What results are provided from the proposed solution?

A. The proposed solution produces the required result only.

B. The proposed solution produces the required result and the optional desired result.

C. The proposed solution does not produce the required result.

3. You are implementing LMHOSTS files for name resolution on your small LAN. Which tag(s) should you place next to your domain controller entries and why?

A. #PDC—to indicate that the entry represents a primary domain controller.

B. #PRE and #PDC—to indicate that the entry should be preloaded, and that the entry is for a primary domain controller.

C. #PRE and #DOM—to indicate that the entry should be preloaded, and that the entry is for a domain controller.

D. None of the above.

TEST YOURSELF OBJECTIVE 6.02

Understanding WINS

WINS (Windows Internet Naming Service) is Microsoft's implementation of a NetBIOS naming server. When planning a NetBIOS name resolution scheme for your organization, you must include WINS in that plan.

To successfully implement a WINS strategy, you must take into consideration what devices and applications depend on NetBIOS, where those devices and applications are located on the network, and what the topology of the network is.

You must also understand the functioning of the various WINS components, such as WINS servers and clients, WINS proxy agents, and the WINS topology.

■   WINS is a NetBIOS name server used exclusively on Microsoft networks.

■   WINS is a client/server application, wherein the network client must be configured to query a WINS server for NetBIOS name resolution.

- WINS uses a distributed database that allows WINS servers spread throughout the network to contain the same database entries.
- WINS client/server traffic consists primarily of NetBIOS name registrations, NetBIOS name queries, NetBIOS name releases, and NetBIOS name renewals.

exam Watch

When designing a WINS infrastructure, sometimes it seems that the more WINS servers the better. Actually, that is not always the case. By putting too many WINS servers in your infrastructure, you are exposing yourself to the ugly reality that WINS is a headache. The larger your WINS replication network, the more replication traffic—and problems—you will experience. Microsoft recommends having one WINS server per 7,500 to 10,000 users (with a backup server). Of course, your mileage may vary. Work toward having the right number of WINS servers, and don't follow the rule of "Too many is never a bad idea."

QUESTIONS

6.02: Understanding WINS

4. If you allow your WINS servers to autoconfigure their replication method, what method is chosen?

    A. They will configure themselves as push partners.

    B. They will configure themselves as pull partners.

    C. They will configure themselves as push/pull partners.

    D. None of the above.

5. You have a number of clients that are not WINS aware. Furthermore, they are DHCP enabled, so their IP addresses are subject to change. How can you integrate these clients into your overall WINS strategy with the least amount of effort? (Choose all that apply.)

    A. Use an LMHOSTS file on these clients to allow them to find other NetBIOS resources.

    B. Configure DHCP to register the IP addresses of these clients in WINS.

C. Configure a WINS proxy agent on the segment(s) with the non-WINS clients to allow them to query the WINS database.

D. Manually input the non-WINS clients' records into the WINS database.

6. **Situation:** You are designing a WINS infrastructure for a client. The client has a large network consisting of a Windows 2000 Active Directory infrastructure; a single Windows NT 4.0 domain providing Exchange, SMS, and file and print services; and a number of Unix servers providing Oracle database services. The environment is primarily a mix of Windows 2000 Professional clients and Windows 98 clients.

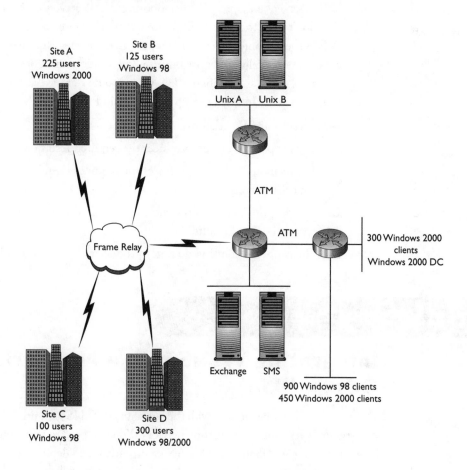

Required Result: You must place WINS servers in this network to adequately support the NetBIOS traffic.

Optional Desired Results:

1. Make sure your design accommodates any non-WINS clients.

2. Determine what replication strategy will best suit this network. You do not have the authority to modify any of the switches or routers in the network.

Proposed Solution: After reviewing the network architecture, you decide to place a WINS server at each of the Frame Relay–connected sites (sites A–D), as well as placing multiple WINS servers on the segment with 1,350 clients and placing a single WINS server on the segment with 300 Windows 2000 clients. You configure the clients to use the WINS server closest to them as the primary WINS server, and one of the neighboring WINS servers as the secondary server. You don't need to set up WINS proxy clients because you do not have any non-WINS clients (only servers, and you can manually register their records). You choose to manually configure push/pull replication on all of your WINS servers, instead of using autoconfiguration, since you do not have access to change the routers to allow Internet Group Membership Protocol (IGMP) traffic.

What results are provided from the proposed solution?

A. The proposed solution produces the required result only.

B. The proposed solution produces the required result and one of the optional desired results.

C. The proposed solution produces the required result and both of the optional desired results.

D. The proposed solution does not produce the required result.

TEST YOURSELF OBJECTIVE 6.03

Integrating WINS into a Network Design Plan

Once you have become familiar with the concepts of WINS, you need to understand how to integrate WINS into your existing network. You will need to know the differences between putting WINS in a simple LAN environment and deploying it throughout a large multisegment network that may contain thousands of clients worldwide.

When implementing WINS, you must address the following issues: reducing the number of failed WINS queries and the number of actual servers on the network, and handling the replication between WINS servers. You must look at WINS client configuration, as well as the support for non-WINS clients.

- NetBIOS clients on a single-segment network can be configured as WINS clients or use broadcasts to resolve NetBIOS names.

- Minimize the number of WINS servers on the network to reduce the chances of WINS replication errors.

- Do not use excessive numbers of secondary WINS servers for WINS clients. This will prevent excessive delays in NetBIOS name resolution when WINS servers cannot be contacted.

- A WINS proxy agent allows non-WINS clients to resolve NetBIOS names by querying a WINS server for a non-WINS client.

- Use static WINS database entries for non-WINS clients when those non-WINS clients share NetBIOS resources.

- Design a WINS replication network using the hub-and-spoke model to allow for the most reliable WINS database replication scheme.

exam
ⓦatch
WINS proxy agents are configured by making a change in the registry. There is no GUI interface that allows you to create a WINS proxy agent, but any Windows computer can be configured as one by editing the registry as follows: set the value of the EnableProxy registry entry to 1 (REG_DWORD). This entry is located in the following registry subkey:

HKEY_LOCAL_MACHINE\SYSTEM\CurrentControlSet\Services\Netbt\Parameters

QUESTIONS

6.03: Integrating **WINS** into a Network Design Plan

7.   You are the network administrator for a company that has 20 small sites connected by 512-Kbps circuits into a Frame Relay cloud. You currently are

using Windows 98 as your desktop operating system, and have Windows 2000 servers providing file and print services. You have an Active Directory domain, and you are using Dynamic DNS for client name resolution. Each of the small sites has between 25 and 75 clients, and has at least one Windows 2000 server.

Recently, you purchased a new backup program for your enterprise. You will be using it to back up both your Windows 2000 servers and certain folders from your Windows 98 PCs. Once you installed and configured it on your servers, you found out through testing that the program depends on NetBIOS to locate the backup agents on target machines. To successfully use this program (which meets all of your specifications, except for using NetBIOS), you will need a NetBIOS infrastructure. In order to keep the NetBIOS traffic to a minimum on your network, where should you place WINS servers in your environment to resolve the NetBIOS requests from the backup application?

A. Place a WINS server at every site.

B. Place two WINS servers at the largest location, and configure your routers to allow the broadcast traffic to pass.

C. Place a WINS server at five or ten of the largest sites, and configure WINS proxy agents on the segments that do not have a WINS server.

D. Place a WINS server at the largest site, and configure WINS proxy agents at the remaining sites.

8. To accommodate your non-WINS clients, you decide to place WINS proxy agents on the segments with the non-WINS clients. How many WINS proxy agents should you have on a segment if it has 300 non-WINS clients?

A. One

B. Two

C. Three

D. Five

9. **Situation:** You are preparing to design a WINS replication topology for your network. You have a fairly complex network infrastructure, as shown in the following illustration:

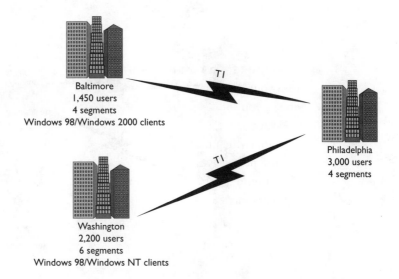

From your early estimates, you determine that you will need at least three WINS servers per site, based on the number of users, segments, and existing network traffic. You also have a number of Linux workstations scattered throughout the network, with at least 30 machines per site.

Required Result: You must pick a replication topology for the network that will generate the least amount of network traffic between the three main sites.

Optional Desired Results:

1. Accommodate the Linux workstations' need for NetBIOS name resolution with the least amount of network overhead.

2. Ensure that the WINS database is properly replicated for failover purposes.

Proposed Solution: You decide to use the replication topology shown on the following page for your WINS databases.

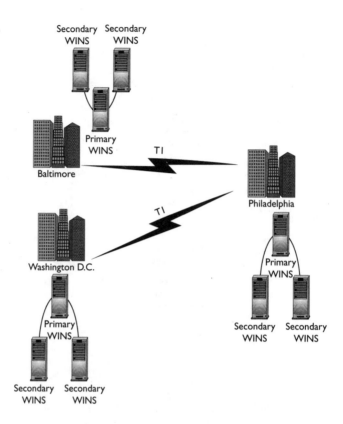

You configure a primary WINS server at each site. You then configure multiple secondary WINS servers at each site. The Philadelphia site will be the master site. Each of the secondary servers will be configured as push/pull partners with the primary server at the site. Next, the primary WINS servers will be configured as pull partners with the Philadelphia primary server. This is done so that replication traffic can be scheduled.

By having multiple WINS servers at each site, you ensure redundancy in the WINS design.

What results are provided from the proposed solution?

A. The proposed solution produces the required result only.

B. The proposed solution produces the required result and one of the optional desired results.

C. The proposed solution produces the required result and both of the optional desired results.

D. The proposed solution does not produce the required result.

Questions 10–11   This scenario should be used to answer questions 10 and 11.

You are working for a telemarketing company whose primary network operating system is Windows 2000. The company has an Active Directory infrastructure. There are four major locations: Atlanta, Miami, Jacksonville, and Houston. These call centers house between 600 and 800 employees. There is also a data center in Orlando, with 200 employees. Up until recently, this company has been using an AS/400-based computer-telephony integration (CTI) application to run their business. However, they have recently decided to implement a new client/server application that runs on a Windows NT and SQL Server back end. It unfortunately has not been certified to run on Windows 2000, but the benefit of replacing the legacy system with this new NT-based solution far outweighs the cost of deploying Windows NT instead of Windows 2000.

The following illustration depicts the network infrastructure at this company:

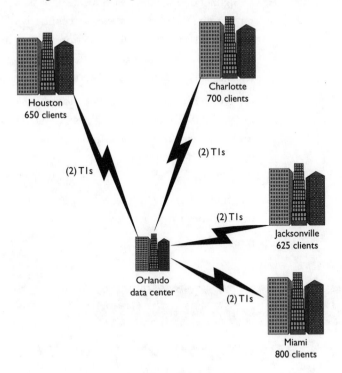

The new application requires that at least ten NT servers be placed at the data center to handle the bulk of the processing. There will also be one NT server dedicated to the application located at each call center.

10. Now that this company is bringing legacy Windows NT servers back into their network, they will have to implement WINS. Where should they place WINS servers to best serve the needs of the clients?

    A. Put one WINS server at each location.

    B. Put one WINS server for every 200 users at the major locations, and put one WINS server at the data center.

    C. Place two to three WINS servers at each of the major locations, and put two WINS servers in the data center for redundancy.

    D. Place three WINS servers at every location.

11. Assuming that the company has implemented the recommendation given in the answer to the prior question, how should they configure their replication topology?

    A. Designate one server at each location to be a primary WINS server. The remaining WINS servers will be secondary WINS servers. Configure the primary servers with pull replication to both of the WINS servers at the data center. Configure the secondary servers with push/pull replication to the other secondary servers throughout the network.

    B. Designate one server at each location to be a primary WINS server. The remaining WINS servers will be secondary WINS servers. Configure the secondary servers with push/pull replication with the primary server at each location. Then, configure the primary server at the data center to pull from the primary WINS servers at the major locations on a schedule.

    C. Configure every WINS server to push/pull replicate with every other server in a full-mesh arrangement.

    D. None of the above.

TEST YOURSELF OBJECTIVE 6.04

Designing Security for WINS Communications

When planning a WINS network that spans WAN links, you need to consider whether you should secure WINS-related traffic over the link. If your WINS replication network is entirely contained within the private LAN environment, there is little reason to incur the overhead of securing the communications, since all machines on the network have access to the WINS database in the normal course of NetBIOS name resolution.

- WINS replication and name resolution traffic that crosses public networks should be secured to protect the internal network namespace from intrusion.

- If your internal WINS servers use public IP addresses, you can use Internet Protocol Security (IPSec) to secure data communications between the servers.

- If you use private IP addresses for your WINS servers and clients, you can use Layer Two Tunneling Protocol/Internet Protocol Security (L2TP/IPSec) or Point-to-Point Tunneling Protocol/Multilink Point-to-Point Protocol (PPTP/MPPP) tunnels to secure your data.

exam
Watch

Although L2TP/IPSec is the preferred method of securing data traversing a public internetwork, there are some limitations. You cannot secure data end to end if you are using network address translation (NAT) on your internal network. If you are using NAT for your internal network clients, IPSec will not protect the data as it moves through the internal network, only as it moves from tunnel endpoint to tunnel endpoint. If you require end-to-end protection, you will need to encrypt the data by other methods.

QUESTIONS

6.04: Designing Security for WINS Communications

12. Your Web design company has two small offices on the West Coast. Both have between 35 and 50 client computers, running a mix of Windows 98, Windows 2000, and Windows NT. You want to set up WINS and configure it to replicate its database between the two offices. You currently have a cable modem connection to the Internet in both offices, but you don't have a

dedicated connection between the two. How can you securely replicate your WINS data between the two offices?

A. Just point the WINS servers at each other's IP addresses. WINS encrypts the data before it sends it.

B. Set up a tunnel between the offices using L2TP and have the servers initiate a virtual private network connection before replicating.

C. Configure your NT 4.0 servers to use IPSec to encrypt the communications between the two WINS servers.

D. None of the above.

13. Which of the following scenarios would suggest that you should secure the communications between your WINS servers?

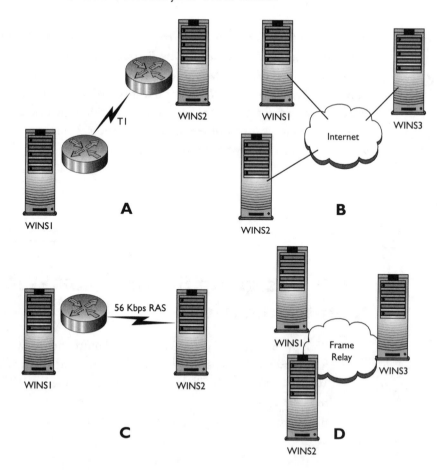

A. WINS replication between two servers on a private network

B. WINS replication between multiple partners across the Internet

C. WINS replication between a server on the corporate network and another server connected via a RAS connection

D. WINS replication between multiple servers connected through a Frame Relay cloud

TEST YOURSELF OBJECTIVE 6.05

Designing a Fault-Tolerant WINS Network

If your network uses mission-critical NetBIOS applications, you must design fault tolerance and availability into your WINS solution. Simply providing secondary WINS servers provides a certain measure of redundancy because you are providing a second copy of the WINS database on the network. However, sometimes your network will require more redundancy and availability. Windows 2000 Clustering is the solution to this problem.

■ WINS database replication provides a measure of fault tolerance for the WINS database when network clients are configured to use multiple WINS servers for NetBIOS name resolution.

■ Microsoft Cluster Server provides a way to provide real-time failover for WINS servers.

exam
ⓦatch

When designing redundancy and high availability into your WINS plan, you will certainly entertain the idea of using Windows Clustering. However, you must also look at the cost of implementing this solution. It does provide failover for a WINS server, but at what cost? You might be better off (and more frugal) by designing a very effective replication strategy and ensuring that it works properly.

QUESTIONS

6.05: Designing a Fault-Tolerant WINS Network

14. Which of the following techniques will provide the best availability for a WINS infrastructure?

    A. Have multiple network interface cards in your WINS servers connected to different subnets.

    B. Have your WINS database replicated across the network to multiple WINS servers.

    C. Ensure that the primary WINS server has redundant power supplies, is running RAID5, and is connected to an uninterruptable power source (UPS) for backup power.

    D. Cluster two or more servers together and host the WINS database from this cluster IP address.

15. **Situation:** You are preparing to design a WINS replication topology for your network. You have a fairly complex network infrastructure, as shown in the following illustration:

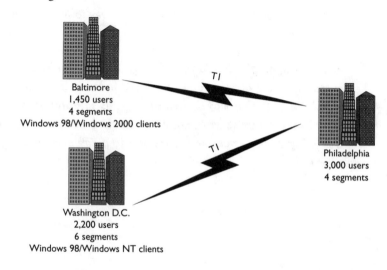

Baltimore
1,450 users
4 segments
Windows 98/Windows 2000 clients

T1

Philadelphia
3,000 users
4 segments

T1

Washington D.C.
2,200 users
6 segments
Windows 98/Windows NT clients

From your early estimates, you determine that you will need at least three WINS servers per site, based on the number of users, segments, and existing network traffic. You also have a number of Linux workstations scattered throughout the network, with at least 30 machines per site.

Required Result: You must design your WINS infrastructure so that it provides the maximum redundancy and availability without incurring huge expense.

Optional Desired Result: You must accommodate the Linux workstations' need for NetBIOS name resolution with the least amount of network overhead.

Proposed Solution: You decide to use the WINS infrastructure in your organization to provide redundancy and availability, as shown in the following illustration:

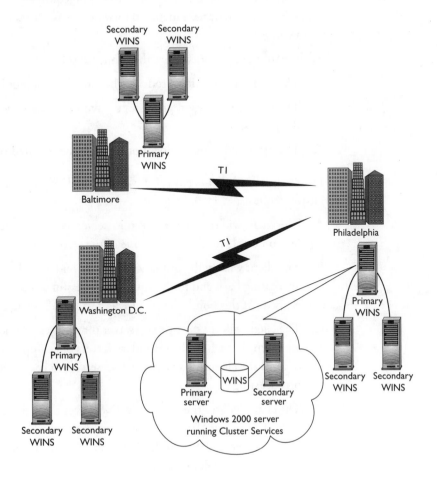

You configure a primary WINS server at each site. You then configure multiple secondary WINS servers at each site.

The Philadelphia site will be the master site. The primary server will be two Windows 2000 Servers clustered together that share the WINS database.

Each of the secondary servers at all three sites will be configured as push/pull partners with the primary server at the site. Next, the primary WINS servers will be configured as pull partners with the Philadelphia primary server. This is done so that replication traffic can be scheduled.

By having multiple WINS servers at each site, you ensure redundancy in the WINS design.

To accommodate the Linux workstations, you configure WINS proxy agents on each of the physical segments to forward the WINS traffic to the proper recipient.

What results are provided from the proposed solution?

A. The proposed solution produces the required result only.

B. The proposed solution produces the required result and the optional desired result.

C. The proposed solution does not produce the required result.

16. How will WINS clients react if the primary WINS server is not available to answer requests?

A. The client will try each server in its server list three times in a round-robin fashion until either it reaches one of the servers or five minutes elapse.

B. The client will try the primary and the secondary WINS servers three times, alternating back and forth, until it is successful or until 30 seconds have elapsed. At this point, the client will start broadcasting for name resolution.

C. The client will try the primary server three times, 750 milliseconds apart, and then try each of the secondary servers once until the query is successful or until the client runs out of WINS servers to try. Then it will resort to broadcasting.

D. The client will try the primary WINS server three times, 750 milliseconds apart. If the query fails, it will repeat this process for each server in the WINS server list. If all of these attempts fail, the client will resort to broadcasting for name resolution.

TEST YOURSELF OBJECTIVE 6.06

Tuning a WINS Network

Your primary goal in tuning your Windows 2000 WINS network is to improve the response time for WINS clients seeking to resolve NetBIOS names. You can break down the problem by approaching it from two directions: improving the responsiveness of the server running WINS, and improving the WINS network design. By focusing your tuning efforts on these two factors, you can improve the overall NetBIOS name resolution responsiveness for the entire network.

■ You can improve WINS server response by upgrading hardware components, including the disk subsystem, memory, and the network interface.

■ You can also improve NetBIOS name resolution response times by improving the WINS network design architecture.

exam
ⓦatch

Pay attention to the convergence time and hop count for your WINS replication. You may be thinking that this refers to routing, but convergence is very important to WINS database replication. Depending on the design of your WINS infrastructure, you could have three or more hops between two WINS servers. In some cases, this could mean that a change on one WINS server will take an hour to reach another WINS server on the other end of the network. This is called convergence. Slow convergence could translate to more help desk calls because users will not be able to reach the resources they are looking for.

QUESTIONS

6.06: Tuning a WINS Network

17. A few months after implementing your WINS design, you notice that your servers are struggling to keep up with the load of name resolution requests. What can you do to improve your servers' performance?

    A. Improve the network infrastructure.

    B. Add processors to the server.

    C. Improve the disk subsystem.

    D. Increase the amount of memory on the server.

    E. All of the above.

18. The following illustration shows your network's WINS topology. How long will it take for a client record change on one of the secondary servers at the Atlanta site to reach the New York site's secondary servers?

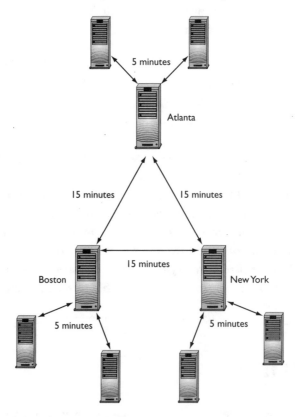

    A. Up to 5 minutes

    B. Up to 10 minutes

    C. Up to 15 minutes

    D. Up to 20 minutes

    E. Up to 25 minutes

19. After designing your WINS infrastructure, you calculate that the worst-case scenario for convergence times is 45 minutes. What is the ramification of having long convergence times?

   A. The time stamps on the records in the database become out of sync.

   B. Clients may not receive the correct information when they query WINS.

   C. Active Directory replication may not function properly.

   D. None of the above.

LAB QUESTION

Objectives 6.01–6.06

You have been called in to help a client who is experiencing network sluggishness. The client, BHC Software, has a fairly diverse client mix—Windows 95, Windows 98, Windows NT, and Windows 2000. In some parts of the building, the clients are organized into large workgroups of 40 to 50 machines, and there is also an NT 4.0 domain. A handful of Linux workstations are being used to mimic Windows functionality for the company's software development projects. There are a total of 600 workstations in the facility.

The network is newly upgraded from 10BaseT to Fast Ethernet. They have used switches to segment off the various floors, but everyone is on VLAN1. The client's network staff was more inclined to install and play with the equipment than to implement it correctly. They only recently began using DHCP to assign addresses—they had been using BOOTP on one of the Unix servers to manage the IP addresses.

The majority of the PCs have both a HOSTS and an LMHOSTS file (which are identical) to provide name resolution to the Unix hosts. They still don't have a DNS server for internal name resolution (they installed NetBIOS support on the Unix servers a while ago).

Based on what you have observed, answer the following questions:

1. Could excessive NetBIOS broadcasts be causing the network sluggishness that the client has reported?

2. Could this problem be associated with the HOSTS and LMHOSTS files on the client PCs?

3. If excessive NetBIOS broadcasts are the problem, how can you resolve this problem?

4. How can you allow the Linux systems to take advantage of your solution in question 2?

5. If you chose to implement WINS, do you need to design an elaborate replication scheme for this office? If so, how would you do it?

A QUICK ANSWER KEY

Objective 6.01
1. C
2. C
3. C

Objective 6.02
4. C
5. C and D
6. C

Objective 6.03
7. C
8. A
9. B
10. C
11. B

Objective 6.04
12. B
13. B

Objective 6.05
14. D
15. C
16. D

Objective 6.06
17. E
18. E
19. B

IN-DEPTH ANSWERS

6.01: Understanding NetBIOS Name Resolution

1. ☑ **C.** A computer will first check its NetBIOS Remote Name Cache for a match when trying to establish communication.

   ☒ **A, B, D, E,** and **F** are all incorrect because they are not the *first* method that a computer tries when attempting to establish communication with another NetBIOS computer. They are, however, all valid methods of name resolution.

2. ☑ **C.** The proposed solution does not produce the required result. It was on the right track, however. To provide a backup to WINS name resolution, you should place LMHOSTS files on the PCs, rather than HOSTS files. LMHOSTS files contain NetBIOS-to-IP-address mappings, whereas HOSTS files contain domain-name-to-IP-address mappings. To provide even more redundancy, it is correct to allow traffic from UDP ports 137 and 138 to pass through your routers.

   ☒ **A** and **B** are incorrect because the proposed solution does not produce the required result.

3. ☑ **C.** The correct tags to place next to the entries for the domain controllers would be #PRE and #DOM. For example:

   ```
   192.168.1.2    PDC01    #PRE    #DOM
   192.168.1.3    BDC01    #PRE    #DOM
   ```

   The #PRE tag informs your PC to preload this entry into the cache at startup. The #DOM tag indicates that the entry is a domain controller. You should place these entries at the bottom of your LMHOSTS files because they are preloaded; if they are at the top of the list, they will degrade the performance of the LMHOSTS lookup.

☒ **A** is incorrect because #PDC is not a valid LMHOSTS tag. **B** is incorrect because #PDC is not a valid LMHOSTS tag. In both instances, you should have used #DOM.

6.02: Understanding WINS

4. ☑ **C.** Autoconfigured WINS partners will become push/pull partners. When you enable automatic partner configuration, your WINS server will use multicast to discover other WINS servers. If you have not configured your routers to allow IGMP forwarding, then autoconfiguration will be limited to a single segment. Otherwise, you could allow WINS servers on multiple segments to find and configure replication with each other.

☒ **A** and **B** are incorrect because autoconfiguration uses push/pull replication. The WINS servers have a pull interval of two hours, with a push interval of zero, indicating that no push triggers will be sent.

5. ☑ **C** and **D** are correct. This is a tough question because there really isn't an easy way to both allow the non-WINS clients to use the WINS database for resolution *and* have their records registered in the WINS database. The WINS proxy agent will intercept the NetBIOS broadcasts and send them to the WINS server for resolution on behalf of the non-WINS clients. However, the proxy agent will not register the client's information. Thus, you will have to do this manually.

☒ **A** is incorrect. You will be required to maintain an LMHOSTS file that contains all of the records that the WINS database maintains. This will be an administrative headache. **B** is incorrect because DHCP cannot register WINS clients; it can only register DNS clients.

6. ☑ **C.** The proposed solution produces the required result and both of the optional results. First, a conservative number of WINS servers was placed throughout the network. If a segment had more than 250 to 300 clients, then a second WINS server was used on that segment. Segments that had only servers were not given a WINS server. WINS proxy agents were not needed, because the Unix servers would not be generating any NetBIOS traffic and would not need to resolve NetBIOS names. Finally, the actual method of replication was not critical for this scenario; the only critical factor was that autoconfiguration

could not be used throughout the network, since you did not have the ability to allow IGMP traffic to flow between segments.

☒   **A**, **B**, and **D** are incorrect because the proposed solution produces the required result and both of the optional results.

6.03: Integrating WINS into a Network Design Plan

7.   ☑   **C.** The best solution would be to limit the number of WINS servers to the least amount possible. You do not need to place a WINS server at each of the small sites. (That would be overkill!) You can then configure WINS proxy agents to help the WINS queries get across the WAN links. Microsoft strongly recommends that you limit the number of WINS servers to twenty or less. Because WINS is a replicated database, you want to decrease the risk that the data will be corrupted during replication among a large number of partners.

☒   **A** is incorrect because you would be putting in well over the recommended number of WINS server for any size network. **B** is incorrect because you would be saturating your WAN links with broadcast traffic. **D** is incorrect because you need to have redundancy, and one server would not provide redundancy of the database.

8.   ☑   **A.** You only need one WINS proxy agent on a segment. It will listen for NetBIOS broadcasts and relay them to a WINS server on behalf of the non-WINS clients.

☒   **B**, **C**, and **D** are all incorrect. When you place more than one WINS proxy agent on a segment, you end up increasing the load on the WINS server. Each proxy agent listens for NetBIOS broadcasts. When you have more than one proxy agent, you will have multiple requests being sent to the WINS server, because each proxy agent tries to perform the name resolution on behalf of the client.

9.   ☑   **B.** The proposed solution produces the required result and one of the optional desired results. The replication topology that was proposed is a hub-and-spoke arrangement. The hub, Philadelphia, has been configured to pull WINS data from its two spokes, Baltimore and Washington D.C., at

preconfigured times. The spokes continuously gather information from the local WINS servers via push/pull replication. This arrangement will reduce the amount of WINS traffic over the WAN, and also reduce the number of replication partners in your organization. Instead of having a full-mesh replication topology, you have a full mesh at each site, and a single replication path between the spokes and the hub. The multiple-server approach also adds a measure of redundancy to the plan. Nothing was done to accommodate the Linux workstations, such as configuring WINS proxy agents.

☒ **A**, **C**, and **D** are incorrect because the proposed solution produces the required result and one of the optional desired results.

10. ☑ **C.** The best answer would be to place two to three WINS servers at every location, and then place two WINS servers at the data center. This will align your WINS implementation for a hub-and-spoke replication topology.

☒ **A** is incorrect because this does not provide any redundancy at the major locations should the WINS server go down. **B** is incorrect because a single WINS server can handle far more than 200 users. You should be looking at fault tolerance more than capacity for this size segment. **D** is incorrect because it seems that the company is just haphazardly throwing WINS servers on the network without justifying their necessity.

11. ☑ **B.** The most efficient replication topology for this network environment is the hub-and-spoke model. You designate one WINS server to be the primary server at each location. This is also called the *intersite hub*. The remaining WINS servers become secondary servers. All of the servers at a location will be configured with push/pull replication among each other. This ensures that all of the servers at one location have the same data at roughly the same time (very low convergence time). Next, you configure the primary server at the hub (in this case, the data center) to pull from the primary servers at all of the locations on a schedule. This minimizes the traffic over the WAN—you only have four communication channels, instead of one for each WINS server.

☒ **A**, **C**, and **D** are incorrect because the most efficient replication topology for this network environment is the hub-and-spoke model.

6.04: Designing Security for WINS Communications

12. ☑ **B.** The best way to obtain secure communications between the offices would be to set up a tunnel through the Internet between the two offices. Then, using a virtual private network (VPN) connection, the WINS servers can use IPSec between the two offices.

   ☒ **A** is incorrect because WINS does not encrypt the data before sending it. **C** is incorrect also, because Windows NT 4.0 does not use IPSec for its IP communications.

13. ☑ **B.** You should definitely secure the replication data between multiple partners across the Internet. This example would represent the greatest threat to your company's data.

   ☒ **A** is incorrect because the two servers are on a secure, private network. You should not have to worry about intruders intercepting your replication data in this example. **C** is incorrect because a RAS connection has a certain degree of security built in. **D** is also incorrect, because a Frame Relay cloud is a collection of VPNs, which are not accessible except under very unusual circumstances.

6.05: Designing a Fault-Tolerant WINS Network

14. ☑ **D.** The technique that provides the best availability is the cluster server solution. This ensures that if the primary server in the cluster fails, the secondary server picks up and begins servicing WINS requests immediately. No matter how many servers are in the cluster, they all work with the same database.

   ☒ **A**, **B**, and **C** are all incorrect because they do not provide the same level of availability as answer **D** does. Multiple network interface cards do not address the failure of the server hardware. As for replicating the WINS database, this is more of a redundancy issue than one of availability.

15. ☑ **C.** The proposed solution does not produce the required result. Everything here would be perfect, except that you cannot use Windows 2000 Server for clustering. You must use Windows 2000 Advanced Server or Data Center Server. Otherwise, the replication topology that was proposed is a hub-and-spoke arrangement. The hub, Philadelphia, has been configured to pull WINS

data from its two spokes, Baltimore and Washington D.C., at preconfigured times. The primary server at Philadelphia (if it had been configured using Windows 2000 Advanced Server) would be a highly available solution.

The spokes continuously gather information from the local WINS servers via push/pull replication. This arrangement will reduce the amount of WINS traffic over the WAN, and also reduce the number of replication partners in your organization. Instead of having a full-mesh replication topology, you have a full mesh at each site, and a single replication path between the spokes and the hub. The multiple-server approach also adds a measure of redundancy into the plan. The Linux workstations were accommodated correctly by configuring WINS proxy agents.

☒ **A** and **B** are incorrect because the proposed solution does not produce the required result.

16.   ☑ **D.** The client will try the primary WINS server three times, 750 milliseconds apart. If the query fails, it will repeat this process for each server in the WINS server list. If all of these attempts fail, the client will resort to broadcasting for name resolution. Obviously, this will take some time (up to 30 seconds) for the client to try up to 12 servers (the maximum allowed in Windows 2000).

☒ **A** is incorrect because the correct method is to try each server three times before moving on to the next one on the list. **B** is incorrect, again because the client will try each server three times before going to the next server on the list. **C** is incorrect because the client will try all of the servers three times before resorting to broadcasting.

6.06: Tuning a WINS Network

17.   ☑ **E.** To improve your WINS server's performance, you can implement any or all of these measures. If you are running an Ethernet 10-Mbps network, upgrade the WINS server and WINS clients, and migrate devices to Ethernet 10/100. WINS is able to take advantage of a multiprocessor system; adding processors can result in up to a 20 percent improvement in performance. If you are using IDE drives, upgrade them to SCSI drives. If you are using simple volumes to house the WINS server and WINS database, move them to a striped array. Adding RAM to a server always helps performance of server

services. Additional RAM can help circumvent the number of calls made to the page file during periods of system stress.

☒ There are no wrong anwers.

18. ☑ **E.** It will take up to 25 minutes for a WINS record change on one of the secondary servers in Atlanta to reach the secondary WINS servers in New York. It will take five minutes for the change to reach the intersite hub, 15 minutes for it to travel from the intersite hub in Atlanta to the intersite hub in New York, and an additional five minutes to reach the secondary servers in New York. Thus, 25 minutes is the worst-case scenario.

☒ **A, B, C,** and **D** are incorrect because it will take up to 25 minutes for a WINS record change on one of the secondary servers in Atlanta to reach the secondary WINS servers in New York.

19. ☑ **B.** The effect of having long convergence times is that the information in your distributed WINS database may not be consistent across the enterprise. A record may have changed on one WINS server, but because of an inefficient replication topology, the WINS servers at the other end of the network may not learn about this change for 20, 40, or even 60 minutes (maybe longer, depending on your settings).

☒ **A** is incorrect because convergence does not affect time stamping on WINS records. **C** is incorrect because WINS replication convergence has nothing to do with Active Directory replication.

LAB ANSWER

Objectives 6.01–6.06

1. Yes, excessive NetBIOS broadcasts would be the prime suspect in this network scenario. The client has 600 workstations that mostly depend on NetBIOS to find network resources. Although the company has implemented a switched network, it has all of their clients on one VLAN. This effectively nullifies the benefits of having switches—all of the machines are still in the same broadcast domain.

2. Not really. The HOSTS and LMHOSTS files are used to provide name resolution for domain name and NetBIOS name hosts. The client has mistakenly used the same file for both domain name and NetBIOS name resolution. This will cause a problem with the client trying to resolve a name to an address, but won't appreciably add to the broadcast traffic. It certainly doesn't minimize the broadcast traffic. Over time, performance will degrade using these files, since DHCP will be changing workstation IP addresses as time goes on.

3. To resolve the NetBIOS broadcast problems, you should implement a WINS solution. In this environment, you would only need two or three servers to service the entire facility. You could easily configure the clients that utilize the WINS server by configuring the WINS address in the DHCP scope options.

4. You can configure a WINS proxy agent to help the Linux workstations use the WINS database information. You only need one proxy agent per network segment, or in this case, VLAN.

5. You really don't need to design an elaborate replication scheme. Because all of the servers are in one building, and there are only two or three servers, you could use push/pull replication between the servers to ensure a low convergence time.

MICROSOFT CERTIFIED SYSTEMS ENGINEER

7

Designing Distributed Data Access Solutions

TEST YOURSELF OBJECTIVES

I n any network, reliability, stability, and high availability are primary concerns. As companies begin to deploy robust networking services such as Web server farms and enterprise client/ server database applications, the need for distributed data access solutions within the network architecture will grow. Designing a distributed data access solution is the process of determining what applications and services within a network are mission-critical and building an infrastructure to support applications that are distributed across an enterprise to provide reliability and availability.

This chapter discusses design and planning considerations for deploying distributed data access solutions within a Windows 2000 network. It looks at services native to Windows 2000, including the Windows 2000 Advanced Server Clustering service, the Windows 2000 Advanced Server Network Load Balancing service, the Windows 2000 Distributed File System service, and Windows 2000's support for multiprotocol environments.

Understanding Distributed Data Access Solutions

The purpose of building a distributed data access solution is to provide availability to critical data at all times. All systems are inherently prone to failure; thus, you need to plan for this failure.

Distributed data access solutions are built using highly available systems, which are composed of RAID arrays and redundant network interface cards (NICs), power supplies, and processors. These features try to keep a single point of failure from existing in the system hardware.

These solutions also include clustering and load balancing, which attempt to keep a single system from being a point of failure.

Finally, you can use Distributed File System (Dfs) to prevent single points of failure from existing in your data. Dfs allows you to have redundant copies of critical data distributed throughout your network.

■ A distributed data access solution is a deployment solution that provides for highly available and fault-tolerant systems and services.

■ Windows 2000 Server includes multiprotocol support and Dfs.

■ Windows 2000 Advanced Server and Windows 2000 Data Center Server
include Network Load Balancing and Clustering services.

exam
ⓌＡＴＣＨ

Make sure you know which of the distributed data access features are available on each of the Windows 2000 server versions. For instance, Clustering is only available on Advanced Server and Data Center Server, whereas Dfs is available on all of the server products.

QUESTIONS

7.01: Understanding Distributed Data Access Solutions

1. **Situation:** You are preparing to build an e-commerce Web site for your client. You expect to have a million hits per week to start, and your calculations indicate that you may receive up to a million hits per day within a few months. You will be using Windows 2000 Advanced Server as your operating system, with Internet Information Services (IIS) 5.0 as your Web server.

    Required Result: You must recommend a solution that can handle the number of incoming requests that you are anticipating.

    Optional Desired Result: Recommend hardware features that will allow for 100 percent uptime.

    Proposed Solution: You propose to use Network Load Balancing to evenly distribute the Web requests to a number of Web servers, as opposed to building one very large Web server with multiple processors and a lot of memory. You ensure that the Web servers have redundant power supplies and NICs, as well as having a shared disk array to store the Web pages.

    What results are provided from the proposed solution?

    A. The proposed solution produces the required result only.

    B. The proposed solution produces the required result and the optional desired result.

    C. The proposed solution does not produce the required result.

2. What distributed data access technology allows you to create a logical view of a file system that is physically hosted on numerous servers?

   A. Network Load Balancing

   B. Distributed File System

   C. Windows Clustering

   D. Multiprocessor servers

3. The following illustration shows a high-availability solution that includes two or more servers that share a common drive array:

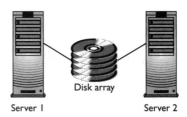

   What type of high-availability solution does this illustration represent, and what Windows 2000 products support it?

   A. Load balancing; only Windows 2000 Advanced Server

   B. Clustering; all Windows 2000 server products

   C. Clustering; only Windows 2000 Advanced Server and Datacenter Server

   D. Distributed File System; only Windows 2000 Server and Advanced Server

TEST YOURSELF OBJECTIVE 7.02

Designing a Multiprotocol Strategy

Windows 2000 was designed with flexibility in mind with regard to multiprotocol support. From a network protocol standpoint, Windows 2000 supports TCP/IP, NetBEUI, IPX (NWLink), AppleTalk, and SNA. From a routing protocol standpoint, Windows 2000 handles many more protocols than its predecessor, accommodating RIP, RIP v2, OSPF, RIP and SAP for IPX, ICMP, RADIUS, L2TP, IPSec, and NAT.

With all of these protocols, or languages, traveling across your network, you must have a good plan for managing them. This diversity can lead to chaos if not handled properly.

- Windows 2000 allows you to implement sophisticated routing and filtering of network protocols on your network using the Routing and Remote Access Service (RRAS).

- Windows 2000 supports RIP, version 2, for IP, OSPF, ICMP Router Discovery, RADIUS, RIP for IPX, SAP for IPX, L2TP, PPTP, NetBEUI, IPX/SPX, TCP/IP, and AppleTalk.

- Windows 2000 supports direct hosting and can be configured to run without NetBIOS support using DNS.

- Windows 2000 includes Gateway Services for NetWare, a service that allows Microsoft clients to connect to NetWare resources as Windows 2000 shares.

- Windows 2000 utilizes Microsoft SNA Server (Host Integration Server) for connectivity to IBM host systems.

Although Windows 2000 can handle a myriad of routed and routing protocols, that doesn't mean you need to implement all of them at once. The more routing protocols you use, such as RIP, OSPF, and so on, the more load you place on your routers as they try to manage multiple routing tables. The old adage of Keep It Short and Simple applies here. Use only what you need to accomplish the mission.

QUESTIONS

7.02: Designing a Multiprotocol Strategy

4. You are the network manager for a midsized corporation that has just completed the migration to Windows 2000 Server from Windows NT 4.0. You have not migrated all of your clients, which are running a mix of Windows 98 and Windows 2000. You only have TCP/IP and NetBIOS bound to your network cards.

Recently, your company announced plans to acquire a competitor. After conducting a site survey of their facility, you noted that they are a NetWare shop running NetWare 3.12. They have a mix of Windows 95 and Windows 98 clients, and they all have NetWare Client32 loaded with IPX/SPX bound to the NIC. They do not use TCP/IP.

Once the deal has been finalized, how can you allow the clients on your Windows 2000 network access to the data that is stored on the NetWare 3.12 servers at your newly acquired division without adding IPX/SPX to your clients?

A. You can go to each NetWare server and add TCP/IP and move it to the top of the binding order.

B. You can implement gateway services for NetWare to allow your Windows 2000 servers to share the NetWare resources.

C. You can implement File and Print Services for NetWare to make your Windows 2000 resources available to your IPX/SPX clients.

D. You can add NWLink as the primary protocol on your Windows 2000 servers so that they can communicate with the NetWare servers on behalf of the clients.

5. **Situation:** You are the network architect for an insurance company with a substantial investment in IBM mainframe technology. Your company has 25 offices connected via a Synchronous Data Link Control (SDLC) network to a data center housing the mainframe. Each branch office has 20 to 50 employees, each with a 3270 terminal. Because of a need to utilize the Internet, plus the desire to move to a Windows platform for increased productivity, you have decided to deploy Windows 2000 Professional PCs to all of your employees. You will still have a need to access your mainframe programs after the deployment. The Internet connection will be located in the data center.

Required Result: Determine how you can access the mainframe using the existing SDLC network with your Windows 2000 PCs.

Optional Desired Result: Determine the type of WAN that will best suit the defined needs of the company.

Proposed Solution: After running through a few scenarios, you decide to implement Microsoft Systems Network Architecture (SNA) server in a branch deployment model (see illustration).

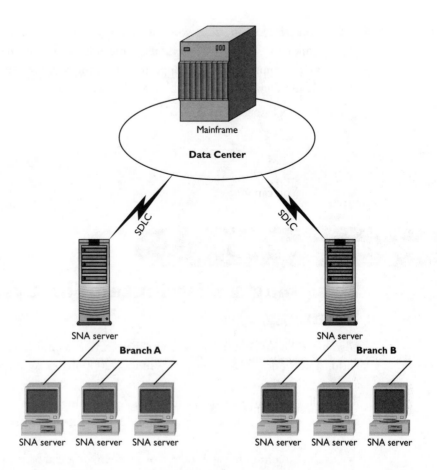

This will allow your client PCs to contact the local SNA server, which will in turn communicate with the mainframe over the existing SDLC network. Since you already have an investment in the SDLC network, you choose to route your Internet traffic through the SNA servers as well to the data center.

What results are provided from the proposed solution?

A. The proposed solution produces the required result only.

B. The proposed solution produces the required result and the optional desired result.

C. The proposed solution does not produce the required result.

6. You are designing a network for a cutting-edge digital editing company in New York City. They wish to send real-time video and audio across their WAN to two design groups on the opposite side of the city. What network protocol should they use to enable this real-time technology?

   A. High-speed Frame Relay

   B. X.25

   C. ATM

   D. SDLC

TEST YOURSELF OBJECTIVE 7.03

Designing a Distributed File System Strategy

Distributed File System (Dfs) is a service that provides a unified namespace for all shares within a network. This can include Windows 2000 shares, Windows NT 4.0 shares, and even Unix shares.

Dfs allows you to provide the following features: high availability for file shares, a unified namespace, load sharing, and the ability to extend data shares transparently to the user.

Dfs can be configured as a stand-alone system, or it can be integrated into the Active Directory, whereby you can use many of the fault-tolerant features and site awareness of Active Directory.

- The Dfs can be configured as a domain-based service or a stand-alone service.

- Dfs provides end users with a single unified namespace for all network file storage.

- Dfs security is based on the existing share and file system permissions set on network resources.

- Dfs clients use Active Directory sites and services to determine the proximity of resources on the network.

exam
⚙atch

Distributed File System uses the File Replication Service (FRS) to replicate its data among fault-tolerant shares. Although for the most part this works very well, you may run into situations where the replication fails due to a lack of space. FRS uses a temporary area on the SYSVOL to queue the data to be replicated. If your SYSVOL is low on space, you may actually use up all of the remaining space when FRS begins the process of replicating the SYSVOL and Dfs data among the servers.

QUESTIONS

7.03: Designing a Distributed File System Strategy

7. You are the webmaster for a growing sports news site. It is hosted on Windows 2000 Server and IIS 5.0. The increased traffic to your site has prompted you to find an inexpensive way to replicate the site's data to two additional Windows 2000 Servers and load balance the requests from your Web server. Which of the following technologies will provide the cheapest way of achieving the goal?

   A. Use domain-based Dfs to replicate the Web site's data to shares on the two other servers, and point IIS to the new Dfs root.

   B. Use load balancing that's built into the operating system to level the requests against three servers.

   C. Cluster the three servers together to provide load balancing.

   D. None of the above.

8. **Situation:** You have recently migrated your Windows NT 4.0 domain to Windows 2000 Active Directory. Although most of your network is now Windows 2000 Professional clients, you still have 50 Windows 98 clients. You are managing three locations that are connected by 128-Kbps leased lines. Thus, they are each in their own Active Directory site. Each location has four standard shares: tools, apps, data, and market-info. For the most part, each of these shares is read-only to the clients. The login script maps a drive letter to

each of these shares. Users constantly complain about how hard it is to find important information quickly. The data in each share is updated from the headquarters on a daily basis; this operation takes anywhere from 15 to 60 minutes, depending on the traffic and the amount of data needing updates. It is cumbersome to manage these shares.

Required Result: You must make it easier for users to access the data in the four standard shares.

Optional Desired Results:

1.   Make the share update process more efficient for the administrative staff.

2.   Reduce the number of drive mappings that are set up with the login script.

Proposed Solution: You propose to implement domain-based Dfs in your new Windows 2000 environment. You create a Dfs root called \\domainname\Dfs, and add shares called tools, apps, data, and mktinfo under the root. You modify the login scripts for all of the clients to map a single drive letter to \\domainname\ Dfs. This will allow all of your users to navigate through a single namespace to find the data or files they are looking for. To help the administrative staff, you create replicas of the four shares in each of the locations and configure FRS to replicate the data between them. This allows the administrative staff to update the data in one place and have FRS replicate it throughout the network.

What results are provided from the proposed solution?

A.   The proposed solution produces the required result only.

B.   The proposed solution produces the required result and one of the optional desired results.

C.   The proposed solution produces the required result and both of the optional desired results.

D.   The proposed solution does not produce the required result.

9.   Which of the following guidelines are limitations of Windows 2000 Dfs? (Choose all that apply.)

A.   The maximum number of Dfs roots per domain is 64.

B.   The maximum number of Dfs roots per server is 1.

C.   The maximum number of Dfs links within a Dfs root is 5,000.

D.   The maximum number of characters in a path is 260.

Questions 10–11   This scenario should be used to answer questions 10 and 11.

You are an architect for an international pharmaceutical company. You are responsible for the Windows 2000 network design for the entire organization, which consists of over 50,000 employees in 120 countries. Currently, you are focusing on desktop management for your desktop and laptop clients. You would like to implement Systems Management Server (SMS), but cannot afford the time and resource investment to bring the project to the table. Thus, you are investigating the use of Dfs to provide similar features at a fraction of the cost.

Your Active Directory site design has identified 40 sites that will be implemented. Per your architectural definition, these are locations that have over 50 users and at least one domain controller. They can have as many as 7,000 users and ten domain controllers.

Your plans currently are indicating that you will have four subdomains under the company's root domain. These subdomains are based on the company's business units, and are named rd.drugcompany.com, mfg.drugcompany.com, hq.drugcompany.com, and sales.drugcompany.com.

Your company has standardized on the following desktop applications: Office 2000 Professional, Internet Explorer 5.0, Outlook 2000, and Acrobat Reader 4.0. Many of the business units have custom MSI packages that are unique to their sections.

The largest WAN links are the T3s that connect the U.S. headquarters, the U.K. headquarters, and the French headquarters. Most of the 40 sites are connected with 128-Kbps to 256-Kbps Frame Relay circuits. A few sites use 128-Kbps B-ISDN circuits.

10. One of the requirements that the CIO has specified is that you must provide a central location worldwide from which employees can install software. That is, users should be able to go to one recognizable network location to find the applications that they are trying to install. How can you use Dfs to meet this requirement?

   A. You can create a domain-based Dfs root in each of the subdomains, and create a share named Software that points to an existing network share in the domain.

   B. You can create a domain-based Dfs root in the forest root domain, and create a share called Software. This share points to multiple shares out in the enterprise where application software is located.

    C. You can create a domain-based Dfs root in the forest root domain, and create a share named Software that points to a network share on a server in the root domain. You can then create a network share called Software on every domain controller in the enterprise (at least one per site). You can then create replicas of the initial Software share, and point them at the network shares worldwide.

    D. None of the above.

11. Which of the following best describes the algorithm by which a client chooses a Dfs replica when a user accesses a Dfs share?

    A. When the user contacts the Dfs for the first time, the client computer transmits its IP address, and Dfs uses DHCP to find the replica that is closest to the user.

    B. When the user contacts the Dfs for the first time, the Dfs root server and the Dfs client have a conversation to exchange the site information about where the client is located.

    C. The Dfs server can tell the site at which the Dfs client is located by looking at the Dfs client's packet header; the Dfs server then refers the local replicas to the client.

    D. The client receives a copy of the Partition Knowledge Table (PKT), which lists shares, their locations, and the time to live. This information is placed in order by site. The client then chooses the share or replica on its own site, or another random location if there are no shares or replicas on the same site.

TEST YOURSELF OBJECTIVE 7.04

Designing a Load-Balancing Strategy

Windows 2000 Network Load Balancing (NLB) service is a feature that allows you to distribute incoming client requests to multiple servers configured in a cluster. Not to be confused with Windows Clustering, NLB can support up to 32 servers, of differing capacity, on the same network segment.

    You need to understand how Network Load Balancing works, the requirements and parameters for implementing NLB in your organization, and how to optimize

NLB. Properly implemented, it can greatly extend the capacity and availability of your enterprise application.

■ *Load balancing* is the process of distributing client requests for an application or service across multiple nodes (or machines) to minimize the chance of overworking one particular server.

■ All nodes within an NLB cluster must be connected to the same network segment.

■ Windows 2000 Network Load Balancing supports up to 32 machines within a cluster.

■ You cannot use Network Load Balancing on token ring networks.

■ Servers involved in an NLB cluster can also be used for other functions by simply using the permanent IP address of the server. Requests to this address will not be load balanced by the NLB service.

exam
ⓦatch

An important concept to understand about NLB is affinity. Affinity is used for managing state—for example, you have probably gone to an e-commerce Web site that seems to remember where you've been and what you have been viewing, without using cookies. This is state. There are three affinity settings: None, Single, and Class C. If you are using NLB to balance an e-commerce site, you should use an affinity setting of Class C to make sure that your Internet customers are able to maintain state while they are surfing through your Web site.

QUESTIONS

7.04: Designing a Load-Balancing Strategy

12. You are preparing to implement NLB in your environment. You have an enterprise scheduling and collaboration application that services 85,000 users on your intranet. The front end for the application is a Web site that is hosted

on IIS 5.0. The back end is a large SQL Server database. This application needs to be available 24/7, since your operation has a worldwide presence. You have already decided to use Windows 2000 Advanced Server on the back end, and use Windows Clustering to create a two-node cluster for the SQL Server database. On the front end, you are going to use four multiprocessor servers running Windows 2000 Advanced Server and IIS 5.0. These servers will have two network interfaces apiece, and will be running the Network Load Balance service. You are going to place these servers on your DMZ segment with the mail server and primary intranet server. These servers, plus your four NLB servers, will be on a 12-port 10/100 switch that is connected to the network core, which is running 100-Mbps Ethernet. The following illustration shows your network configuration:

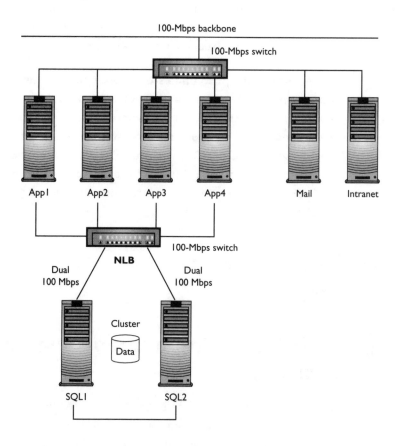

Which of the following illustrates a characteristic of the configuration that does not meet Microsoft's recommendation for using NLB?

A. There is a bottleneck where the traffic comes off the 100-Mbps backbone and goes to the load-balanced cluster.

B. You have servers other than the Network Load Balanced servers on the same segment.

C. You cannot place Network Load Balanced servers on a switch—they must be on a hub in order for the heartbeat to function properly.

D. There aren't any problems with this arrangement.

13. You are preparing to implement a Windows 2000/IIS 5.0 Web site for your company. It will be a support site for your software product, and you anticipate having a high load during 75 percent of the day. The site will have mostly static content, with a few Java-based applets and Active Server Pages. You will use cookies to record the experience of each user. You will start out having three servers running Windows 2000 Advanced Server, and you will use NLB to help distribute the user requests between the three servers. What affinity setting would best serve your implementation?

A. None

B. Single

C. Class C

D. A mixture of all three on the servers

14. **Situation:** You have been hired as a consultant for LotsOfToys.com. Your assignment is to build a fault-tolerant, highly available, and highly scalable network for the company's new e-business Web site. The company's IS staff has begun the work by bringing an OC/3 circuit to the data center. They have a Gigabit Ethernet core, and they are using high-end switches and routers to deliver the traffic to the Web servers. They need your help in bringing the same features to the Web servers and database applications.

Required Result: Recommend a Microsoft technology that will spread the Web site traffic across a number of servers and that can be scaled to meet the demand of the site traffic.

Optional Desired Results:

1. Recommend a failover solution for the technology that you recommend for the required result.

2. Recommend a solution for providing high availability for the SQL Server databases running on Windows 2000 Server that hold the company's catalog and e-commerce application.

Proposed Solution: You recommend that LotsOfToys.com use Windows Network Load Balancing to provide load distribution across the Windows 2000 Advanced Servers that will host the Web application. This will provide the ability to have up to 32 servers in a single NLB cluster. For failover and redundancy, they can have two or more Network Load Balance clusters, and use round-robin DNS to route requests to the multiple cluster IP addresses. To provide high availability for the SQL Server database on Windows 2000 Server, you recommend that they use Windows Clustering to create a four-node cluster. This will provide an immense amount of failover protection for the database should something go wrong.

What results are provided from the proposed solution?

A. The proposed solution produces the required result only.

B. The proposed solution produces the required result and one of the optional desired results.

C. The proposed solution produces the required result and both of the optional desired results.

D. The proposed solution does not produce the required result.

TEST YOURSELF OBJECTIVE 7.05

Windows 2000 Server Clustering

A Windows 2000 *cluster* is a group of servers that are connected together to run an application or share data and act as a single server to clients. This provides for high availability and redundancy that is not readily available with one server hosting an application.

When planning a server cluster, you must look at the hardware requirements, paying attention to the Hardware Compatibility List (HCL), because not all Windows 2000–certified hardware works with clustering; you must identify the needs of the applications that will be clustered; you must determine which clustering technology is required and what clustering model to use; and you must create an implementation plan.

- A *fault-tolerant system* is a system that has no single point of failure.
- Microsoft Clustering Service allows up to four machines to be configured to share hard disk space and work together to seamlessly provide a service to clients.
- Microsoft clustering technology uses a share-nothing cluster methodology, in which a particular machine owns each disk resource. In the event of a failure, the ownership of an application can be transferred to surviving nodes. No disk resource is owned by more than one machine at any time.

exam ⚠️ 𝖂atch

For the most part, it's hard to justify buying two high-end servers and have one sit idly by waiting for a failure. If you have two equally spec'd servers in a cluster, you can have each one provide a separate application, such as email on one, and a database application on the other. You can then configure the opposite server in the cluster to be the failover node. This allows you to increase the utilization of your servers while still keeping all the benefits of using cluster technology.

QUESTIONS

7.05: Windows 2000 Server Clustering

15. Which of the following are benefits of implementing clustering in your network environment? (Choose all that apply.)

   A. More efficient use of equipment

   B. Reduced system or application downtime due to hardware failures

C. Easy deployment of application upgrades

D. None of the above

16. **Situation:** Your supervisor, the director of network services, has asked you
to provide a high-availability solution for four mission-critical data shares on
two existing Windows NT 4.0 servers. He wants to ensure that this data is
available 24/7 to the employees in the organization. He reminds you that the
engineering and customer service departments are working with this data
around the clock, and a server failure can cost the company tens of thousands
of dollars per hour if left unresolved. He also wants to move away from the
Windows NT 4.0 servers and use Windows 2000 because of the information
he has reviewed concerning its new redundancy and high-availability features.
He is reluctant to spend a significant amount of capital funds to make this
move a reality. How do you propose to solve this problem?

Required Result: The four critical data shares must be available 24 hours a
day, with no downtime.

Optional Desired Result: Solve the problem using the least number of servers
possible.

Proposed Solution: You, too, have been reading about Windows 2000, and
decide to implement the following solution. You perform a few calculations,
and determine that you will need four servers to meet the requirements. You
purchase four new servers that have fully redundant subsystems—multiple
power supplies, multiple NICs, internal RAID5 arrays with five disks, and so
on. You install Windows 2000 Advanced Server on these machines, and
configure them to be a four-node cluster. You put one critical share on a server,
and configure the Clustering Service to use the remaining three servers as the
failover nodes for this share. You duplicate this configuration on each of the
remaining servers, using a different critical share on each server.

What results are provided from the proposed solution?

A. The proposed solution produces the required result only.

B. The proposed solution produces the required result and the optional
desired result.

C. The proposed solution does not produce the required result.

17. You are creating a cluster that will host a Web application and WINS. You have an external disk array that is connected to the two servers in the cluster, which are running Windows 2000 Advanced Server. How should the disk array be configured to support these two applications?

    A. Make the entire disk array one partition, and format it using FAT32.

    B. Make the entire array one partition, and format it with NTFS.

    C. Create two partitions on the array, and format them with NTFS.

    D. Create three partitions on the array, and format them with NTFS.

LAB QUESTION

Objectives 7.01–7.05

You have been placed in the position to design and build a fault-tolerant network infrastructure for your company. You are the network engineer for a young company that manufactures wireless networking equipment. You are rapidly outgrowing your current office, and the company is moving to a new, larger facility. Your company has just been granted a large venture capital investment, so funding will not be a problem for your design.

Your new facility will have redundant T3 circuits for Internet connectivity. You will have a switched infrastructure, using both 100-Mbps and Gigabit Ethernet. Your Web presence will start with four servers, possibly expanding to eight. The Web designers have chosen Windows 2000 as the Web platform for your company. You will be hosting your own e-commerce site from your facility to sell your products, as well as to provide technical and customer support.

Your back-end database will be hosted on SQL Server 7.0. This database needs to be available 24/7, and you should also design the connectivity to the database so that it deters attacks from the Internet that somehow defeat the firewall's protection.

You have a business partner that will provide customer data to you directly from their mainframe system. You will need to devise a method of reaching this data interactively.

How can you support all of the needs described for this network?

A QUICK ANSWER KEY

Objective 7.01
1. B
2. B
3. C

Objective 7.02
4. B
5. A
6. C

Objective 7.03
7. A
8. D
9. B and D
10. C
11. D

Objective 7.04
12. B
13. A
14. B

Objective 7.05
15. B and C
16. C
17. D

IN-DEPTH ANSWERS

7.01: Understanding Distributed Data Access Solutions

1. ☑ **B.** The proposed solution produces both the required result and the optional desired result. The decision to use NLB will spread the crush of the hundreds of thousands of hits across multiple Web servers. NLB presents a single, logical IP address to the Internet, while in the background it distributes the incoming traffic across all of the members of the NLB cluster. By distributing the load among multiple servers, you increase the aggregate load that your Web site can handle. Next, by specifying that the Web servers have fully redundant system components, you are reducing the risk that a power supply or network card outage will take a server offline. One important note, though, is that no matter what you do, you cannot guarantee 100 percent uptime.

   ☒ **A** and **C** are incorrect because the proposed solution produces both the required result and the optional desired result.

2. ☑ **B.** Dfs is the technology that allows you to create a logical file system that is physically hosted on numerous servers.

   ☒ **A** is incorrect because NLB is the technology that distributes incoming client requests among multiple servers. **C** is incorrect because Windows Clustering is the technology that allows two or more servers to share a common data source and act as one server. **D** is incorrect because multiprocessor servers are simply servers with more than a processor.

3. ☑ **C.** This diagram represents clustering, a technology that is only available on Windows 2000 Advanced Server and Datacenter Server. These products will support server clusters ranging from two nodes in Advanced Server to four nodes in Datacenter Server.

☒   **A** is incorrect because load balancing is a technology that balances the incoming connections, such as to a Web site, across multiple servers. Load balancing is available on both Advanced Server and Datacenter Server. **B** is incorrect because clustering is not available on Windows 2000 Server—only Advanced Server and Datacenter Server. **D** is incorrect because Dfs is a technology that allows you to create a logical view of multiple physical server shares.

7.02: Designing a Multiprotocol Strategy

4.   ☑   **B.** The key to interoperating between Windows 2000 and NetWare is to implement gateway services for NetWare. This will allow you to connect to the NetWare file resources and publish them as Windows 2000 shares. The clients with TCP/IP can connect to the Windows 2000 shares, and you can slowly begin to remove NetWare Client32 from the acquired company's computers. Ultimately, you can migrate all of the data off the NetWare servers to the Windows 2000 servers to complete the process.

☒   **A** is incorrect because your NetWare servers are currently only running IPX/SPX. By adding TCP/IP and changing the binding order, you are potentially affecting the connectivity to your NetWare servers by the Client32 PCs. **C** is incorrect because File and Print Services for NetWare is a tool for sharing Windows 2000 resources with NetWare clients. **D** is incorrect because you are taking a step away from migrating to TCP/IP by using NWLink as your primary protocol.

5.   ☑   **A.** The proposed solution only produces the required result. By implementing SNA Server, you can continue to utilize your legacy SDLC network for SNA traffic to the mainframe. Unfortunately, you cannot use the SDLC network for your wide area traffic (i.e., Internet, file service, etc.), because Windows 2000 does not recognize SNA as a routable protocol. You must choose a wide area network protocol such as TCP/IP and use a networking technology such as Frame Relay, T-carriers, or ISDN for your WAN links.

☒   **B** and **C** are incorrect because the proposed solution only produces the required result.

6. ☑   **C.** This company should use Asynchronous Transfer Mode (ATM) to transfer their audio and video across town to the design groups. ATM is a dedicated-connection switching technology that organizes data into 53-byte cells and transmits them over the wire. ATM moves data at either 155 Mbps or 622 Mbps, usually over fiber optic lines. It is very well suited for use with real-time video distribution.

☒   **A** and **B** are incorrect because they are "brothers" in the protocol world—well, maybe more like father and son. These are both packet-switching technologies. X.25 employs error checking, which significantly reduces its throughput and makes it worthless for use with video. **D** is incorrect because SDLC is a protocol that is used for mainframe communications.

7.03: Designing a Distributed File System Strategy

7. ☑   **A.** The cheapest way to obtain load balancing would be to use Dfs. If you create a domain-based Dfs, you can create fault-tolerant replicas on other servers that are replicated using FRS. Once that is done, redirect your IIS server to use the Dfs root as its root. Requests coming into the Web server will be load balanced across the three replicas.

☒   **B** and **C** are incorrect because you cannot do clustering in Windows 2000 Server. You must use Windows 2000 Advanced Server or Datacenter Server.

8. ☑   **D.** Believe it or not, the proposed solution does not produce the required result. By implementing Dfs and modifying the login scripts to map a single drive letter to the Dfs root, you cut off the Windows 98 users from the data shares. Windows 95 and 98 clients cannot access Dfs shares without having an add-on utility installed. Once this is installed, they can access the Dfs root or Dfs shares by mapping a drive letter to the resource. Everything else in the proposed solution is correct. The domain-based Dfs will make it easier for users to find the information they are looking for by presenting them with a single unified namespace. It will also make life easier for the administrative staff by allowing them to update a single location and have the files replicated via the FRS.

■ **A**, **B**, and **C** are incorrect because the proposed solution does not produce the required result.

9. ☑ **B** and **D** are correct. The maximum number of Dfs roots that can be configured on an individual server is one. This means that only one root can be hosted on an individual server. This limitation is set to reduce the load that the Dfs root places on the server. The maximum number of characters in a Dfs path is 260. This includes everything from the double slash to the .exe at the end. This really becomes important if you have nested Dfs roots within other Dfs roots. You can easily exceed the 260-character limit in this situation.

■ **A** is incorrect because you can have an unlimited number of Dfs roots per domain. The only limitation is based on the number of servers you have: you can only host one root per server. **C** is incorrect because the maximum number of Dfs links within a Dfs root is 1,000.

10. ☑ **C.** The way to accomplish this task is to create a Dfs root on a domain controller in the forest root domain. Users around the world can access this Dfs by typing **\\drugcompany.com\Dfs**. Next, you can create a share called Software, and map this to a network share on a server in the forest root domain. Preferably, this share will be readily accessible by the users who will maintain the software. In this share you will copy or install the application software. Users can access this by typing **\\drugcompany.com\Dfs\Software**. To make it easier for remote users to access this data, and to build in some redundancy, you can go on to create replicas of the Software share and map these replicas to network shares on domain controllers around the world. Using the File Replication System, the data in these shares will replicate around the world.

■ **A** is incorrect because you still have the problem of users looking to multiple locations to find data. **B** is incorrect because you don't configure a Dfs share to point to multiple shares on the network—this is what replicas are for.

11. ☑ **D.** The Partition Knowledge Table (PKT) lists all of the Dfs shares and includes the site locations for these shares. It is presented in order—all of the shares on the client's site first, and then everything else. The Dfs client will then choose the share or replica closest to home.

■ **A**, **B**, and **C** are incorrect because they don't represent the proper method of picking the local site share.

7.04: Designing a Load-Balancing Strategy

12. ☑ **B.** It is highly recommended that you place NLB clusters on their own segment or dedicated switch. Every client request that is received by the switch will cause a switch flood—the broadcasting of the request to all ports—because the request will have the MAC address of the virtual server, not a real server. Because the switch cannot determine the location of the virtual server, it will flood all of its ports with the request. Thus, every device on the switch will receive the request. For this reason, you should keep servers that are not a member of the NLB cluster off this segment or switch.

    ☒ **A** is incorrect because there isn't a bottleneck coming off the backbone. It's actually the other way around—you have a number of 100-Mbps devices that are ready and willing to overwhelm the switch that's on the edge of the backbone. **C** is also incorrect because you can place Network Load Balanced servers on a switch.

13. ☑ **A.** The best affinity setting for this environment would be None. Affinity is used to manage state on your Web application. Since you are planning to have primarily static content, with cookies to manage the user experience, you really don't need NLB to keep track of the server used to process the request. Thus, you don't need affinity.

    ☒ **B** is incorrect because when the affinity setting is set to Single, your servers will manage state for a particular IP address. This means that all requests from a particular IP address will be routed to the same server in the NLB cluster. This also means that your NLB cluster's efficiency will diminish, because you are managing state for an application that doesn't require it. **C** is incorrect because when you set affinity to Class C, the servers will go a step further and manage state based on 24 bits of the client's IP address. This setting is meant mainly for servers hosting Internet applications, because many firewalls and proxies use a different IP address for each request (but usually on the same subnet). **D** is incorrect because you must have the same affinity setting on every server in your NLB cluster.

14. ☑ **B.** The proposed solution provides the required result and one of the optional results. Microsoft's solution for load distribution is NLB. You are

correct in this recommendation. Also, using round-robin DNS to distribute requests to multiple NLB clusters is a good solution either to get around the 32-server limit on NLB cluster membership or to provide redundancy.

You cannot use Windows Clustering with Windows 2000 Server to provide high availability for the SQL Server databases. You must use either Windows 2000 Advanced Server (two nodes) or Datacenter Server (four nodes).

   ☒   **A**, **C**, and **D** are incorrect because the proposed solution produces the required result and one of the optional results.

7.05: Windows 2000 Server Clustering

15.   ☑   **B** and **C** are correct. Clustering technologies provide for reduced system and application downtime due to failures by providing a failover server to service requests should the primary server go down. Clustering also allows for easy deployment of application upgrades because you can sequentially update each server in the cluster, while the end user never sees a loss of service.

   ☒   **A** is incorrect because clustering is a deliberate duplication of hardware, not a more efficient use of it.

16.   ☑   **C.** The proposed solution does not produce the required result. You made a number of fatal errors in your calculations for this solution. First, the hardware configuration for the cluster will not work. Clustering requires a shared disk array, connected by a shared SCSI or fiber channel. You did not configure this. Second, in order to have a four-node cluster, you need to install Windows 2000 Datacenter Server. Third, you placed the critical shares on separate machines, which cannot be done. Finally, you overcalculated your requirements by a factor of two—you can do this job efficiently with just two servers.

You should have built two servers with Windows 2000 Advanced Server, and connected them to a shared disk array. You should have then copied the data shares to the array on separate partitions. Next, you should have configured each server to host two of the four shares; that is, server1 has share1 and share3, while server2 has share2 and share4. In configuring the failover parameters, you can have server1 failover its two shares to server2, and server2 failover its two shares to server1. Unless the entire cluster is brought down, or you have a massive hardware failure, this will work fine. This also meets the optional results, because you have only purchased two new servers instead of four.

☒ **A** and **B** are incorrect because the proposed solution does not produce the required result.

17. ☑ **D.** You should create three partitions on the disk array, and format each of them as NTFS. According to the guidelines, you should have one partition for each application you are using (in this case, the Web application and WINS), plus a partition for the quorum resource. This is the area the cluster server will use to communicate status information to the other nodes in the cluster. This gives you a total of three partitions.

☒ **A** is incorrect because you need one partition for each application. You also must use NTFS with clustering. **B** and **C** are incorrect because of the need for one partition for each application.

LAB ANSWER

Objectives 7.01–7.05

Let's start with the Web servers. You know that the Web designers want to use Windows 2000. Spec these servers as Windows 2000 Advanced Server so that you can use Network Load Balancing and/or Windows Clustering if necessary. You will want to build these servers with redundant components and hardware RAID5 for availability. To provide load balancing for the e-commerce site, you should implement NLB. Place these four servers on a separate switch just off the corporate backbone. Configure the NLB cluster for Class C affinity to accommodate the state information for the Internet e-commerce application.

You should use high-end servers for the SQL Server database—in fact, you should probably use two servers configured as a failover cluster. Remember to use a shared disk array for the database. These servers must be running Windows 2000 Advanced Server or Data Center Server. To protect the link between the SQL Server cluster and the Web servers, you could configure the network connections to use NWLink: traffic coming to the Web servers on TCP/IP wouldn't be able to cross the links using NWLink. (This is a solution that has been around since Windows NT 4.0.)

Finally, to utilize the partner's mainframe data, you could design a small SNA network for access. You would need a dedicated SDLC circuit to the partner's data center, and you would need to install SNA Server. You will also need to install the SNA client on those PCs that need to access the data.

MICROSOFT CERTIFIED SYSTEMS ENGINEER

8

Designing Internet Connectivity Solutions

TEST YOURSELF OBJECTIVES

W indows 2000 provides much more support for Internet solutions than previous versions of Windows NT. You must know how these technologies fit together in order to effectively plan your network design.

You must understand how firewalls work and how they are implemented in a network infrastructure. You also need to know how to develop routing and remote access strategies for your Windows 2000 network. You need to be familiar with Windows 2000 Network Address Translation (NAT) and how it is implemented. You will have to demonstrate knowledge of Internet Connection Sharing (ICS), which is very similar to NAT. Finally, you need to understand how to integrate Windows 2000 with Proxy Server, Internet Information Server (IIS), and Exchange Server.

TEST YOURSELF OBJECTIVE 8.01

Designing Internet Connectivity Solutions

When designing Internet connectivity solutions, you must take into consideration all of the variables that are present in providing access for your company, while being extremely aware of the associated risks.

When you prepare your design, you should perform a number of steps to gather the information required. These steps include conducting an audit of the existing environment, taking an inventory (hardware and software, user and application access needs, remote access, and security), and then formulating a plan. Your plan should include diagrams that detail the physical connectivity of your network. Other factors that will influence your design are the use of firewalls, remote access, and Internet connectivity for workstations.

- An audit of the existing network is important in putting together a solution for Internet connectivity. Some of the things you have to consider in devising a design are applications, user needs, email, and Web servers.

- Creating diagrams helps organize the planning steps and is useful for providing network documentation after your solution is in place. The documentation can serve as a foundation for proposals and presentations. Diagrams also assist nontechnical management personnel in understanding the solution.

exam

atch

With the Internet becoming more and more pervasive in our everyday lives, it also has become standard in most workplaces. Having access to the Internet is one thing—having secure access is another. You should expect to see a few questions about firewalls and Microsoft's implementation of NAT. These are both good mechanisms for keeping unwanted users off your network.

QUESTIONS

8.01: Designing Internet Connectivity Solutions

1. Up until recently, your company has not provided Internet access to its employees. Those who needed access were given a modem and an analog phone line for connectivity through a local ISP. However, the number of users who need access is exceeding the cost savings of not having Internet access through the LAN. If you were asked to design an Internet connectivity solution now, what question would you ask in order to make a decision about the capacity needed to serve your company's needs?

   A. How many users will be served by this connection?

   B. What applications or services need access to the Internet?

   C. Will a Web presence be hosted from our location?

   D. All of the above.

   E. None of the above.

2. What security technology can you implement on your network that has the capability to block traffic on a port-by-port basis both coming into and leaving your network?

   A. Firewall

   B. NAT

   C. Switch

   D. Terminal Server

3. **Situation:** You have been hired by a company to design a new Internet connectivity solution for them. They have been connected to the Internet for three or four years, by many methods—56-Kbps leased line, ISDN, DSL, and DirectPC. Their business has been expanding fairly steadily, and none of these Internet access methods will provide the bandwidth necessary to support the operation. The following illustration (prepared by the network administrator) shows the current network architecture:

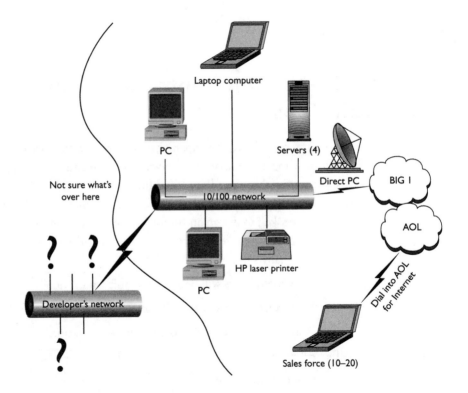

The company is prepared to spend some time and money on developing a realistic Internet access plan. How are you going to develop this plan?

Required Result: You must develop a plan for building a new Internet access solution for this company. Describe how you will obtain the information required to support your plan.

Optional Desired Result: Describe how you will bring the sales force into the corporate network.

Proposed Solution: Your first step is to conduct a detailed hardware and software inventory for the company. It is apparent from the network diagram that was presented to you that the IS staff doesn't have a clue about the state of their network. Once this audit is complete, you use Visio to rediagram the network to see exactly how everything is interconnected. Your next steps are to interview the users to see how they currently use the Internet and to determine what applications they have that may be dependent on the Internet connection. You interview the staff to uncover what applications and services (email, WWW, FTP, etc.) need Internet access. Once you have compiled all of this information, you begin to put the plan together.

The sales force should be using Remote Access Service (RAS) to connect to the corporate network for Internet connectivity. This will provide an additional means of security for the data on the laptops, as well as allow the sales force to utilize corporate services such as email without having to use a third-party email package to get messages back to their co-workers.

What results are provided from the proposed solution?

A. The proposed solution produces the required result only.

B. The proposed solution produces the required result and the optional desired result.

C. The proposed solution does not produce the required result.

TEST YOURSELF OBJECTIVE 8.02

Implementing Firewall Solutions

A *firewall* is a device on a corporate network used to keep unwanted traffic off the network. It can be either hardware based, such as Cisco's PIX line, or software based, such as Checkpoint's products. Both methods have their strengths, and they both have the ability to block or deny traffic.

A firewall can be selective going about its duties—most firewalls can block traffic on a port basis or an IP address basis. This granularity is good for allowing only certain hosts or types of traffic onto your network.

- There are two types of firewalls: software firewalls and hardware firewalls. The advantages of hardware firewalls include out-of-the-box readiness (most of the time) with no extra hardware needed. The advantages of software firewalls include seamless integration with the OS; the disadvantages include the fact that hardware must be purchased separately and that both software and hardware configuration is required.

- Firewalls can allow access via IP address or IP port number. When configuring your network, you may use a combination of these two. This will generally make your environment that much more secure.

- The key to configuring a firewall is to deny all traffic first, and then explicitly allow only the traffic you want to come through the firewall. Do not start by allowing all traffic and then trying to block traffic. You will inevitably miss the port that the hacker is trying to use.

exam
ⓦatch

When considering firewalls for your network, don't rule out Microsoft ISA Server—Proxy Server's latest revision. It contains many of the benefits of a good hardware firewall, at a fraction of the cost. Just remember that a software-based firewall will never perform as well as a hardware-based firewall.

QUESTIONS

8.02: Implementing Firewall Solutions

4. You are the network administrator for a small liberal arts college. You are responsible for 2,500 users on a 10/100-Mbps Ethernet network. You currently have a firewalled 10-Mbps Internet connection (multiple T1s). In recent months, you have watched your available Internet bandwidth dwindle from 40 percent to 10 percent. In reviewing your network logs, you notice a tremendous increase in traffic from a host called server.napster.com:8875. You also see a lot of traffic

coming from 208.49.239.242, 208.49.239.247, and 208.49.239.248, ports
4444, 5555, 6666, 7777, and 8888. ("A lot of traffic" means between 500MB
and 1GB per day from these hosts.) Obviously, this is causing a huge problem
because normal users wanting to check their email or the market conditions are
being crippled by this traffic to and from server.napster.com and its associated IP
addresses. What can you do about this traffic nightmare without affecting the rest
of the college's Internet access? (Choose all that apply.)

A. You can block all traffic from server.napster.com from passing into your
college network at the firewall.

B. You can block all traffic on ports 4444, 5555, 6666, 7777, and 8888 from
entering your network at the firewall.

C. You can block the outbound traffic from users who are known to download
from Napster (you identify these users from the logs).

D. You can block all traffic from the suspect IP addresses (as documented
above) from entering your network.

5. You are in the process of designing an Internet connectivity strategy for your
company. You have a fairly complex design because you plan on using a virtual
private network (VPN) across the Internet to connect ten of your remote offices
to the corporate network. You also will have a demilitarized zone (DMZ) that
will hold the Web, FTP, and mail servers. The following illustration shows this
environment:

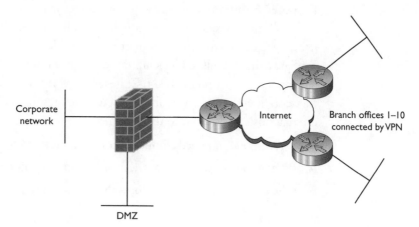

You haven't decided on what type of firewall to use for your network. Which type of firewall will provide the best performance for this network?

A.   Hardware based with at least three interfaces

B.   Software based (Windows NT) with at least two interfaces

C.   Hardware based with at least two interfaces

D.   Software based (Microsoft ISA Server) with at least three interfaces

6.   **Situation:** You are the network manager for a company in the midwestern United States. Your CIO has asked you to implement firewalls on your network to keep unauthorized traffic from the Internet from coming onto the corporate LAN. You currently have a 256-Kbps Internet connection. Your design should allow traffic from anyone on the corporate LAN to travel out through the firewall to the Internet. She wants to restrict incoming traffic to Web, Telnet, and FTP traffic, and to restrict outgoing traffic to just Web and FTP traffic.

Required Result: Design a firewall access policy that will accomplish the CIO's directives.

Optional Desired Results:

1.   Identify what method you will use to block the traffic coming through the firewall.

2.   Recommend a firewall product for your network that will handle the expected volume of traffic.

Proposed Solution: You choose to implement Microsoft's ISA Server to act as a firewall for your company. Although it's a software-based firewall, it should handle the expected volume without much problem. As for your design, you configure the firewall to block all traffic except for ports 20, 25, and 75 from passing into the corporate LAN. This will allow the Web, FTP, and Telnet traffic to flow through. You also configure the firewall to allow all traffic from internal hosts to flow out to the Internet.

What results are provided from the proposed solution?

A.   The proposed solution produces the required result only.

B.   The proposed solution produces the required result and one of the optional desired results.

C.   The proposed solution produces the required result and both of the optional desired results.

D.   The proposed solution does not produce the required result.

TEST YOURSELF OBJECTIVE 8.03

Developing Routing and Remote Access Strategies

Routing and Remote Access Service (RRAS) is fully integrated within Windows 2000. This objective focuses on the remote access features of RRAS—primarily the ability for a remote user to dial in to an RRAS server to make a network connection.

The Windows 2000 version of RRAS provides stronger security and authentication and more options than previous implementations. Microsoft Challenge Handshake Authentication Protocol (MS-CHAP) was supported in Windows NT 4.0, but a new version, MS-CHAP v2, comes with Windows 2000. MS-CHAP v2 provides a higher level of security for logon authentication. Also supported are Remote Authentication and Dial-In Services (RADIUS) and Extensible Authentication Protocol (EAP). As in NT 4.0, you can configure callback options for additional security.

- Supported authentication protocols in Windows 2000 RRAS include Password Authentication Protocol (PAP), Shiva PAP, Challenge-Handshake Authentication Protocol (CHAP), MS-CHAP, MS-CHAPv2, and EAP.

- Another security feature is the callback mode, which can be set to No Callback, Callback Set by Caller, or Callback Preset. The Callback Preset mode allows you to specify a number entered that the server will automatically call back when a user dials in. With Callback Set By Caller, the dial-in user enters a phone number at which he or she will be called back by the server.

exam
ⓦatch

Routing and Remote Access Service is a very complex feature set for Windows 2000. It encompasses a number of key networking features of the OS, which had been separate entities in earlier versions of NT. You can be certain to see a question or two on RRAS on this test, especially because of the breadth of technical knowledge needed to design an effective RRAS environment.

QUESTIONS

8.03: Developing Routing and Remote Access Strategies

7. You are configuring RRAS to allow your remote branch offices to connect to the corporate network via a dial-in connection. You want to ensure that only certain users have permission to connect to the RRAS server, and, once connected, you want to have an additional measure of security that only allows calls from a known telephone number. How would you configure this in RRAS?

   A. In the RRAS management console, choose the Remote Access Services properties, and under Authorized Users, add the names of the users who will receive access.

   B. In the Properties dialog for each authorized user, go to the Dial-In tab and choose Allow Access. Also, choose Set By Caller under Callback Options.

   C. In the Properties dialog for each authorized user, go to the Dial-In tab and choose Allow Access. Also, choose Always Callback To under Callback Options and type in a phone number.

   D. In the RRAS management console, create a remote access policy to control user access to the server. In the Properties dialog for each authorized user, go to the Dial-In tab and choose Control Access Through Remote Access Policy. Also, choose Always Callback To under Callback Options and type in a phone number.

8. You have designed and implemented an RRAS network under Windows 2000. The majority of your clients are running Windows 2000 Professional, but you have 20 to 30 clients that are still running Windows 95. When you configure

RRAS for authentication, which protocols can you use that will provide encryption or a challenge token and work across all the clients?

A. Extensible Authentication Protocol (EAP)

B. Password Authentication Protocol (PAP)

C. Microsoft CHAP (MS-CHAP)

D. Microsoft CHAP version 2 (MS-CHAP v2)

E. All of the above

9. **Situation:** Your company has just made the decision to move the sales force out of the corporate office and into home offices. You have a relatively large sales force of 350 employees, so this could have a large impact on your remote access network infrastructure. These employees already have laptops with Windows 2000 Professional installed. You need to design your RRAS network to accommodate these employees and to provide security for the connection between the sales users and the corporate network.

Required Result: Conduct an analysis to determine how many dial-in ports you will need to accommodate these users.

Optional Desired Results:

1. Choose an authentication protocol that is secure and provides encryption of the user information.

2. Determine if any security needs to be in place for the RRAS connection.

Proposed Solution: You performed an analysis of your users, and determined that you would need thirty-two dial-in ports to start. Although you will have nearly 350 remote users, they will probably not all try to connect at the same time. You choose MS-CHAP, version 2, for authentication because of its secure nature and use of a challenge token to secure the authentication. Since these users will be calling in from home, you really don't think any additional security will be required.

What results are provided from the proposed solution?

A. The proposed solution produces the required result only.

B. The proposed solution produces the required result and one of the optional desired results.

C. The proposed solution produces the required result and both of the optional desired results.

D. The proposed solution does not produce the required result.

TEST YOURSELF OBJECTIVE 8.04

Understanding Windows 2000 Network Address Translation

Network Address Translation (NAT) is a new feature with Windows 2000. NAT allows for secure connections behind your firewall, using one public IP address to access the Internet for every workstation on your network. The addressing scheme behind the NAT server can be whatever you want it to be. However, you should use the range of addresses set aside as nonroutable on the Internet.

You will be required to know how to install the NAT service in your network environment, how to configure it, and how to implement it.

■ Dynamic NAT uses different ports based on the workstation sending the information. The NAT-configured server keeps track of its clients by using these port numbers.

■ You can configure static NAT ports for specific machines behind your NAT server. For example, you could use port 80 for a Web server or port 25 for a mail server. You would assign the static port to the address of the server on your network.

exam
ⓦ*atch*

If you look at the IP addressing designs of most large corporations, they are using NAT behind their firewalls. The reason for this is twofold: they are able to use any address they want, and they can have as many addresses as they want. By hiding their hosts behind one address, they can expand their internal network to practically an infinite number of hosts (16 million versus 254 for a Class C public address).

QUESTIONS

8.04: Understanding Windows 2000 Network Address Translation

10. You have decided to use NAT on your corporate network. What are the guidelines for IP addressing on your private internal network?

   A. You can use any address range on the inside, but you must have a valid, assigned IP address range on the public side of your NAT server.

   B. You must use an address from the 192.168.x.x private network range on your internal network.

   C. You can use any address from the 10.x.x.x private address range on your internal network, as long as you have a valid, assigned IP address for your external interface.

   D. None of the above.

11. Why would you want to use NAT on your network?

   A. You don't want the actual IP addresses of your hosts exposed to the outside world.

   B. You have a large number of hosts, but you cannot get a contiguous block of IP addresses from your ISP to assign to them.

   C. You only have a small number of valid addresses from your ISP, but you want to provide Internet access to all of your users.

   D. All of the above.

12. **Situation:** You are designing a new network for a marketing firm. They currently have 400 users running Windows 95 and 98, and they use Windows 98 ICS for shared Internet access through a cable modem. They have email and a Web server, but both of these services are hosted by their ISP. They would like you to implement a Windows 2000 network at their office in Houston. Once this

network is constructed, they would like to bring the email and Web servers back to their office and host them from there. They will continue to use the default Domain Name System (DNS) servers at the ISP for name resolution.

Required Result: You must provide an NAT network design that will allow the company to host their Web and email servers in the Houston office.

Optional Desired Results:

1. Determine how many valid IP addresses will be needed to support this network design.

2. Determine how you will offer name resolution services for your clients.

Proposed Solution: Once you build the new Windows 2000 domain, you configure the domain controller with the cable modem connection. Since this is a simple design, you configure the cable modem connection to be shared with the rest of the Windows 2000 clients. This will provide basic NAT services to the clients. You build the new email and Web servers, and configure them with 10.10.10.5 and 10.10.10.6. You also configure Dynamic Host Configuration Protocol (DHCP) on the Windows 2000 server and create a scope of 10.10.20.1 through 10.10.21.254 for the clients. DHCP will also configure the DNS setting to point to the ISP's DNS server. This will accommodate all of the existing clients. By using ICS NAT, you will only need one valid address from the ISP.

What results are provided from the proposed solution?

A. The proposed solution produces the required result only.

B. The proposed solution produces the required result and one of the optional desired results.

C. The proposed solution produces the required result and both of the optional desired results.

D. The proposed solution does not produce the required result.

Questions 13–14 This scenario should be used to answer questions 13 and 14.

You are the network administrator for a small firm that specializes in Internet law. You have a Windows 2000 network, with a mix of Windows 98 and Windows 2000 clients, configured as an Active Directory domain. You have an

Exchange server that is configured to pull the messages down from a POP3 server at the ISP's location.

When you first began offering Internet access to your users, you gave them modems and ordered analog phone lines for them. This worked for a while, but the company's growth has outpaced this solution, making it both a costly and inefficient method for providing Internet access.

You are now faced with having to get a full-time connection to the Internet for the office. Your ISP is going to charge a hefty fee to give you a full Class C address for your office, and based on the growth, you may outgrow this address space in a year or so, forcing you to readdress your network soon.

13. How can you provide Internet access to your users without spending the majority of your budget on the monthly IP address fee?

   A. You can configure RRAS to provide demand-dial access to the Internet for your entire network.

   B. You can configure your Windows 2000 Server to use ICS to share a single IP address for all of your users.

   C. You can configure NAT to share a single address with the entire organization. You can also use DHCP to manage your IP addressing.

   D. None of the above.

14. If you transition your network to NAT, will this cause any problems with your Exchange server? What will have to be done to allow the messages to flow to and from the ISP?

   A. Nothing. The Exchange server will continue to work as it did in the past.

   B. You will need to tell the ISP the new IP address of the server. Once that is done, everything should work fine.

   C. You will need to create a static route on the NAT server to allow the traffic to flow in and out through the NAT server.

   D. You will need to create a static NAT port on the NAT server to translate a single valid IP address to the internal address of the Exchange server.

Utilizing Windows 2000 Internet Connection Sharing

Windows 2000 Internet Connection Sharing (ICS) allows you to share a single Internet connection with a number of computers. This represents a good cost savings for small offices that need Internet access for more than one PC but do not want to pay for multiple cable modems. ICS is basically a simple implementation of NAT, plus DHCP and DNS.

For this objective, you will need to understand how ICS functions, how it is installed and configured, and when and how it should be implemented in your network.

- Little configuration and administration are required for ICS. When installed, the simple DHCP allocator uses network addresses in the 192.168.0.0 Class C network. The address of the ICS-bound adapter gets changed to 192.168.0.1.

- As with NAT, you can set up static mapped ports for your ICS services. This allows you to have servers behind your ICS connection for specific purposes, such as Web servers, FTP servers, or mail servers.

exam
ⓦatch

ICS is a neat technology for a small network. It works fairly well in environments of up to 40 or 50 users. Your mileage may vary, especially if your users are addicted to the Internet or if you are trying to share a 56-Kbps modem. If you are looking for a solution for larger environments, you may wish to look at Proxy Server.

QUESTIONS

8.05: Utilizing Windows 2000 Internet Connection Sharing

15. You have a medium-sized network with 280 users and three Windows 2000 servers. You want to provide inexpensive Internet access for these users. You

don't expect to have more than 100 to 125 users accessing the Internet connection at any one time. Based on this, you choose to install an ADSL connection from your local telephone company (telco) provider with 1-Mbps upstream bandwidth. Your telco will only provide one free IP address for your use, but you can lease additional IP addresses at a cost of $4.95 per month per address. What is the most economical way of providing Internet access to your users?

A. Lease enough IP addresses for 125 concurrent connections to the Internet.

B. Use network address translation on your Windows 2000 server and, combined with DHCP, use a private IP addressing scheme on your network. Then configure NAT to use the one free IP address from the telco on the external interface.

C. Use ICS on the Windows 2000 server that is connected to the ADSL modem to provide access to your network.

D. None of the above.

16. You are designing a small network for a doctor's office. It will consist of a Windows 2000 PC and five Windows 98 PCs. The office will be using this network primarily for managing patient records, as well as for accessing the Internet to submit insurance claims online to the major providers. You have chosen to implement ICS to provide Internet access. Which of the following services are required on the Windows 2000 PC to support ICS?

A. DHCP

B. DNS

C. NAT

D. None of the above

TEST YOURSELF OBJECTIVE 8.06

Integrating Windows 2000 with Microsoft Proxy Server, Internet Information Server, and Exchange Server

Designing an Internet solution for a Windows 2000 network often includes deployment of various Internet services. Your organization could require the Web page caching and filtering capabilities of a proxy server. You might want to provide a Web presence via a Web server. Furthermore, it is almost certain that you will need to provide email for your users. Microsoft products such as Microsoft Proxy Server, Internet Information Server, and Exchange Server are easier to integrate into your Windows 2000 network if you plan for their deployment.

- Internet Information Server, version 5, is included with Windows 2000 Server. When designing your Internet solution, you should consider whether you will be running IIS on your network. If you will be, you must consider security factors and integration with other network components.

- Port 80 is the common HTTP port used by IIS for Web services. IIS also uses port 443 for Secure Socket Layer (SSL) connections. If you use NAT or ICS for your Internet connectivity, static port mappings should be used for these types of services.

- When using the Exchange mail server, you must make sure your firewall is configured to allow traffic through the different ports used to communicate with other mail servers (typically 25 for SMTP and 110 for POP3).

- If you are using NAT or ICS in conjunction with Exchange, you must make sure you have the appropriate static port mappings in place to allow communication through the NAT server to the mail server on your network.

exam *Watch* *If you are implementing these technologies in your existing network environment, make sure that your firewall is configured to allow traffic to pass to the servers. Make sure you understand which port numbers map to which services. You will probably have a question on IP ports on the test.*

QUESTIONS

8.06: Integrating Windows 2000 with Microsoft Proxy Server, Internet Information Server, and Exchange Server

17. What advantages does Microsoft Proxy Server give you over using network address translation or ICS? (Choose all that apply.)

    A. It allows you to share a single IP address among a number of internal clients.

    B. Proxy Server can cache Web content to increase the performance of the Internet connection.

    C. Proxy Server can perform many of the duties of a software-based firewall.

    D. Proxy Server, like ICS, requires the use of the 192.168.0.0 network.

18. You have implemented a hardware-based firewall between your Internet connection (a T1) and your corporate network. You have an Exchange server and an IIS server behind the firewall. What ports must you allow to pass through the firewall for these services to continue to operate properly? (Choose all that apply.)

    A. 80 and 443

    B. 25 and 110

    C. 20 and 21

    D. 23 and 88

19. **Situation:** You have just completed designing your basic Windows 2000 network. You will have two subnets connected by a Layer 3 switch. The switch will connect to a router by way of a hardware-based firewall. The entire network will be connected to the Internet via a 128-Kbps circuit. You will be placing an

Exchange 2000 server on the network, as well as an IIS server. The following illustration shows the network configuration:

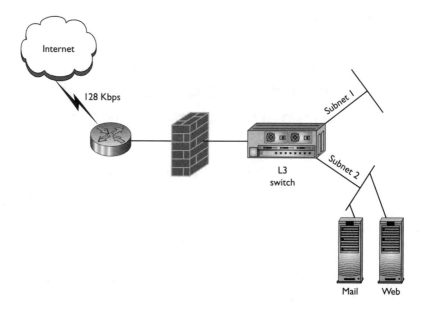

The Web server will be used primarily for hosting a simple corporate Web page. It will also host the Outlook Web Access service. Exchange will be configured to receive mail that has been routed from the ISP. The DNS server on your network contains the MX record for your email server. Are there any security issues that need to be addressed by having these two servers on the network?

Required Result: You must identify any security risks associated with having your Web server and Exchange server on the internal network.

Optional Desired Results:

1. Describe any means of making these servers more secure on your network.

2. Redesign your network to reflect these changes.

Proposed Solution: Conventional wisdom suggests that you shouldn't allow traffic onto your network that doesn't need to be there. By adding the Web server and the mail server, you are introducing two hosts that will be receiving traffic addressed to them, as opposed to being sourced by them. After conducting your analysis, you feel that these servers should be placed on a separate interface on the firewall to keep them somewhat separated from the internal network. You decide to configure the firewall to only allow HTTP, HTTPS, SMTP, and POP3 traffic into the two servers on the DMZ, while allowing any traffic that originates from either the DMZ or the internal network to go out. The following illustration shows the new configuration:

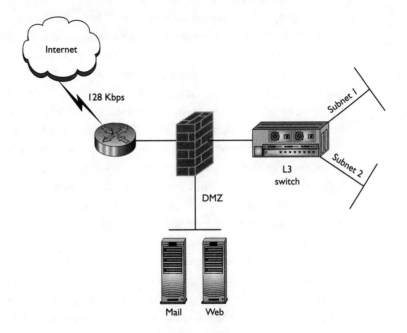

What results are provided from the proposed solution?

A. The proposed solution produces the required result only.

B. The proposed solution produces the required result and one of the optional desired results.

C. The proposed solution produces the required result and both of the optional desired results.

D. The proposed solution does not produce the required result.

LAB QUESTION

Objectives 8.01–8.06

You are working with a large insurance company to redesign their network from a NetWare 3.1 and SNA infrastructure to a Windows 2000 network.

The company has 14 branch offices and a headquarters facility. There are a little over 1,700 employees. They are running Windows 95 and Windows 98 on the desktop, and most of the management team have laptops with Windows 98 running on them. The executives dial in to receive their mail when they are on the road for business.

The company does not provide Internet access to its employees at this time, but they realize that it could provide a significant business advantage to have this access. Thus, they would like to design this access when the network is rebuilt.

Another significant area of improvement will be the addition of a Web server farm at the headquarters location, which will be used in part to provide online rate quotes for prospective customers. This segment will need to be isolated from the rest of the network, but it must also have the ability to get traffic out to the Internet.

Finally, the company wants to ensure that Internet security is at the forefront of the design. Being a relatively conservative company, they want to maintain their reputation in the market—not have their name all over the news with reports of a break-in.

Your assignment is to determine what kind of Internet connectivity would best suit this company, design the infrastructure to support the Internet connectivity, and come up with a plan to accommodate their Internet hosting activities. Answer the following questions during your planning:

1. How will you determine the amount of bandwidth that will be required for this company?

2. Do they need a firewall? Where on the network will a firewall best support their activities?

3. Do you need to use network address translation? How would you implement this? What about ICS or Proxy Server?

4. Are there any issues with having the Web server farm on the corporate network?

5. Do you need to design an RRAS network solution?

A QUICK ANSWER KEY

Objective 8.01

1. D
2. A
3. B

Objective 8.02

4. A, B, and D
5. A
6. D

Objective 8.03

7. D
8. C
9. C

Objective 8.04

10. A
11. D
12. D
13. C
14. D

Objective 8.05

15. B
16. D

Objective 8.06

17. B and C
18. A and B
19. C

IN-DEPTH ANSWERS

8.01: Designing Internet Connectivity Solutions

1. ☑ **D.** All of the above. When you begin planning to provide Internet access to the masses, you need to ask a lot of questions to determine the type of Internet connection you are going to purchase. Some questions are obvious: how many users are going to be using this connection? What applications or services (such as Exchange) need access? Will there be a Web server that uses this connection? All of these questions attempt to paint a picture about the needs of the company.

   ☒ There are no wrong answers since they are all correct.

2. ☑ **A.** A firewall is a hardware or software device that has multiple network interfaces and is used to block traffic from entering or leaving your network. It normally works on a TCP and UDP port basis, allowing you to effectively keep unwanted packets from entering your network. It is regarded as a critical component of any contemporary network design that includes connectivity to the Internet or a third-party network, such as that of a vendor or business partner.

   ☒ **B** is incorrect because NAT is used to hide multiple invalid IP addresses, such as those from the 10.x.x.x range, behind a valid address. It is widely used to expand the number of IP addresses that can be used on a private network. **C** is incorrect because a switch is a Layer 2/3 connectivity device that is used to provide network access to client or server machines. **D** is incorrect because a Terminal Server is used to provide multiaccess solutions to network clients.

3. ☑ **B.** The proposed solution produces the required result and the optional desired result. When designing an Internet connectivity scheme, you need to have accurate data on which to base your conclusions (just like with any other type of design project). Once this data is in hand, you can go about diagramming your findings, and then diagramming your future network. It is very important to uncover exactly how the Internet connection will be used, both now and in the future.

The recommendation to bring the sales force onto the corporate network is a good one. This allows them to take advantage of the corporate data network as well as access the corporate email server. Currently, they must use AOL Mail to get messages to their coworkers. To bring these users onto the network, you can either use RAS or stick with AOL and use a VPN to provide access to the network.

☒ **A** and **C** are incorrect because the proposed solution produces the required result and the optional desired result.

8.02: Implementing Firewall Solutions

4. ☑ **A**, **B**, and **D** are correct. This question addresses a very common problem at many colleges and companies—how to restrict access to a popular network service without affecting the valid traffic on the network. By configuring your firewall to deny certain types of traffic from entering your network, you can bring some peace and order back to your Internet connection. You can block traffic into or out of your firewall based on domain name, IP address, and port number.

    ☒ **C** is incorrect because you have not addressed the traffic inbound to your network. This solution would be an administrative headache to maintain.

5. ☑ **A.** A hardware-based firewall with at least three interfaces will provide the best performance for your network. This type of firewall is designed to do nothing else but process packets as they cross from one interface to another, much like a hardware-based router. This network has design elements that will put a tremendous load on the firewall. First, each of your ten remote offices will need a conduit through the firewall so that the authorized traffic can flow to the inside network. Second, the firewall has two inside interfaces: the internal network and the DMZ. Both of these elements require that the firewall do more than just deny or allow the packet to flow—it must read more of the packet, which will slow down the flow of data. It would take a huge server with a software-based firewall to equal the performance of a lower-end hardware firewall.

    ☒ **B** is incorrect, both because it doesn't have enough interfaces and because a software-based firewall is not the best choice for a complex DMZ/VPN strategy. **C** is incorrect because it doesn't have enough interfaces to support the design. **D** is incorrect because a software-based firewall will not keep up with a hardware-based firewall unless you build a very large server.

6. ☑ **D.** The proposed solution does not produce the required result. The CIO wants to allow only Web, FTP, and Telnet traffic to enter the corporate LAN

through the firewall. You configured the firewall to allow ports 20, 25, and 75 to enter. Unfortunately, these ports do not correspond to the required traffic. You should have allowed ports 20 and 21 for FTP, 23 for Telnet, and 80 for HTTP. Also, you configured the firewall to allow traffic from any internal host to flow to the Internet. You needed to restrict this traffic to only Web (port 80) and FTP (ports 20/21). You did correctly identify the type of firewall that would be appropriate for this network. The amount of traffic (256 Kbps) should not overwhelm the firewall in the near future.

☒ **A**, **B**, and **C** are incorrect because the proposed solution does not produce the required result.

8.03: Developing Routing and Remote Access Strategies

7. ☑ **D.** The best way to configure this access policy is to (1) create a remote access policy in the RRAS management console, (2) ensure that each authorized user's properties reflect that their dial-in permissions are controlled by a remote access policy, and (3) configure the callback number for each user. The following illustration shows the dial-in permissions for a specific user:

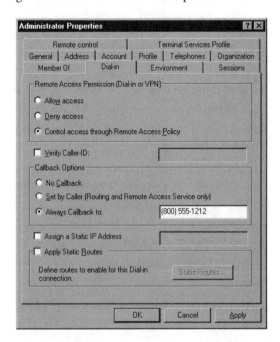

You can configure RRAS to check the Caller ID to match phone numbers, but it's more secure to set the callback number on a per-user basis.

☒ **A** is incorrect because you cannot grant or deny access to RRAS in this manner. **B** is incorrect because the user will be responsible for providing a callback number. This doesn't provide any security—just a means for an employee to save money on the dial-in call. **C** is incorrect only because it is not as efficient as **D**. This method will work on a small scale, but it's better to use a remote access policy in a corporate environment.

8. ☑ **C.** Microsoft CHAP is the only authentication method from the given list that uses either encryption or a challenge token (CHAP uses a challenge token) and works across all the products.

☒ **A** is incorrect because EAP is a new protocol in Windows 2000 that is designed to enable developers to create new authentication methods that are compatible with Windows 2000. **B** is incorrect because although both Windows 2000 and Windows 95 support PAP, this protocol sends passwords in clear text across the network. **D** is incorrect because Windows 95 doesn't support MS-CHAP, version 2.

9. ☑ **C.** The proposed solution produces the required result and both of the optional desired results. In order to determine how many RAS ports you will need, you have to understand how the users will be using the network. In this case, you are designing access for a sales force who will be working from home. This might lead you to believe that you need a large number of ports, but because of the nature of sales, you probably won't have more than 30 or 40 users connecting at any one time. Their use will primarily be for messaging, but your analysis will uncover any other needs, such as a sales automation tool that may need a connection on a daily basis as well. Your mileage may vary, and you can always add more lines and modems later if you need to. The choice of MS-CHAP, version 2, is an acceptable solution for this RAS network. The clients and servers are all running Windows 2000, so this protocol will work fine. Your remote users probably don't need any additional security for dialing in from home. A better choice would be to use one of the dial-back options so that you can reduce the charges that are incurred by dialing in from home, allowing the company to take advantage of the corporate rate that you would get from calling the user back.

☒ **A**, **B**, and **D** are incorrect because the proposed solution produces the required result and both of the optional desired results.

8.04: Understanding Windows 2000 Network Address Translation

10. ☑ **A.** When you are designing a network to use NAT, technically you can use any address range that you want on your internal network. That means that if you want to use Microsoft's public address range on your internal network, you can. You *must* have a valid, assigned IP address for the external interface on your NAT server. It is highly recommended that you stick with the private address ranges for your internal network:

Class A range: 10.0.0.0 to 10.255.255.255

Class B range: 172.16.0.0 to 172.31.255.255

Class C range: 192.168.0.0 to 192.168.255.255

☒ **B** is incorrect because you can use any address range that you want, not just the 192.168.x.x private address range. **C** is incorrect also, because you can use any address range that you want on your private network behind the NAT server. You just must have a valid address on the external address.

11. ☑ **D.** Network address translation can be used for all of these reasons. **A** describes a situation in which you may not want the outside world to know the IP addresses of your internal hosts and servers. By using NAT, you can hide these hosts behind one or more valid IP addresses. **B** describes a situation in which you have a large number of hosts, say 1,000 or so, and your ISP can only give you multiple Class C addresses to reach the appropriate number required. Here you would use a Class A or Class B private range for your internal network, and just use a few Class C addresses for your external interfaces. **C** describes the opposite situation, in which you only have a handful of addresses and you have a large number of hosts needing access to the Internet. Here you can hide all of your internal hosts behind a single valid address using NAT.

☒ There are no wrong answers.

12. ☑ **D.** The proposed solution does not produce the required result. If you were just going to use NAT to share an Internet connection with your users, this solution would be fine. However, you have brought two public servers behind the NAT server and given them private addresses. In this scenario, you have cut them off from the outside world. Also, ICS only uses the Class C

private range of 192.168.x.x, so by assigning the servers addresses from the 10.x.x.x range, you have cut them off from the inside network as well.

The correct solution would be to configure NAT in the RRAS console. You can use one valid IP address to share among your users, and then you can configure two static NAT ports for the email and Web servers. These static ports map a valid IP address with an invalid private address, allowing traffic to flow through the NAT server from both the external interface and the internal interface. To support this simple arrangement (sharing and static NAT ports), you will need at least three valid IP addresses—one for the sharing and two for the static ports. (You will also need valid addresses for your router's interfaces.) To provide name resolution, you can have your internal clients go to the ISP, or you can have NAT do the resolution on the client's behalf. This is done by configuring NAT to resolve IP addresses for clients using DNS, as shown in the following illustration:

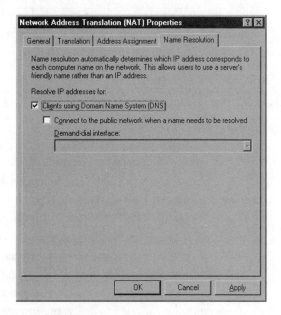

☒   **A**, **B**, and **D** are incorrect because the proposed solution does not produce the required result.

13.   ☑   **C.** The best way to avoid paying the monthly bill is to switch to NAT. You can set up NAT to share a single valid IP address with the entire network. Although you have a number of hosts, it's easier to readdress your network now

to take advantage of NAT, which will give you practically unlimited address space for the future.

☒ **A** is incorrect because you are actually incurring more fees and charges: you will have a dial-up line that will probably be active 20 hours a day. **B** is incorrect because once you implement ICS on the network segment, you can no longer use DHCP or DNS—ICS handles this. ICS also changes the default gateway to 192.168.0.1 and expects that all clients will have a 192.168.0.x address.

14. ☑ **D.** In order to have your email continue to flow, you will need to configure a static NAT port on the NAT server that maps the valid external IP address to the internal IP address. This IP address is separate from the one used for the clients to share the connection.

☒ **A** is incorrect because if you do nothing, the email will not come to the Exchange server. **B** is incorrect because your ISP doesn't need to know the IP address—it's a nonroutable address, and you pull your mail from them rather than having them push it to you. **C** is incorrect because you do not need to create a static route—you need a static NAT port.

8.05: Utilizing Windows 2000 Internet Connection Sharing

15. ☑ **B.** All of the information that is provided seems to lead toward using ICS, but you must remember the IP addressing that ICS uses. When you install ICS on a PC, that PC's IP address changes to 192.168.0.1. ICS will provide IP addresses via an AUTODHCP utility, and these addresses will fall in the 192.168.0.2 to 192.168.0.254 scope. In the case of your network, you have 280 hosts, plus three servers. You will exhaust your supply of ICS addresses well before you run out of clients. Using NAT in this example is thus the only way to go. You can use any IP addressing scheme and still use only one valid IP address from the telco to access the Internet.

☒ **A** is incorrect because it is not an economical way of providing access. Plus, you don't have enough addresses for your entire network. **C** is incorrect for the reason described in the previous paragraph. Basically, you cannot use ICS on networks with more than 253 hosts (one address for the ICS machine, plus 253 for the clients).

16. ☑ **D.** You don't need any additional services on the ICS PC to provide shared Internet access to the clients on the network. It comes with its own DHCP server (AUTODHCP) as well as preconfigured DNS settings.

☒ **A** is incorrect because DHCP is provided by the ICS service. You don't need an additional DHCP server on the same network. **B** is also incorrect, because you do not need DNS to implement ICS. ICS provides its own settings, utilizing the ISP's DNS servers to resolve domain names. **C** is incorrect because ICS is another version of NAT—you can look at ICS as the automatic version of NAT.

8.06: Integrating Windows 2000 with Microsoft Proxy Server, Internet Information Server, and Exchange Server

17. ☑ **B** and **C** are correct. Microsoft Proxy Server takes all of the features of NAT and ICS, and adds a few that make it invaluable in today's networked environment. First, Proxy Server will cache content from Web sites. This caching will increase the performance of your network. When a client PC requests a Web page, Proxy Server checks its cache first. If it already has the page in memory, it will return that cached page. If not, it goes on the Internet to get the page. The second advantage that Proxy Server has over NAT and ICS is firewall functionality. Proxy Server can filter packets based on predefined criteria, acting like a firewall.

☒ **A** is incorrect because it's not a benefit that Proxy Server has over ICS or NAT—all three technologies will allow you to share a single IP address among multiple clients. **D** is incorrect because Proxy Server does not require you to use the 192.168.0.0 network.

18. ☑ **A** and **B** are correct. In order to allow your Exchange server and IIS server to continue to send and receive packets through the firewall, you will need to allow ports 80 and 443 (HTTP and HTTPS) and ports 25 and 110 (SMTP and POP3) to pass through. You may also need to allow ports 143 and 995 through if your email server is using IMAP or secure POP3.

☒ **C** is incorrect because ports 20 and 21 correspond to those used by FTP. **D** is incorrect because port 23 is used by Telnet, and port 88 is used by Kerberos.

19. ☑ **C.** The proposed solution produces the required solution and both of the optional results. You properly identified a number of the risks that are associated with having mail and Web services on your internal network. The best way to handle these services is to place them on a demilitarized zone (DMZ) off your firewall. Here, you can place very restrictive filters on the traffic that is allowed to enter and leave the segment (not that you won't have restrictive filters on your internal interface as well). The initial port filtering will work fine. You may find after a short period of time that an application needs another port opened in order to function properly.

☒ **A**, **B**, and **D** are incorrect because the proposed solution produces the required result and both of the optional results.

A LAB ANSWER

Objectives 8.01–8.06

1. You must take a multiphase approach to gathering this information. You know some of the details just from the initial planning process. You have a number of users and a number of services that would like or require Internet access. You will need to interview the network services team to determine the remaining services that need access.

2. Absolutely! These days, every company that is connected to the Internet should have a firewall. You should have a firewall located at every entrance point to the network from the outside. For example, if you have one Internet connection, you should have at least one firewall. This company needs to have a firewall with multiple interfaces. Their Web server farm should be placed on its own segment (called a DMZ) that is isolated from the rest of the network.

3. They will need NAT if they don't have enough valid IP addresses to support the users and devices on the network. Remember, they are a NetWare shop migrating to Windows 2000. They probably have IPX, so this would be a perfect opportunity to design their IP network around NAT. You could use the Class A private address range (10.0.0.0) and subnet it as much as you need. You will need to configure static NAT ports for any host on the internal network that needs to have access to the outside using its own valid IP address (i.e., mail, Web, FTP, etc). You cannot use ICS in this type of environment because the environment is too large. A proxy server might help later on when you need to optimize the traffic going to the Internet. It's probably not needed at this point.

4. There aren't any issues unless you put the farm on the same segment as the rest of your office. If you keep it separated on a DMZ, you shouldn't have a problem.

5. You will need to implement an RRAS dial-in network for the executives. They will need to have dial-in access to the network for email and Web access.

MICROSOFT CERTIFIED SYSTEMS ENGINEER

9

Designing Internet Connectivity Using Microsoft Proxy Server 2.0

TEST YOURSELF OBJECTIVES

Microsoft Proxy Server 2.0 is a full-featured proxy server and firewall product. When you integrate Proxy Server 2.0 into your Windows 2000 network design, you can provide Internet connectivity for your internal network users and protect the internal network from undesired Internet users.

To successfully implement Proxy Server 2.0, you need to understand how the product works. Once you have done this, you can design a Proxy Server network implementation. Your design will need to address security and fault tolerance of the proxy servers. Finally, you need to be able to optimize your Proxy Server implementation so that it gives the maximum performance for your network.

Understanding Proxy Server 2.0

Microsoft Proxy Server 2.0 will provide your organization with a secure Internet access solution for your internal network clients. It can also protect your internal network from Internet intruders.

For this exam you will need to know the basics about how Proxy Server operates. You need to know how to install and configure it on both Windows NT 4.0 and Windows 2000 servers. You need to understand the design considerations for implementing Proxy Server in various network configurations (single site, multiple sites, and segmented network). You must understand the advantages that Proxy Server gives you, such as high security, performance, and application compatibility. Finally, you need to understand how to integrate Proxy Server with Windows 2000.

- Microsoft Proxy Server 2.0 provides a way to secure the internal network from Internet intruders and to exercise control over what content internal users can access on the Internet.

- Microsoft Proxy Server 2.0 was not designed with Windows 2000 in mind. However, you can download a setup program from the Microsoft Web site that will allow Proxy Server 2.0 to be installed and integrated with Windows 2000 services, including the Active Directory.

- Microsoft Proxy Server 2.0 is installed "on top of" Internet Information Server 5.0.

- Proxy Server 2.0 includes three separate and distinct services: the Web Proxy Service, the WinSock Proxy Service, and the Socks Proxy Service.

- The Web Proxy Service is used by CERN-compliant browsers and provides access to resources via the HTTP, HTTPS, Gopher, and FTP protocols.

- The WinSock Proxy Service is used to replace the native WinSock driver on the proxy client's TCP/IP protocol stack.

- The Socks Proxy Service is for Sockets applications that run primarily on Unix and Macintosh systems that do not support the WinSock Session Layer interface.

exam
Watch

Remember that private IP address ranges (10.0.0.0, 192.168.0.0, etc.) are not accessible over the Internet because Internet routers do not route these IP addresses. All requests for resources located on machines with private IP addresses will be dropped by Internet routers.

QUESTIONS

9.01: Understanding Proxy Server 2.0

1. You have decided to use proxy services on your corporate network. You have a relatively small connection to the Internet (128 Kbps), and the number of users in your organization that have requested access is constantly increasing. When you begin to design your implementation of Proxy Server, what questions should be addressed?

   A. Does the organization center around a single physical site, or is it spread across multiple geographical sites separated by WAN links?

   B. Is the network segmented? If so, will different segments need to have different levels of access to the Internet?

   C. Do you plan to use access controls to limit what users can do with their Internet connection, or will users be free to access whatever they like, whenever they like?

   D. Will users on the Internet require access to any internal resources on the network?

   E. All of the above.

2. You have just begun upgrading your Windows NT 4.0 network to Windows 2000. Everything has been going very smoothly. You are now ready to upgrade the servers that are running Proxy Server 2.0. What must you do in order to upgrade these servers to Windows 2000 and allow Proxy Server to continue to run properly? (Choose all that apply.)

   A. You must uninstall Proxy Server, upgrade your server to Windows 2000, and then reinstall Proxy Server from the CD.

   B. You must back up the Proxy Server configuration to floppy disk. After you upgrade the server to Windows 2000, you must restore the Proxy Server settings to the server.

   C. You must back up the Proxy Server settings, and then uninstall Proxy Server. After you have upgraded your server to Windows 2000, you must reinstall Proxy Server 2.0 using the updated installation utility available on the Internet. Once that is complete, you can restore the settings that you previously backed up.

   D. After you upgrade from NT 4.0 server to Windows 2000, you will need to reinstall Proxy Server in the same location as it had been installed on NT 4.0.

3. **Situation:** You are consulting for a firm that wants to implement Proxy Server 2.0 on their Windows 2000 network. However, they are concerned that this product won't be worth the money, compared with just implementing the NAT service that is included in Windows 2000. This firm has four sites, with over 1,700 users throughout the organization. Three of the sites are connected to the headquarters with 56-Kbps Frame Relay circuits. The company has a 256-Kbps circuit to the ISP for Internet access. Some of their other requests are as follows: they want to be able to restrict which Web sites can be accessed over the corporate network, they want their Macintosh clients to be able to access the Internet through the proxy, and they want to be able to restrict which users have access to the Internet connection.

   Required Result: You must describe the main features of Proxy Server that make it a better choice than NAT for implementation on this customer's network.

   Optional Desired Result: Describe which features of Proxy Server will help with their other requests.

   Proposed Solution: You inform the client that the primary feature of Proxy Server 2.0 that makes it a better choice than NAT for their network is its ability to provide firewall functionality. This will give them much better security for their network than NAT will. The features of Proxy Server that will address their other requests are its ability to filter objectionable material and even to block access to specific URLs, its ability to control access by using Windows 2000 user and group membership, and its ability to provide access for non-Windows clients with the WinSock Proxy component.

What results are provided from the proposed solution?

A. The proposed solution produces the required result only.

B. The proposed solution produces the required result and the optional desired result.

C. The proposed solution does not produce the required result.

Designing a Proxy Server Network Implementation

The implementation of Proxy Server on your network can be very simple or very complex, depending on how you design the network. This should not be looked at as a drawback of the product, because this complexity can produce incredible performance increases for clients on slow WAN links.

You need to determine where you will place your proxy servers for the optimum benefit to your organization. You also need to understand the implications of integrating Proxy Server into an existing network. Finally, you must know how your clients should be configured in order to take advantage of Proxy Server's features.

■ When designing a proxy networking implementation, you need to consider where to locate proxy servers on your network, and the implications of doing so.

■ A proxy server can be located on the "edge" of a network. These edge proxy servers have at least one interface exposed to the Internet. This interface will have a public IP address that is accessible from any host location on the Internet.

■ A proxy server can also be located internally and have no interfaces exposed to the Internet. These proxy servers are used primarily to manage Web caching. However, you can also use them on the edges of subnets to provide increased security for particular segments.

■ Bandwidth requirements must be considered along with hardware requirements. External interfaces will have slower interfaces that are dependent on the WAN technology being used.

e x a m
ⓦ a t c h

Proxy servers can be placed either on the edge of a network, where the proxy server provides firewall functionality, or on a non-Internet segment, where it can provide caching and packet filtering between internal segments.

QUESTIONS

9.02: Designing a Proxy Server Network Implementation

4. **Situation:** You are preparing to deploy Proxy Server throughout your Windows 2000 network to provide Web caching and access control for your organization. The following illustration shows your current infrastructure:

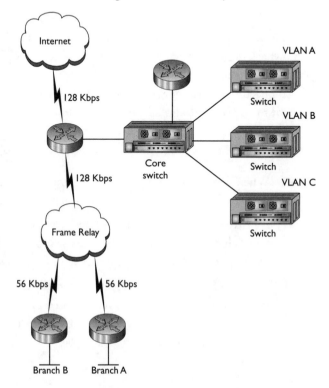

There are 40 employees at Branch A, 65 employees at Branch B, and 750 employees distributed across VLANs A through C. All of your employees are using either Windows 2000 or Windows 98. You have addressed your network using the 10.0.0.0 private address range. You are slowly moving toward opening the Internet up to all of the employees, but you haven't been able to get the senior management to catch on. Thus, your bandwidth between sites and the Internet is relatively low. Management wants to be able to control who has access to the Internet, and they would like to be able to block access to the major employment Web sites on the Internet.

Required Result: How would you place the proxy server(s) in this network to optimize the bandwidth?

Optional Desired Results:

1. Configure Proxy Server to control who gets access to the Internet.

2. Configure Proxy Server to block the undesired Web sites.

Proposed Solution: You want to employ multiple proxy servers in your environment. You will place one proxy server on each VLAN, one attached to the core switch, one in each branch office, and one between the Internet router and the core switch. The following illustration shows your plan:

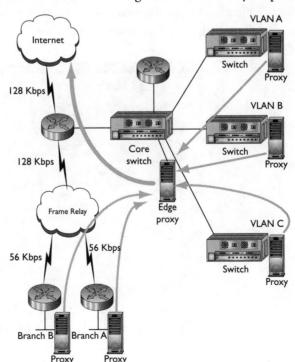

You configure the edge proxy server to deny access to the major employment sites as shown in the following illustration:

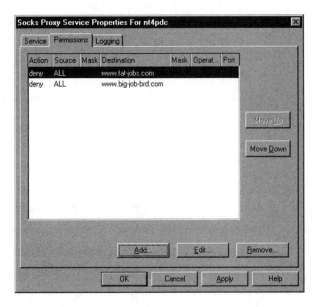

Finally, to control who has access to surf the Internet, you configure the Web Proxy Service as shown in the following illustration:

What results are provided from the proposed solution?

A. The proposed solution produces the required result only.

B. The proposed solution produces the required result and one of the optional desired results.

C. The proposed solution produces the required result and both of the optional desired results.

D. The proposed solution does not produce the required result.

5. Your company is implementing a Proxy Server solution. What is the easiest way to provide fault tolerance for your proxy servers?

A. Install a single proxy server and configure multiple interfaces, each connected to a different Internet connection.

B. Build two Windows 2000 Advanced Server machines, install Proxy Server 2.0 on each one, cluster the two servers together, and configure Proxy Server on each machine to be a single proxy array.

C. Deploy a minimum of two proxy servers in your organization. Configure one proxy server to direct upstream routing to another proxy server. Provide the name of your second proxy server. Configure the second proxy server to direct upstream routing to the Internet via a direct connection.

D. Deploy a minimum of two proxy servers in your organization. Configure these servers to be a proxy array.

6. You have designed and implemented your basic Proxy Server configuration throughout your Windows 2000 network. You have an Active Directory domain, and you are running in native mode. You have 200 clients, all of which are running Windows 2000 Professional. How can you quickly configure your clients to use the proxy server instead of the default route to make a WWW connection to the Internet?

A. Send a message to each user and have them change the settings in Internet Explorer to point to the proxy server.

B. Go to each machine and install the WinSock Proxy Client software, and then configure it to use the correct proxy server.

C. Configure a group policy to manage the Internet settings for your domain computer. Have this group policy set the correct proxy server address for the computers in your domain.

D. None of the above.

TEST YOURSELF OBJECTIVE 9.03

Ensuring Proxy Server Security

After you have determined how you will integrate Proxy Server 2.0 into your organization's network, you will need to configure the proxy server's security parameters. If you choose to use Proxy Server for Web caching only, this section is not applicable.

Proxy Server has a number of security measures that you can implement to protect your internal network from intruders and to keep unauthorized users from accessing resources on the Internet. These measures are as follows: client access control, packet filtering, domain filters, and Web publishing/reverse hosting.

- Proxy Server 2.0 provides both inbound and outbound security for the internal network.

- Outbound security can be enforced for all three proxy services (Web Proxy, WinSock Proxy, and Socks) in a slightly different manner. Access controls based on user or group membership allow you to control which users can access what particular content on the Internet.

- Inbound security can be enabled by the firewall-like capabilities of Proxy Server 2.0's packet filters. Packet filtering allows the proxy server to examine all packets coming to the external interface prior to any processing. If the packet is not of an allowed protocol or port type, it is rejected without further processing.

- You can limit the visibility of potentially harmful domains on the Internet by using domain filters.

You can configure the Web Proxy and the WinSock Proxy services to allow and deny access via user and security group permissions. You cannot control access to the Socks Proxy via user-based or security group–based access controls. Per-server security that extends across all users and security groups can be set for domain filtering and packet filtering.

QUESTIONS

9.03: Ensuring Proxy Server Security

7. **Situation:** You manage an infrastructure that utilizes a single proxy server at the edge of your network. The CIO of your company has mandated that all Internet users must be authorized by their department managers to have access to the Internet. He also wants to ensure that temporary employees and contractors do not have access to the corporate Internet connection. For those employees who are authorized to use the Internet, the CIO wants their access to aol.com, msn.com, espn.com, and msnbc.com to be blocked. He wants these restrictions implemented as soon as possible and as efficiently as possible.

Required Result: Devise a method to restrict access to the Internet to only those employees who have been authorized by the department managers.

Optional Desired Results:

1. Block Internet access for temporary employees and contractors.

2. Block access to the Web sites listed by the CIO.

Proposed Solution: First, you create a domain global group called Authorized Internet Users. This is where you will add the authorized users. You go into the Proxy Server management console and choose the properties of the Web Proxy object. You choose Permissions, and grant access to the Authorized Internet Users group for the WWW protocol and the Secure protocol. Next, in order to block Internet access for temporary employees and contractors, you create another security group called Temp Users and put your contractors and temporary employees in this group. Finally, to deny access to the listed domains, you go into the properties of the Web Proxy, choose the Security button, and then choose the Domain Filters tab. You configure this dialog box as shown in the illustration on the following page.

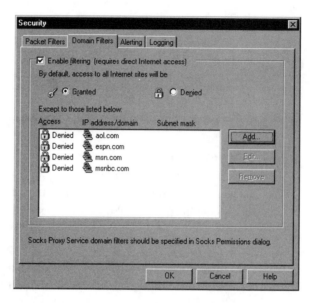

What results are provided from the proposed solution?

A. The proposed solution produces the required result only.

B. The proposed solution produces the required result and one of the optional desired results.

C. The proposed solution produces the required result and both of the optional desired results.

D. The proposed solution does not produce the required result.

8. You want to use Proxy Server 2.0 as a firewall for your small network. How do you configure it to perform this function?

A. This feature is enabled by default.

B. You need to turn on packet filtering on the Security tab.

C. You need to configure routing from the Routing tab.

D. None of the above.

9. Your help desk has been receiving calls on a daily basis complaining about Internet sluggishness in the afternoon. You have Proxy Server installed behind your firewall for Web caching, so you're sure you can track down the problem. You monitor your network for a week or so, and after examining the log files,

you notice that a few users are downloading gigabytes of files from an online music-sharing service. After conferring with the director of networking, she instructs you to block access to the service and to prevent any packets from the service's network servers from entering through your proxy server. How will you do this?

A. Note who the users are from the logs, and then remove their access to the Internet.

B. Add the domain name of the music-sharing service to the Domain Filters list.

C. Add a custom packet filter to block access to the music service's TCP port in the Web Proxy properties.

D. Define a protocol for the music service in the WinSock Proxy, and disable access to that protocol for the users who have been downloading from the service.

Questions 10–11 This scenario should be used to answer questions 10 and 11.

You are a consultant working for a large client in the Southeast. They have a multisegment network with redundant T1 Internet connections. They are using a hardware-based firewall, simply because it meets the capacity requirements of the network.

The client has 11,000 users, many in three campus facilities in Charlotte. The remainder are in a multistory building in Raleigh. Charlotte and Raleigh are connected by a dedicated T3 circuit, and each location has a T1 Internet connection. The two locations are actually separate business units: Accounting Solutions is housed in Charlotte, and IT Business Solutions is located in Raleigh.

The network is a mix of Windows 95, Windows 98, and Windows 2000 clients, all running on a Windows 2000 Active Directory infrastructure. The entire network will be on Windows 2000 by the end of the year.

The company is implementing Microsoft Proxy Server 2.0 so that they can provide Web content caching, user access control to the Internet, and domain filtering.

10. How can this company restrict access to the Internet using Proxy Server?

A. They can configure Proxy Server to perform packet filtering and then restrict access via the packet header.

B. They can configure Proxy Server to restrict access based on a user's membership in a security group.

C. They can use the Socks Proxy to perform per-user or per-group access restriction.

D. None of the above.

11. It was mentioned that this company would like to restrict certain Web sites from the users who connect through the proxy server. The company's CIO does not want any sites that portray pornography to be allowed on his network. How should you configure this site restriction?

A. Go to the Security button, choose Domain Filters, and enter the domains to which you want to restrict access.

B. Go into Packet Filters under the Security button, and make sure that the HTTP-P protocol is disabled.

C. Under the Caching tab, choose Advanced, and then choose Cache Filters. Enter the Web sites that you don't want to cache.

D. Purchase an add-in to Proxy Server that manages the restricted domain list for you.

TEST YOURSELF OBJECTIVE 9.04

Designing a Fault-Tolerant Proxy Network

The proxy server is central in your Internet access and security solution. It is important to ensure consistent and reliable availability of Proxy Server services around the clock. Windows 2000 allows several methods for increasing the reliability of your proxy services, such as proxy server arrays, multiple DNS entries to accommodate DNS round robin, and Windows 2000 Network Load Balancing. You can use these methods individually or in tandem to increase the fault tolerance of your proxy network.

■ Proxy server arrays provide a measure of fault tolerance as well as of load balancing. An array allows groups of proxy servers to function as a single server entity for a number of server-related functions. All servers share the same Web cache. Clients are directed to the appropriate server that contains the sought-after object in the cache.

■ DNS round robin can be used to provide fault tolerance for proxy server arrays. You enter the name of the array in the DNS for each server in the array. When clients query DNS, they will receive a randomized list of IP addresses to access for the proxy service required.

■ Network Load Balancing is an extension of the Microsoft Clustering Service, which allows the entire server cluster to share a single IP address. When a client request is made for proxy services located on a cluster, a member of the cluster will respond. If a member of the cluster becomes disabled, the remaining cluster member automatically handles requests.

exam
ⓦatch

Two of the methods for providing Proxy Server fault tolerance are proxy arrays and Network Load Balancing. It is important to understand that proxy arrays will run on any version of Windows 2000, but Network Load Balancing is only supported on Windows 2000 Advanced Server and Data Center Server.

QUESTIONS

9.04: Designing a Fault-Tolerant Proxy Network

12. You have a Windows 2000 network infrastructure. You want to implement a fault-tolerant Proxy Server implementation to increase the performance of your client's Internet experience. You'd like this solution to offer caching. How would you implement a solution using three servers running Windows 2000 Advanced Server? (Choose all that apply.)

  A. Configure Proxy Server on all three servers, create a proxy array called "Proxy," and then add the three servers to the array.

    B. Configure Proxy Server on all three servers, and configure Network Load Balancing to distribute the traffic going to the NLB cluster.

    C. Configure Proxy Server on all three servers, and chain the servers so that if one server cannot fulfill the request from its cache, the next one can.

    D. None of the above.

13. You host a heavily used Web site on your network behind a redundant proxy server array. This site, www.new-kitchen-tools.com, uses four Web servers and a clustered SQL Server. How can you provide a level of fault tolerance for the Web servers so that when a client requests the site, it will be directed to one of the four Web server addresses?

    A. DNS round robin

    B. Proxy array

    C. Windows Clustering

    D. Proxy chaining

14. **Situation:** You are the network administrator for Smith Calibration Tools. You have a medium-sized network, with three locations and 1,100 users. You have implemented two proxy servers in the main location to help improve the performance of Internet access for your users. The following illustration shows the structure:

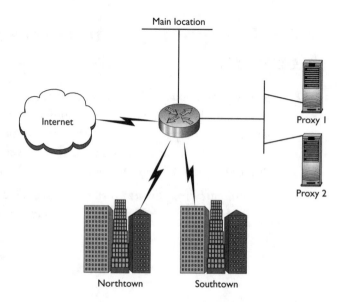

Recently, users at your Southtown location have started to complain that they cannot access the Internet. You check the client settings and note that you have manually configured these users to access the Internet through Proxy2.smithcal.com. You check the proxy server and discover that it is down. How can you keep this from happening again?

Required Result: Provide a solution to solve the problem of users losing access to the Internet if a proxy server goes down.

Optional Desired Result: Describe how you can quickly reconfigure these users to implement your solution to the problem.

Proposed Solution: You propose to create a proxy array using the two existing proxy servers. You name the proxy array "Proxy." You then add two Host records in DNS for "Proxy," using the IP addresses of each proxy server. This round-robin configuration will redirect clients to the two proxy servers, rather than having only one proxy server configured for a specific proxy client. To rapidly bring your users in compliance, you create a group policy to send the new proxy server address to the client machines.

What results are provided from the proposed solution?

A. The proposed solution produces the required result only.

B. The proposed solution produces the required result and the optional desired result.

C. The proposed solution does not produce the required result.

TEST YOURSELF OBJECTIVE 9.05

Maximizing Proxy Server Performance

After you have designed and configured your basic Proxy Server configuration, you need to investigate the options for increasing its performance. There are a couple of technologies that will improve the user experience: Web content caching and proxy server chains.

You can configure Proxy Server to perform either passive or active caching. Proxy server chains allow you to create a hierarchy of proxy servers to reduce the overall number of requests from clients going across the WAN to the Internet.

- You can improve user experience when accessing Web objects by implementing the Web Proxy caching capability. The Web cache on the proxy server will automatically place all objects accessed via the proxy server into the cache. For security reasons, only objects that are not secured by a password or accessed via SSL will be placed in the cache.

- Passive caching occurs when the proxy server places objects in the Web cache after they have been requested by a proxy client. No matter what type of caching you implement, passive caching is always in effect.

- Active caching improves the speed of Web object access for end users. Not only does it take advantage of the passive caching capabilities of Proxy Server 2.0, but the proxy server will also seek out popular and frequently accessed Web objects on its own during times of low processor use on the proxy server.

- Although active caching does provide a speed advantage for the end user, it consumes more bandwidth on the Internet connection. It also requires more disk space for the Web Proxy cache, and there is an overall increase in the amount of processor use.

exam
ⓦatch

Web content caching is the strength of Proxy Server. When choosing between passive and active caching, you must look at the amount of free disk space that you have available. Active caching will update cache content during periods of low utilization, which could put a serious load on your hard disk space.

QUESTIONS

9.05: Maximizing Proxy Server Performance

15. You have implemented Proxy Server in your environment as a means of controlling access to the company's Internet connection. The users have started to call the help desk to express concern that their Internet access seems to be getting slower on a daily basis. How can you increase the performance of your Internet connection using Proxy Server?

  A. Add a second proxy server to your environment.

  B. Configure your proxy server to perform passive and active content caching.

  C. Configure your proxy server to use domain filtering.

  D. None of the above.

16. Your company uses reference material from a business partner's Web site. Is there any way you can configure Proxy Server to always cache content from this heavily used (but not popular) Web site? (Choose all that apply.)

  A. Simply turn on active caching—it can determine what needs to be cached by examining the history files.

  B. On the Caching tab, choose Cache Filters (under Advanced Caching Options). Here you can add sites from which you want to have content cached.

  C. You cannot configure Proxy Server to cache specific Web sites.

  D. On the Caching tab, choose the radio button for Faster User Response Is More Important (under Enable Active Caching).

17. **Situation:** You have a small but very dispersed network. There are eight sites in your Windows 2000 network, which is operating a single Active Directory domain. All of your clients are running Windows 2000, and you have at least one Windows 2000 Server in every location. The sites are connected to the headquarters using demand-dial 56-Kbps links. The following illustration shows the structure:

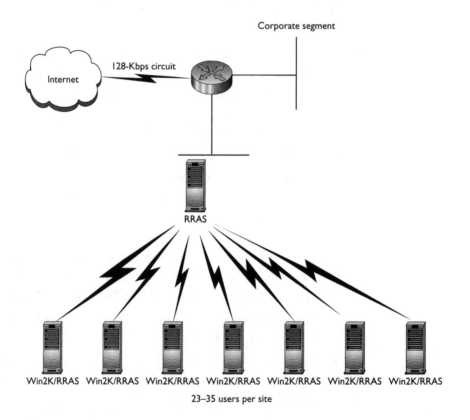

You want to implement Proxy Server to help increase the performance of your Internet connection. You are thinking of using a hierarchical design.

Required Result: Provide a Proxy Server design for the network that uses hierarchical proxy chaining and is economical.

Optional Desired Result: Suggest any other configuration options that may improve the Internet experience for the users in the small sites.

Proposed Solution: You propose to implement Proxy Server on three of the seven sites that are connected to the headquarters network via demand-dial routing. The remaining sites will connect to one of the three proxy servers for Internet access. The three proxy servers will be configured to send unfulfillable requests to a proxy server on the headquarters LAN, which will be configured to contact the Internet. You will also configure caching to help speed up the Internet experience.

What results are provided from the proposed solution?

A. The proposed solution produces the required result only.

B. The proposed solution produces the required result and the optional desired result.

C. The proposed solution does not produce the required result.

LAB QUESTION

Objectives 9.01–9.05

Please refer to the following illustration for this lab exercise:

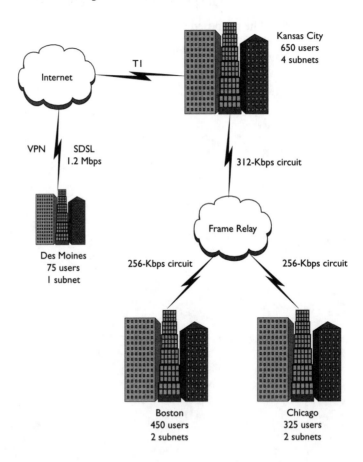

The BlaTech Corporation is an e-business software firm. It has four locations. Kansas City is the location of the company headquarters. Boston and Chicago are both sales/marketing/development offices. The Des Moines location is a Web development firm that was acquired six months ago to expand the corporation's e-commerce software line.

BlaTech has a mixed environment of Windows 98, Windows NT 4.0, and Windows 2000. They have a Windows 2000 Active Directory infrastructure in place.

The three large sites—Boston, Chicago, and Kansas City—are all interconnected with a Frame Relay cloud. Des Moines is connected to the Internet via an always-on SDSL connection and then a connection to the corporate network with a virtual private network (VPN). The Kansas City location is connected to the Internet with a T1.

BlaTech would like to implement Microsoft Proxy Server in their environment for a number of reasons. First, they would like to utilize its firewall capabilities, because the company has yet to buy a firewall. Second, they would like to use its Web caching technology to increase the performance of the Internet at all of their sites. Third, they would like to block access to three major Web sites that seem to be very popular with the employees for most of the day. Finally, BlaTech would like to restrict access to certain protocols and services by security group.

You have been hired to implement Proxy Server for the BlaTech Corporation. Please describe the steps in the design and implementation that you will follow. Also, answer the following questions during your design:

1. Does this network need to have fault-tolerant proxy servers? If so, how would you implement fault tolerance?

2. How will you allow the users in Des Moines to connect to a proxy server to gain access to the Internet?

3. What ports or protocols need to be allowed to come into the network from the Internet?

4. Can you use proxy chaining effectively in this environment?

5. How will you block the restricted Web sites?

6. What caching method will you choose for this environment?

QUICK ANSWER KEY

Objective 9.01

1. E
2. C and D
3. C

Objective 9.02

4. B
5. D
6. C

Objective 9.03

7. C
8. B
9. B
10. B
11. D

Objective 9.04

12. A and B
13. A
14. B

Objective 9.05

15. B
16. A and B
17. C

IN-DEPTH ANSWERS

9.01: Understanding Proxy Server 2.0

1. ☑   **E.** When you begin to design your Proxy Server implementation, you need to ask all of these questions. The answer to the question in **A** will determine how many proxy servers you need on your network, and what configuration they will need to be placed in. The answer to **B**'s questions will help to determine if you need to provide more security for some segments and less for others. A good example is a DMZ, where you may not want very much security due to the exposure to the Internet. If you plan to use access controls, this will require that you set custom security on the proxy server to control user access to the resources protected by the server. Finally, if you answer Yes to the question in **D**, you may need to provide a separate interface for VPN users to access your internal network.

   ☒   There are no wrong answers.

2. ☑   **C** and **D** are correct. Proxy Server 2.0 was not designed for use with Windows 2000. Microsoft had to create a special installation wizard to allow the product to properly install on Windows 2000. The best solution is to back up your Proxy Server configurations and then uninstall the product. After you have upgraded to Windows 2000, you can reinstall the product using the special installation program. Then you can restore the Proxy Server configuration, as shown in the following illustration:

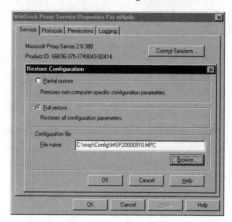

If you upgraded from NT 4.0 to Windows 2000 without uninstalling Proxy Server, you will need to reinstall Proxy Server using the special wizard once the OS upgrade is complete. Using this wizard along with the CD for Proxy Server 2.0, you can reinstall the product. Your settings will migrate properly.

☒   **A** is incorrect because you do not have to uninstall the product before upgrading the server to Windows 2000. This might cause you to lose your proxy settings from Windows NT 4.0. **B** is incorrect because the installation of Proxy Server will not be valid once you upgrade the OS to Windows 2000. You still need to reinstall the product.

3.   ☑   **C.** The proposed solution does not produce the required result. The key feature of Proxy Server 2.0 that makes it a much better choice than NAT for this client is Proxy Server's ability to cache Web content. This client has a network that contains slow links to the main headquarters. By using Proxy Server at the boundaries between the remote office and the headquarters, you can increase the performance of HTTP requests by actively caching content from popular Web sites. The customer is not immediately concerned with using Proxy Server or NAT for security at this point. Proxy Server can also address the client's other requests by providing the ability to limit access to the Internet by group membership, as well as to block objectionable content by filtering. The feature that allows non-Windows clients to have the ability to access the firewall is the Socks Proxy, not the WinSock Proxy.

☒   **A** and **B** are incorrect because the proposed solution does not produce the required result.

9.02: Designing a Proxy Server Network Implementation

4.   ☑   **B.** The proposed solution produces the required result and one of the optional desired results. By placing a cascading Proxy Server arrangement on your network, you are able to control the amount of Internet traffic that is on your network. The clients on each VLAN and in each branch office are configured to use the proxy server on their own segment. These proxy servers are configured to try to fulfill the request from their caches, and then pass unfulfilled requests up to the edge proxy server. If this server cannot fulfill the

request from its cache, it will contact the Internet to get the page. It might also make sense to have the edge proxy server perform active caching in order to process more requests from its own cache. This, of course, will require much more disk space on that server.

The solution for denying access to the employment Web sites is not quite correct. If you'll notice the title bar of the dialog box in the figure, this list is configured on the Socks Proxy. Unfortunately, none of your clients use Socks. This would work perfectly if it had been done under the Web Proxy.

The solution for controlling access to the Internet is right on target. To effectively control access to the Web, create a security group called Internet Access, and then grant that group the right to access the WWW protocol. You might also want to repeat these steps for Secure access (otherwise known as HTTPS).

☒ **A**, **C**, and **D** are incorrect because the proposed solution produces the required result and one of the optional desired results.

5. ☑ **D.** The easiest way to provide fault tolerance with your proxy servers is to configure two or more proxy servers into a proxy array. Not only do you get fault tolerance by having multiple proxy servers available to answer client request, but you also get a performance boost because you now have the collective cache of multiple proxy servers to draw from.

☒ **A** is incorrect because a single proxy server cannot provide fault tolerance. **B** is incorrect because this is a complex and costly solution. Proxy Server runs on both Windows 2000 and Windows NT 4.0. **C** is incorrect because this choice describes chaining, which provides aggregation of Internet requests as they pass higher in the chain.

6. ☑ **C.** Since you are running a pure Windows 2000 network with an Active Directory domain, the quickest way to configure your clients is to use a group policy to set the Proxy Server setting. This gives you manageability now as well as in the future, should your configuration change.

☒ **A** is incorrect because you cannot depend on your users to properly configure their machines, especially if they understand the ramifications of changing to a proxy server. **B** is incorrect because you don't need the WinSock Proxy Client software with the Internet Explorer (IE) 5.0 that is included in Windows 2000. IE 5.0 comes with a Proxy Server client built in.

9.03: Ensuring Proxy Server Security

7. ☑ **C.** The proposed solution produces the required result and both of the optional desired results. Once you enable access control on your proxy server, you will be able to restrict access to the Internet by security groups. After creating a domain local or global security group for the users who will have access, enable this group in the Permissions dialog for the WWW and Secure protocols. You don't need to do anything to keep the temporary employees and contractors from going out on the Internet (users are blocked by default) until you add them to the Permissions dialog. To block access to specific domains, you simply need to add the domains to the Domain Filters list, which is reached from the Security button.

   ☒ **A**, **B**, and **D** are incorrect because the proposed solution produces the required result and both of the optional desired results.

8. ☑ **B.** In order to use Proxy Server as a firewall, you need to enable packet filtering on the Security tab. Packet filters allow you to control access based on protocol and direction; this configuration works across all three proxy services.

   ☒ **A** is incorrect because you need to explicitly enable packet filtering on Proxy Server. **C** is incorrect because the correct setting is packet filtering, which is located on the Security tab.

9. ☑ **B.** By using domain filters, you can add the music-sharing service's domain name to the list. This will prevent users from directly accessing the service via the domain name. If you know the server IP addresses, you can also block access to these. You don't need to do anything to block packets sourced at the music-sharing service: the packet filtering feature blocks all ports that are not explicitly allowed.

   ☒ **A** is incorrect because this solution is too wide reaching to meet the goals of the director. Plus, it keeps these users from accessing valid sites. **C** is incorrect because you don't need to do anything to block access—this is done by default. You need to explicitly allow access through Proxy Server. **D** is incorrect because the solution will not have an impact on the remaining users on the network who are potential users of the service, only those identified as having used the service in the past.

10. ☑ **B.** The easiest way for this company to use Proxy Server to restrict access to the Internet is to configure Proxy Server to check group membership before allowing the connection to go through.

☒   **A** is incorrect because packet filtering is designed to mimic firewall technology, not provide user access. **C** is incorrect because Socks cannot control access at the user or group level.

11. ☑   **D.** This is kind of a trick question. Technically, if you only had a few sites to restrict, you would use the solution in answer **A.** However, there are hundreds of thousands of pornographic Web sites out there, and that number is continuously growing. You should purchase a third-party add-in for Proxy Server that will provide the restriction and that will provide updates to the list through regular network connections.

☒   **A** would be correct if the list of denied Web sites was short. **B** is incorrect because there is no HTTP-P protocol. **C** is incorrect because here you are just telling the server not to cache content rather than to actually refuse connection to the Web site.

9.04: Designing a Fault-Tolerant Proxy Network

12. ☑   **A** and **B** are correct. The best way to create a fault-tolerant Proxy Server implementation is to configure a proxy array using the three servers. Once configured, you can direct all of your clients to use the proxy array name (in this case "Proxy") to access the Internet. If one server fails, the other two will pick up the traffic. Then, teamed with Network Load Balancing, a client will not run into a situation where it cannot reach a proxy server.

☒   **C** is incorrect because chaining does not provide the level of fault tolerance that proxy arrays do.

13. ☑   **A.** DNS round robin is a method that allows multiple IP addresses to be sent to a client based on the host name sent to the DNS Service. This is a common technique for high-availability Web sites.

☒   **B** is incorrect because a proxy array doesn't provide IP addresses or direct clients to specific servers. **C** is incorrect because Windows Clustering provides the ability for two servers (Windows 2000 Advanced Server) to act as one when providing a service to clients. **D** is incorrect because proxy chaining is a technique in which multiple proxy servers are configured to pass requests up through a hierarchy of proxy servers to fulfill a request.

14. ☑ **B.** The proposed solution produces the required result and the optional desired result. First, you should always strive to have fault tolerance in your network for critical systems. In the case of the proxy servers, these devices are the means for Internet access for the organization. You should combine the two servers into a proxy array for additional availability. By adding DNS round robin, you can direct incoming requests to the DNS name of the array, rather than having users point to specific server addresses. The quickest way to roll out this change is to use a Group Policy Object to make the setting for the client.

☒ **A** and **C** are incorrect because the proposed solution produces the required result and the optional desired result.

9.05: Maximizing Proxy Server Performance

15. ☑ **B.** The easiest way to gain additional performance from your proxy server is to enable passive and active caching. The following illustration shows the enabling of passive and active caching:

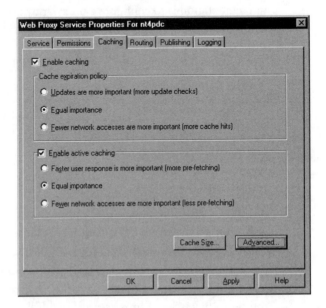

Passive caching will store any content that has been accessed by the proxy server on behalf of clients. Active caching will proactively go out to the Internet and retrieve popular objects during periods of inactivity on the proxy server and then store them in anticipation of client requests.

☒ **A** is incorrect because the addition of a second proxy server will not bring as much performance benefit as enabling caching on your existing server. **C** is incorrect because domain filtering is a security mechanism, not a performance mechanism.

16. ☑ **A** and **B** are correct. Under normal circumstances, Proxy Server uses active intelligent caching to determine what content needs to be cached based on previous requests from clients. You can also configure Proxy Server to explicitly cache content from specific URLs.

☒ **C** is incorrect because you can configure Proxy Server to cache content from specific sites. **D** is incorrect because this setting adjusts the frequency with which Proxy Server updates its cache files.

17. ☑ **C.** The proposed solution does not produce the required result. You were supposed to implement Proxy Server in an economical, hierarchical fashion. By placing only three proxy servers among your demand-dial sites, you are creating even more traffic between the individual sites. You should probably install Proxy Server on a server at every site, and configure each of these to send requests to a proxy server just behind the Internet router. This proxy server can be configured to contact the Internet. Although it's not a required element, you should probably start thinking about getting another means of communication between the sites and the headquarters. You might want to consider DSL or cable modem service. The choice to use caching was correct. If you use active caching, the proxy server will bring down popular content during slow periods.

☒ **A** and **B** are incorrect because the proposed solution does not produce the required result.

LAB ANSWER

Objectives 9.01–9.05

The first step in the design is to determine exactly what type of proxy environment the customer needs. A few questions that need answers are how many users there will be, how much security is needed, and so on.

1. The network doesn't *need* fault-tolerant proxy servers, but they would be nice to have. You should implement two at the Kansas City location, arrange them in an array, and configure round-robin DNS or Network Load Balancing so that users can access a single IP address and get either of the two servers.

2. You should place a proxy server in Des Moines and manage it separately from your other proxy servers. It already has a direct connection to the Internet, and it would be silly to have Web traffic go across the VPN, into the corporate network, and then back to the Internet. Make sure that all of the access rights and filters are in place.

3. You can allow the default ICMP protocols to come in to both Kansas City and Des Moines, plus allow the ports required for the VPN to come in.

4. Yes, proxy chaining would work very well. You could place proxy servers at the Boston and Chicago sites and configure them to use upstream routing, as shown on the following page. The remote sites would send traffic to the Kansas City proxy server. If they cannot connect to Kansas City, then they'll go directly to the Internet.

5. The restricted sites will be blocked by configuring the domain filter and adding the names of the domains that are off-limits.

6. You should use both passive and active caching. This will provide the best performance gain for the end user.

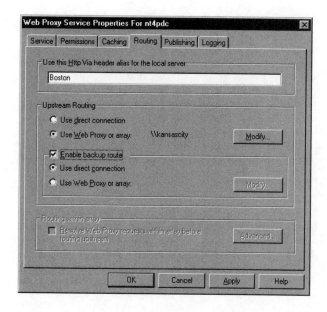

MICROSOFT CERTIFIED SYSTEMS ENGINEER

10

Designing a Wide Area Network Infrastructure

TEST YOURSELF OBJECTIVES

T he term *wide area network* (WAN) is used to describe the connection of two or more local area networks (LANs) within a company, or the connection of a remote office to the mainframe using Synchronous Data Link Control (SDLC). In today's Internet economy, there are a significant number of companies that have WANs simply because they have a connection to the Internet. This type of network fits the technical definition of a WAN, even though it doesn't fit the traditional mold.

To succeed in taking this exam, you must understand the role of Routing and Remote Access Service (RRAS) in Windows 2000. You must know how to design a remote access solution using RRAS, understand how to implement RADIUS with user authentication, design a virtual private network (VPN) strategy, and use demand-dial routing to connect disparate locations.

TEST YOURSELF OBJECTIVE 10.01

Designing a WAN Infrastructure

Designing a WAN infrastructure is more complex than connecting routers at two locations and running a leased line between them. It involves a lot of planning to ensure that traffic can flow where it needs to flow and that everyone who needs access can obtain it.

You should understand all of the various types of wide area network connectivity technologies, such as Integrated Services Digital Network (ISDN), Frame Relay, T-carriers, and the newer Digital Subscriber Line (DSL) and cable. You should also understand the basics behind virtual private networks (VPNs) and remote access. Finally, you should know the differences between WAN protocols such as SLIP, PPP, L2TP, and PPTP.

- WANs consist of any number of LANs connected together.

- Popular WAN connectivity options include T-carriers, such as T1s and T3s. ISDN is another traditional method of connectivity.

- Newer connectivity options include DSL and cable.

- VPNs are becoming more pervasive in companies as they realize the cost savings of tunneling through the Internet instead of spending capital on banks of modems.

■ Virtual local area network (VLAN) connections are typically made over Point-to-Point Tunneling Protocol (PPTP) or Layer Two Tunneling Protocol (L2TP) connections

exam
⑭atch

Microsoft often scrutinizes your understanding of network terminology. For this exam, it is important to fully understand what sets VPNs apart from virtual networks. You can use a virtual networking protocol such as L2TP and create a virtual link between your LANs that are separated over the Internet. However, this link (or tunnel) will not be a VPN until you add an encryption protocol (such as IPSec) that protects the data as it moves through the virtual link.

QUESTIONS

10.01: Designing a WAN Infrastructure

1. You are preparing to connect your two small offices together with a WAN connection. You will be implementing Exchange for email, and you will be using NetMeeting for collaboration among employees at both sites. Which of the following technologies offers the best performance for the least cost in a simple file-sharing and email-exchanging environment?

   A. 56-Kbps analog dial-up

   B. BRI-ISDN

   C. SDSL

   D. 56-Kbps Frame Relay

2. Your client is looking for ways to allow his 30 remote workers to connect to the company's network so they can access the marketing information that is shared on a Windows 2000 file server. The company has an ISDN demand-dial connection to the Internet, and the users connect to the Internet through MCI. How would you suggest that he accommodate these remote users with the least cost?

   A. Purchase two modems and connect them to the COM ports on the server. Then configure RAS to allow the users to dial in to the network.

    B. Configure the Windows 2000 server to become a VPN server in RRAS. Let the users tunnel in to the network through MCI.

    C. Upgrade the remote user's home offices with ISDN lines, and allow them to connect to the company's network from home.

    D. None of the above.

3. **Situation:** You are designing a new WAN to replace your current architecture, which has grown in disjointed segments with widely varied technologies. You have offices around the United States, some connected with DDS leased lines, some with Frame Relay, some with ISDN, and some with analog dial-up lines. There is no rhyme or reason to the choice of technologies. Your company has also recently acquired a competitor, which has a legacy Frame Relay network providing service to its three offices. The following illustration shows the current state of the network:

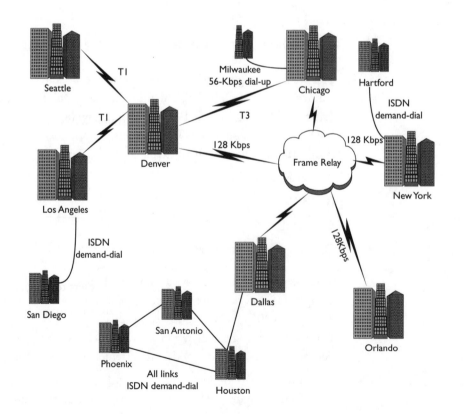

The following table shows the distribution of users and servers by location.

Location	Users	Servers
Chicago	670	18
Dallas	430	15
Denver	560	10
Hartford	85	6
Houston	70	3
Los Angeles	410	17
Milwaukee	90	4
New York	390	31
Orlando	250	20
Phoenix	65	2
San Antonio	50	2
San Diego	70	4
Seattle	230	13

Required Results: You must choose a single WAN carrier (for example, T1 circuits, ISDN) to connect all of the large sites together. Your choice must be able to accommodate a minimum of 1.5 Mbps. You must choose a connectivity option to bring the small sites into the network with the best performance at the least cost.

Optional Desired Results:

1. Choose a Windows 2000–supported routing protocol that will provide the best performance for this network.

2. Decide how you would connect remote users to the network.

Proposed Solution: Your solution is to continue to use Frame Relay as the primary network connectivity solution. All of the major sites will connect to the Frame Relay cloud using 1-Mbps SDSL with bursting to 7 Mbps (which is becoming very popular now). You choose to join the small sites to the network by using 128-Kbps ISDN demand-dial routing to the nearest large site. You choose to use OSPF (Open Shortest Path First) as the routing protocol. For remote users, you decide to partner with a major ISP to allow users to dial in to the local POP and then tunnel in to the network over the Internet.

What results are provided from the proposed solution?

A. The proposed solution produces the required results only.

B. The proposed solution produces the required results and one of the optional desired results.

C. The proposed solution produces the required results and both of the optional desired results.

D. The proposed solution does not produce the required results.

TEST YOURSELF OBJECTIVE 10.02

Designing a Remote Access Solution That Uses Routing and Remote Access Service

Routing and Remote Access Service (RRAS) is the consolidated interface for configuring routing services, Remote Access Services (RAS), NAT, and VPN in Windows 2000. Whether the server is routing dial-up information or routing between two or more network interfaces, it is handled by RRAS.

You will be tested on your knowledge concerning RRAS installation and configuration. You also need to understand how to optimize your Windows 2000 router design for availability and performance. This includes configuring Routing Information Protocol (RIP) and OSPF for routing packets from one network to another. You need to understand the differences between hardware- and software-based routing solutions. Finally, you need to know how to optimize and monitor RRAS to increase performance.

■ RRAS is a program that manages all routing of packets that a router would perform.

■ RRAS is installed and is disabled by default with Windows 2000 server. To enable RRAS, you must first open the RRAS console in Administrative Tools in the Start menu.

■ Windows 2000 does not support Serial Line Internet Protocol (SLIP). It supports Point-to-Point Protocol (PPP) for dial-up accounts.

exam
Watch

RRAS is one of the features of Windows 2000 that deserves a lot of attention. Not only does it contain the configuration for simple routing and RAS, but it also contains the configuration for NAT and VPN.

QUESTIONS

10.02: Designing a Remote Access Solution That Uses Routing and Remote Access Service

4. You are building a small routed network between four of your offices. You don't want to invest a lot of money in hardware-based routers, so you decide to use Windows 2000 servers that are multihomed. The following illustration shows your network architecture:

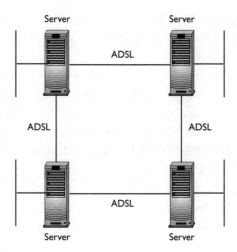

What routing protocol would be the most practical in your environment?

A. RIP, version 2

B. OSPF

C. EIGRP

D. None of the above

5. One of your remote dial-in users has just called the help desk to complain that she cannot dial in to the network. She explains that her connection attempt is getting rejected. The technician who answered the call cannot be sure if it is a user or a network problem. The first step in the help desk's resolution guide is to make sure the RRAS server is up and running properly. What is a quick way of checking to see if the server is functioning properly?

A. Walk back to the server closet and see if the server is still running.

B. Using the RRAS console, connect to the RRAS server and see if the console is showing that the server is up.

C. Using System Management Server, check the status of the RRAS server.

D. Use PING to check the network connectivity back to the RRAS server.

6. **Situation:** You are designing the WAN for your company. You have four remote locations, each with a single Class C subnet. Your headquarters building has five Class C subnets, as well as a core network segment running on Gigabit Ethernet with its own subnet. The remote sites will each have a Windows 2000 server for file and print services. There will be approximately 400 employees at the headquarters, and close to 50 employees at each remote site. The WAN will be used primarily for checking email using Outlook 2000 and Exchange. Your remote sites will be connected to the headquarters with demand-dial ISDN lines, and each remote site will be connected with its neighbor with an ISDN line for redundancy. The illustration on the following page shows the configuration.

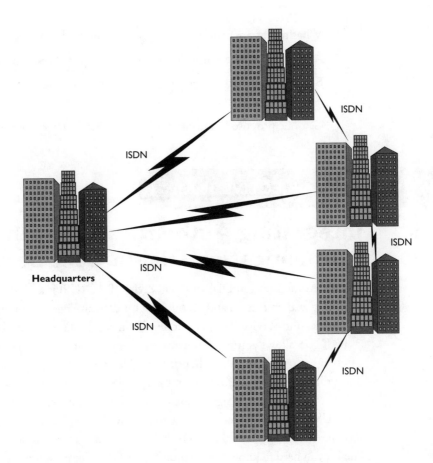

Required Result: Choose the routing protocol that is best suited for this architecture.

Optional Desired Result: Choose the most appropriate routing solution (hardware or software) for this network.

Proposed Solution: You choose to use OSPF as the routing protocol for this network, and configure it with six areas: one for the backbone, one for the remaining subnets in the headquarters, and one for each remote office. You made this choice because of OSPF's robustness and fast convergence. You also feel that all of the offices should have a dedicated hardware router for the WAN. You don't think the Windows 2000 servers can handle the additional load of processing OSPF packets.

What results are provided from the proposed solution?

A.   The proposed solution produces the required result only.

B.   The proposed solution produces the required result and the optional desired result.

C.   The proposed solution does not produce the required result.

TEST YOURSELF OBJECTIVE 10.03

Integrating Authentication with Remote Authentication Dial-In User Service

Remote Authentication Dial-In User Service (RADIUS) is an industry standard for providing authentication and accounting for dial-in services. The Internet Authentication Service (IAS) is Microsoft's implementation of RADIUS.

RADIUS allows you to centralize your RAS accounting and policies, and allows for a tighter control over RAS authentication. Using RADIUS, you are not dependent on the authentication infrastructure of the local ISP into which the user is dialing.

You must be able to design a functional RADIUS solution, know how to secure a RADIUS server, and understand how to improve RADIUS server accessibility. You must also understand how to make RADIUS fault tolerant and how to increase its performance. Finally, you need to know how to monitor RADIUS for preventive maintenance.

- ■ RADIUS works over TCP/IP and requires an IP address to communicate with the RADIUS client.

- ■ RADIUS is a protocol that IAS uses to communicate with RAS clients. This protocol facilitates communication between IAS and the RAS servers throughout your network.

exam
ⓦatch

RADIUS is an up-and-coming protocol that is extremely valuable in helping to manage the authentication of remote users. Even though Microsoft has only recently begun supporting RADIUS, the protocol has been around for a couple of years. One of the most interesting uses of RADIUS is to allow an ISP to use a RADIUS client to authenticate your corporate dial-in users against the Active Directory. This feature makes the process of managing remote users that much easier.

QUESTIONS

10.03: Integrating Authentication with Remote Authentication Dial-In User Service

7.   You would like to outsource your remote access servers to a regional ISP for the corporate LAN. All of your remote users are in the service area of this ISP. You plan on using IAS to authenticate the remote users against Active Directory using the RADIUS protocol. What RADIUS/IAS hardware or software needs to be in place at the ISP to allow this to work properly?

   A.   A properly configured IAS server

   B.   A RADIUS server

   C.   A RADIUS proxy server

   D.   A network access server

8.   You are preparing to configure IAS so that you can use RADIUS to authenticate your remote access clients as they connect to your network. In the IAS management console, you see a folder for Clients, as shown in the following illustration:

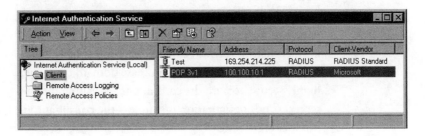

What type of clients must you configure here?

   A.   These clients are network access servers.

   B.   These clients are the dial-in users who have permission to dial in.

C. These clients are users who have authenticated themselves via RADIUS.

D. None of the above.

9. **Situation:** You have been asked to design a RADIUS-based remote access solution for your company. You work for a nationwide solution provider with well over 5,000 consultants on the payroll. All of these consultants are road warriors—they rarely spend any time in the office. The company has an expansive intranet solution that provides a knowledge/solutions database, the time accounting system, human resources information, and expense management. The intranet also provides access to the public folders on Exchange, as well as access to the file shares. You have a limited budget to accomplish this mission, and the end result must be that the consultants get fast, secure access to these resources on the intranet.

Required Result: You must design a RADIUS-based remote access solution that utilizes IAS, RRAS, and Active Directory.

Optional Desired Results:

1. The consultants' connections must be highly secure because of the sensitive nature of some of the information.

2. The solution should be very easy for the consultants to use once it's in place on their laptops—no messy configurations or operating instructions.

Proposed Solution: You decide to outfit a data center with 200 modems, and connect them to Windows 2000 RRAS servers. You configure a toll-free number as the point for a hunt group, which will pick the first open modem on the rack. You also position five Windows 2000 servers configured to be IAS servers in the data center. These servers will handle the requests from the RRAS servers, which are configured to be RADIUS clients. The domain controllers will be at a data center in the next campus building. The IAS servers will authenticate against the Active Directory on these domain controllers. This solution is highly secure because the consultants are calling their own company's RAS servers. The configuration is simple—the consultant just has to dial the same number every time.

What results are provided from the proposed solution?

A. The proposed solution produces the required result only.

B. The proposed solution produces the required result and one of the optional desired results.

C. The proposed solution produces the required result and both of the optional desired results.

D. The proposed solution does not produce the required result.

TEST YOURSELF OBJECTIVE 10.04

Designing a Virtual Private Network Strategy

Virtual private networks (VPNs) allow you to make a connection to your corporate network through the Internet. VPNs provide secure channels through larger internetworks, allowing users to view them as private dedicated links. VPNs provide remote access and routed connections to private networks.

You must understand how to design the use of VPNs in a routed network. You must also know how to maximize VPN availability, how to use PPTP or IPSec/L2TP to secure a VPN, and what events to monitor on your VPNs.

- VPNs allow remote networks or users to connect to another network through the Internet or other large networks.

- Layer Two Tunneling Protocol (L2TP) is a VPN communications protocol that is included with Windows 2000. L2TP relies on Internet Protocol Security (IPSec) to create a secure tunnel for VPN communications.

- It is always a good idea to monitor unauthorized access attempts. Other concerns are also important, such as CPU or network interface card (NIC) use. Monitoring is done through Performance Monitor.

exam
Watch

VPN technology is high on Microsoft's list of important networking services. Because of the significant cost savings afforded to businesses that implement VPNs, Microsoft wants its MCSEs to be thoroughly versed in the concepts and practice of VPN implementation. Be sure you thoroughly understand how VPNs work and how to design cost-effective and efficient VPN solutions before taking the test.

QUESTIONS

10.04: Designing a Virtual Private Network Strategy

10. You are planning your corporate remote access strategy and have decided to use VPNs as a means for your remote workers to connect to the corporate LAN. You have an even mix of Windows 2000 and Windows 98 client laptops. Which tunneling protocol will provide secure communications in this mixed environment?

    A. L2TP

    B. PPTP

    C. SLIP

    D. PPP

11. You have a corporate office and a branch office that you would like to connect via an L2TP tunnel over the Internet. Both offices are running native Windows 2000 servers and clients. Both servers have valid intranet and Internet connections. You configure demand-dial routing connections on both servers to use L2TP tunneling. You configure the static routes that will direct traffic to the appropriate interface on the routers. Finally, you set the L2TP-over-IPSec filters on the corporate office's server. When you initiate the connection, you get an error stating that a valid certificate was not found. What is the problem?

    A. You forgot to configure the IPSec settings on the corporate server's interface.

    B. You did not install an X.509 certificate on the corporate server.

    C. You did not install an X.509 certificate on the branch office server.

    D. You did not configure IPSec correctly on the Ports page in the RRAS console.

12. **Situation:** You are the network administrator for Super Interactive, a Web-design company in the Washington, DC, area. You have 40 users in your Rockville office. You have recently installed a Windows 2000 infrastructure and upgraded the majority of your PCs to Windows 2000. You have a handful of Macintosh systems being used by your graphic artists. You also have another office in Lithicum, which has 50 users on the network and the same mix of Windows 2000 and Macintosh systems. Both offices have 7-Mbps Asymmetric Digital Subscriber Line (ADSL) Internet connections. You would like to connect the offices with a WAN using your existing technology and without spending additional money to do so.

    Required Result: Determine how you can connect the Rockville and Lithicum offices with your existing technology.

    Optional Desired Result: Ensure that you do not isolate the Macintosh systems in your design.

    Proposed Solution: You choose to add a second 640-Kbps ADSL line to each office, and then configure your Windows 2000 server with a demand-dial tunnel over to the other office. You set up the tunnel so that it is continuously up between the two offices. You also make sure that your static routes on the Windows 2000 default gateway will allow traffic to the other office to travel over the tunnel, while the Internet traffic still goes to the Internet on the larger connection. You use PPTP on the tunnel to make sure that your data is encrypted and safe.

    What results are provided from the proposed solution?

    A. The proposed solution produces the required result only.

    B. The proposed solution produces the required result and the optional desired result.

    C. The proposed solution does not produce the required result.

    Questions 13–14   This scenario should be used to answer questions 13 and 14.

    You are consulting for a large company that has an 800-member sales force. They want to modernize their sales team with laptops, Internet access, and corporate file and email access. The company has 17 major locations across the United States, and the sales team works out of their homes.

The corporate network is running a mix of Windows 2000 and Windows NT 4.0 servers. You are in a Mixed-mode Active Directory forest with three domains. The office-based clients are mostly Windows 98, with about 25 percent having been converted to Windows 2000 Professional.

The corporate network, which sits behind a hardware-based firewall, uses the private network address space of 10.4.0.0.

13. The CIO has made the decision to allow the sales force to use VPN connections to access their email and data on the corporate network. He doesn't want to worry about providing dial-up service, so he allows each salesperson to pick his or her own local ISP; your team will then set up the VPN connection on the sales force's Windows 2000 laptops. What type of VPN connection will you use to get back to the corporate LAN through the firewall?

   A. L2TP

   B. PPP

   C. PPTP

   D. PPPoE

14. Given your knowledge of Windows 2000 IAS and RADIUS, how could you save the company some administrative effort if you implemented IAS? (Choose all that apply.)

   A. You could set up IAS on the internal network, and allow the users to authenticate against that server before proceeding to connect via a VPN.

   B. You could contract with local ISPs across the country, provide them with RADIUS proxy servers, and have the users dial in to one of the preferred ISPs. Then, the RADIUS server could authenticate the users.

   C. You can contract with a national ISP that has POPs across the country. You can then configure the laptops with dialer software to pick the POP closest to them. The ISP can use its RADIUS proxy server to direct the authentication calls to your IAS server through the firewall by using the realm information in the packet header. Then the user can make a VPN connection through this Internet connection.

   D. None of the above.

TEST YOURSELF OBJECTIVE 10.05

Designing an RRAS Routing Solution to Connect Locations via Demand-Dial Routing

In some instances, it makes sense to connect offices with just a demand-dial routing solution. This is a connection that is only active when data needs to be passed from one network to the other. Usually, the link is based on ISDN, but it could be DSL or analog.

You should know how to implement and configure demand-dial routing, understand some of the considerations for using demand-dial routing, and know how to monitor your implementation once finished.

- Routing Information Protocol (RIP) is the basic protocol that routers use to communicate. One of the major concerns about RIP has always been a lack of security. This has been fixed with RIP, version 2, which supports password authentication.

- Open Shortest Path First (OSPF) is a much more robust routing protocol. One of the major improvements gained by using OSPF is speed, because it finds and uses the quickest path to transmit data.

- Demand-dial routing allows you to have nonpersistent network links between remote sites in order to pass traffic between them.

exam
ⓦatch
When using a demand-dial connection to establish a link between two offices, you should use ISDN rather than analog modems if possible. ISDN establishes the link in a few seconds, rather than 10 to 20 seconds, and the link tends to be more stable. The higher cost of ISDN can be offset by the stability of the link and the increase in employee productivity.

QUESTIONS

10.05: Designing an RRAS Routing Solution to Connect Locations via Demand-Dial Routing

15. You would like to set up a demand-dial connection between a remote office and the corporate office. Both sites are members of the same Windows 2000 Active Directory domain. You want the link to be established only by the remote office—that is, traffic destined for the corporate office from the remote office will bring up the connection, but traffic destined for the remote office from the corporate office will not. Why would you want to configure demand-dial routing in this manner?

    A. You don't want to pay for a continuous link between the two offices.

    B. You want to maintain control over how the link is used.

    C. You are using the link as a backup to a leased-line connection, and you only want traffic to use this link in an emergency.

    D. All of the above.

    E. None of the above.

16. Your company has two offices that are connected via a VPN tunnel through the Internet. Each office has a T1 link to a local ISP that gives it continuous Internet access. You use RIP, version 2, for a routing protocol. Your Windows 2000 servers act as routers, since they are configured with two network interface cards. You would like to have redundancy on your WAN link in case a link should fail. How can you configure this on your Windows 2000 servers so that the redundant link is only available if the primary link is down?

    A. You can configure the static routing table to send traffic to the other office via an RAS connection if the primary link fails.

    B. You can configure RRAS to initiate a demand-dial connection to the ISP, and then use a VPN tunnel to connect to the other office.

    C. You can have a second continuous circuit connected between the offices in case the primary link goes down.

    D. None of the above.

LAB QUESTION

Objectives 10.01–10.05

As part of their nationwide Windows 2000 network deployment, your client wants to design and deploy a WAN infrastructure. They have seven offices across the country, in New York, Boston, Chicago, Los Angeles, Phoenix, Seattle, and Dallas. Each office has between 200 and 400 employees. There are also 30 to 50 remote users who work out of each of the seven main offices.

Currently, each office is an island—none of the main offices are networked together. The clients in each office have Windows 95 and Windows 98 PCs that are in Workgroup mode on a single LAN segment within the office. The remote users have Internet connectivity from their laptops, but no access to the networks at each facility.

The company is on a limited budget to accomplish this project, so they are not going to use hardware-based routing solutions. Since they will be implementing Windows 2000 domain controllers at each of the offices, they have decided to use software-based routing.

The primary objectives for the project are as follows:

- Connect all of the main offices with a WAN.
- Configure redundancy for all of the links.
- Allow the remote users to access the corporate network by at least two methods.
- Contain the costs of the project.

How would you design this network for the client to meet their objectives?

A QUICK ANSWER KEY

Objective 10.01
1. C
2. B
3. D

Objective 10.02
4. D
5. B
6. C

Objective 10.03
7. C
8. A
9. D

Objective 10.04
10. B
11. B and C
12. C
13. C
14. C

Objective 10.05
15. D
16. B

IN-DEPTH ANSWERS

10.01: Designing a WAN Infrastructure

1. ☑ **C.** In today's market, SDSL will give you the best performance for the least cost. Symmetrical DSL costs approximately $50 per month for 128-Kbps bandwidth. This gives you leased-line characteristics and performance for analog-line costs.

   ☒ **A** is incorrect because 56-Kbps analog dial-up is not well suited for real-time collaboration, in comparison with SDSL. **B** is incorrect because the cost of ISDN is higher than SDSL, with the same performance. **D** is incorrect, again because of the cost and also because of the performance—56-Kbps Frame Relay is only half as fast as SDSL.

2. ☑ **B.** Configure VPN on your Windows 2000 server and allow the users to connect using their existing MCI dial-up accounts. You may need to upgrade your office's Internet connection in the future.

   ☒ **A** is incorrect because you will incur the extra cost of the two analog lines, the slower speed of analog, and the limitation of only handling two users at a time. **C** is incorrect because you would be incurring a huge charge to put ISDN in all 30 users' homes.

3. ☑ **D.** The proposed solution does not produce the required results. The choice to use Frame Relay as the overall connectivity solution is a good choice; however, deciding to use 1-Mbps SDSL is not. SDSL does not burst (like Frame Relay does), and it does not meet the requirement of accommodating 1.5 Mbps. A better choice would be to use traditional 1.544-Mbps circuits from the offices to the Frame Relay cloud. The decision to use ISDN to connect the smaller offices to the larger sites is mostly okay, although a better choice would be to use DSL or a leased line to provide a link that is up all of the time, rather than demand-dial routing. The choice of OSPF will work perfectly, if used in conjunction with the correct choices described previously. OSPF is not a good choice when using demand-dial routing, because the links going up and

down force the routing protocol to continuously run through the link state advertisement (LSA) process. Having your remote users dial in to a national ISP is also a good solution, because it outsources the RAS component of your network to a provider who has the equipment and the capacity to handle it.

☒ **A**, **B**, and **C** are incorrect because the proposed solution does not produce the required result.

10.02: Designing a Remote Access Solution That Uses Routing and Remote Access Service

4. ☑ **D.** None of these protocols is the most practical routing protocol for this infrastructure. You would be better off just using static routes between these sites. You have no overhead of a routing protocol, and with no redundant routes, there's really no need for dynamic route discovery.

    ☒ **A** and **B** are both incorrect, because each of these routing protocols adds too much overhead and complexity to a very simple WAN arrangement. **C** is incorrect because EIGRP is a Cisco proprietary routing protocol, and you cannot use it on a Windows 2000 router.

5. ☑ **B.** A very quick way of determining the status of the RRAS server is to use the RRAS console and connect to the server in question. The server's icon will show either a green arrow pointing up or an X in a red circle to indicate the server's status. The following illustration shows an example of this indicator for a properly functioning server:

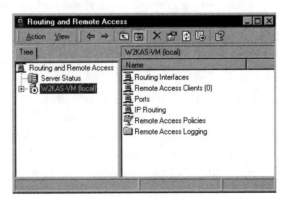

☒ **A** is incorrect because it requires the help desk technician to get up and physically check the server. There are a number of things that can be done right from the desktop to check the server's status. **C** is incorrect because System Management Server won't give you the status of the RRAS service running on the Windows 2000 server. It will only tell you if the server itself is running. **D** is incorrect because PING won't check the status of the RRAS service—only the functionality of the IP stack on the RRAS server.

6. ☑ **C.** The proposed solution does not produce the required result. Although OSPF is a great routing protocol for large and very large networks, it is not a good choice for small networks, especially small networks with dial-up links. To understand this, you must look at how OSPF works. The link state database is the routing table for OSPF. To create this database, each router sends a link state advertisement (LSA) to its neighbors. The LSA tells what the router knows about the routers that are adjacent to itself (that is, whether the links are up or down). Once each router has received the LSA information from every other router in its autonomous system, it determines the shortest paths to all of the networks. When you have a network with links that are constantly going up and down, such as the one in this scenario, this LSA flooding process happens continuously, generating a lot of overhead. A better choice for this network would be to use RIP, version 2. RIP, version 2, supports Variable-Length Subnet Masking (VLSM) and classless interdomain routing (CIDR), as well as encryption of the routing table information. It has much less overhead than OSPF, and you can configure RIP to be quiet; that is, you can configure RIP to not send updates.

As for using hardware-based versus software-based routing, it's probably more cost effective to use the existing Windows 2000 servers at the branch locations, simply because the load from the email users will not cause that much overhead on the servers.

☒ **A** and **B** are incorrect because the proposed solution does not produce the required result.

10.03: Integrating Authentication with Remote Authentication Dial-In User Service

7. ☑ **C.** In order for the RADIUS authentication request to be routed to the IAS server, you need to have a RADIUS proxy server in place at the ISP. This

server will take the RADIUS authentication request and forward it to the proper IAS server by examining the realm name in the request.

☒ **A** is incorrect because the IAS server should be located on the same segment or near the Active Directory server. **B** is incorrect because IAS is a RADIUS server. **D** is incorrect because a network access server is another name for an RAS server or a VPN server.

8. ☑ **A.** The clients that are listed in this folder are RADIUS clients. A RADIUS client is a machine that accepts connections from users, such as a Network Access Server or a Remote Access Server, and then passes the RADIUS authentication request up to the RADIUS server/IAS server, or to a RADIUS proxy server.

☒ **B** and **C** are both incorrect because these clients are not end users. If you had to manage your end-user access accounts from the IAS console, you would be defeating the whole purpose of RADIUS and Active Directory integration.

9. ☑ **D.** The proposed solution does not produce the required result. The solution is technically feasible, but it fails to fulfill the edict to work within a limited budget. Outfitting a data center with the hardware to support 200 modems is not cheap! The better solution would be to team up with a nationwide service provider and allow your consultants to dial in to one of the ISP's local POP numbers. Then, the ISP can use RADIUS to authenticate the client against the Active Directory back in the data center. Once the consultant has a PPP connection, he or she can establish a VPN connection back to the intranet. Again, this would be authenticated using RADIUS. You can use L2TP or PPTP to encrypt the data on this connection, as well as using IPSec. The user experience would be easy if you used the Connection Manager from the Connection Manager Administrators Kit. The consultants could just pick the POP closest to their location.

☒ **A**, **B**, and **C** are incorrect because the proposed solution does not produce the required result.

10.04: Designing a Virtual Private Network Strategy

10. ☑ **B.** PPTP is the protocol that will offer secure communications for both your Windows 2000 and Windows 98 clients. L2TP is not supported by Windows 98.

☒   **A** is incorrect because L2TP is not supported by Windows 98 clients. If you had a native Windows 2000 environment, L2TP would be the best choice because it utilizes IPSec to encrypt the data. **C** is incorrect because SLIP (Serial Line Internet Protocol) is not a tunneling protocol. **D** is incorrect because PPTP is also not a tunneling protocol.

11. ☑   **B** and **C** are correct. In order for IPSec to work properly, you must have installed a computer certificate on both the corporate and branch office servers. This allows IPSec to encrypt the data using the certificate; the protocol fails without it.

☒   **A** is incorrect because there are no IPSec settings on the corporate server's interface. **D** is also incorrect because you don't configure IPSec on the Ports page in the RRAS console.

12. ☑   **C.** The proposed solution does not produce the required result. You didn't need to add another connection to the Internet to get the offices connected. Everything else in your proposed solution will get the job done, *with your existing Internet connection*. The following illustration shows the end result:

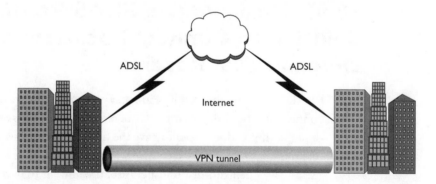

By using PPTP, you ensure that there are no compatibility issues with the traffic being sent by the Macintosh clients.

☒   **A** and **B** are incorrect because the proposed solution does not produce the required result.

13. ☑   **C.** You will have to use PPTP to connect the remote users to the corporate LAN through a VPN. Since the company is using NAT on the corporate network (10.4.0.0 address space), you cannot use L2TP and IPSec because the

packet header gets changed during the NAT process, and IPSec won't accept the return packet.

☒ **A** is incorrect because of the problem with using IPSec and NAT. **B** is incorrect because PPP is not a VPN protocol. **D** is incorrect because PPPoE (PPP over Ethernet) is a commonly used protocol for users who have certain implementations of ADSL—it is not a VPN protocol.

14. ☑ **C.** You could save some administrative effort by (a) using a national ISP to provide network access for the company's users and (b) using RADIUS and IAS to perform the authentication. This way the company's administrative staff won't be forced to administer 800 individual accounts for RAS permissions. IAS can handle all of that.

☒ **A** is incorrect because the users cannot communicate with the IAS server until they make a network connection. **B** is incorrect because the users would not be able to get through the firewall with this scenario. They would need to make a VPN connection after they connect to the Internet.

10.05: Designing an RRAS Routing Solution to Connect Locations via Demand-Dial Routing

15. ☑ **D.** All of the above. There are many reasons to create demand-dial routing connections, but usually cost, control, and redundancy are the main reasons for doing so. If you don't need to have the link up continuously, then use demand-dial routing. If you want to control what traffic can bring up the link, you can use one-way demand-dial routing. Also, if you want to have a backup route available if the primary circuit fails, you can use the one-way demand-dial routing.

☒ There are no incorrect answers.

16. ☑ **B.** If your primary circuit to the Internet (the T1) should fail, you can configure RRAS to make a demand-dial connection to the Internet using an analog or ISDN line. Once you have the Internet connection, you can then use RRAS to set up a VPN connection back to the other office. RIP, version 2,

should adjust the routing table to reflect the new route to the other office, and you'll be set.

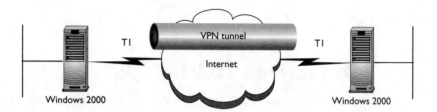

☒ **A** is incorrect because you are not using static routing. **C** is incorrect because you would have two continuous links, rather than one link that is continuous and one that is only available if the primary link is down.

LAB ANSWER

Objectives 10.01–10.05

Based on the criteria and objectives that the client has set forth, you should start by ruling out T1s and other expensive leased-line circuits as the means of connecting all of the offices.

A good game plan for this network would be to use a cheaper broadband technology, such as DSL or cable. You could configure each office to connect to the Internet using DSL—in this case, you should use Synchronous DSL (SDSL) so that the upstream and downstream bandwidth is the same. Once you have all of the offices connected to the Internet, you can configure VPN tunnels using L2TP to connect all of the offices to a hub. In this case, you could use the Chicago office as the hub and have the remaining six offices connect to it through the tunnel. You can use Routing and Remote Access Service to configure a routing protocol, such as OSPF or RIP, version 2, to manage the routes between the seven offices. OSPF would be a good choice because you have a continuous connection between the offices through the DSL and VPN link. You would then need to configure the default gateway on your clients to use the Windows 2000 server in their facility as the default gateway.

To have redundancy for the wide area network connections between the sites, you can configure a demand-dial connection to the Chicago hub. You should connect an analog or ISDN modem to each of the servers. Using RRAS, you can configure these analog connections to (a) dial an ISP and make an Internet connection and (b) set up a VPN connection to the Chicago site if the primary DSL connection goes down. Since you are depending on the Internet for your wide area links, you may want to use a different ISP for your demand-dial connection than you use for your primary link.

To allow your remote users to connect to the network, you can use a number of approaches. Your objective is to have two means of connecting. The users already have Internet access, so the easiest solution would be to configure a VPN connection back to the office with which they are associated. You would need to configure RRAS on a Windows 2000 server in each office to accept VPN connections. If you have a public key infrastructure and you have assigned computer certificates to your clients and servers, you can use L2TP. Otherwise, you will have to use PPTP for the VPN connection. A backup means of connecting would be to use an RAS server—probably at a central location with a toll-free number. This way, users could access the network from anywhere, such as hotel rooms, without incurring extra connection expenses on the road. By having all of your RAS resources in a central location, you can control the hardware more efficiently.

MICROSOFT CERTIFIED SYSTEMS ENGINEER

11

Designing an IPSec Implementation Strategy

TEST YOURSELF OBJECTIVES

W indows 2000 is the first operating system from Microsoft to natively implement Internet Protocol Security (IPSec). Unlike Secure Sockets Layer (SSL), which occurs high in the Open Systems Interconnection (OSI) model, IPSec is implemented at the Network layer and is therefore considered an OSI Layer 3 encryption technology.

To successfully implement IPSec in your Windows 2000 network infrastructure, you need to understand how IPSec operates and how to define the goals of using IPSec on your network. You need to know how to install and configure IPSec for proper operation, as well as how to configure IPSec security policies on your network. Finally, you need to demonstrate knowledge of how to monitor and optimize the use of IPSec.

TEST YOURSELF OBJECTIVE 11.01

Understanding IPSec

IPSec is defined in RFC 2401 as a means of securing IP packets on a network. Its function is to provide data integrity, confidentiality, and authentication at Layer 3 in the OSI model. Windows 2000 IP Security builds on this by mixing public key and private key encryption as well as integrating automatic key management.

Some of the major standards that IPSec either uses or supports are Diffie-Hellman Technique, HMAC, MD5, SHA, DES, and 3DES. In addition, it supports the ISAKMP/Oakley (IKE) standard.

- IPSec has two primary components. Authentication Header (AH) verifies the origin of content, and Encapsulating Security Payload (ESP) encrypts data.

- AH adds an extra series of bytes after the IP header, but routers that don't support IPSec can still handle these packets just like any other payload data.

- ESP is primarily associated with encryption, but you can also support authentication directly within ESP.

Although you will not need to know the contents of the IPSec packet headers for day-to-day administration, you should be familiar with the two main types for the exam—Authentication Header and Encapsulating Security Payload.

QUESTIONS

11.01: Understanding IPSec

1. Imagine that you have two network devices that are exchanging packets using IPSec on your network. Device A is a router, and Device B is a PC. What feature of IPSec lets it know that the packets that are coming from Device A are actually from Device A, instead of from Device C (another PC)?

   A. MD5

   B. AH

   C. ESP

   D. 3DES

2. You have set up IPSec to use 3DES to encrypt data that travels on a link between two Windows 2000 servers on your network. Data is flowing properly between the two servers; however, when you look at the System Monitor on your systems, the processor utilization remains close to 95 percent when the server is sending and receiving network traffic, and the actual throughout from your server is barely exceeding 20 Mbps on your Fast Ethernet network. What is the easiest way to resolve this sluggishness on your servers?

   A. Add more memory to the servers.

   B. Add an additional processor to each of the servers.

   C. Replace the network card with one that can offload the IPSec processing to its own processor.

   D. All of the above.

3. When using IPSec to authenticate data on your IP network, you can choose from a number of methods of authentication. Which of the following authentication methods can be configured for use by IPSec? (Choose all that apply.)

   A. Kerberos authentication

   B. Microsoft Point-to-Point Encryption (MPPE)

   C. Certificate-based authentication

   D. Preshared keys

TEST YOURSELF OBJECTIVE 11.02

Defining the Goals of IPSec on Your Network

Just because you have IPSec at your disposal doesn't mean that you have to use it. Before implementing IPSec to protect your IP traffic, you need to define the goals of your IPSec implementation.

IPSec is used mainly for end-to-end security and virtual private network (VPN) security. End-to-end security covers traffic from one client PC to another, from a client PC to a server, or from a router to a router. VPN security can be broken into two areas: client to gateway and gateway to gateway.

- There are two primary ways to configure IPSec: Tunnel (VPN) mode, or Transport (end-to-end) mode.

- Tunnel mode is more taxing on the server because it requires that all data passing through the gateways be secured via IPSec tunneling.

- If you choose to use IPSec tunneling, you must specify the destination endpoint of the tunnel.

When deciding whether to use IPSec on your network, you need to have clearly defined goals. IPSec is costly in terms of both money and utilization of resources. Unless you have a distinct need for IPSec, you should not haphazardly throw it on your network.

QUESTIONS

11.02: Defining the Goals of IPSec on Your Network

4. You are the IS manager for a small technical college. You have recently completed migrating all of your desktop PCs and servers to Windows 2000.

You have configured an Active Directory domain and are developing a public key infrastructure (PKI) using Windows 2000 Certificate Services. You would like to protect the transmissions between college staff computers and the administrative servers. You are not really concerned about securing the traffic going out to the Internet, because the vast majority of your interesting traffic stays on your network. What type of IPSec security policy should you implement on your network?

A. You should configure IPSec to require secure communications between the administrative PCs and the administrative server.

B. You should configure your servers to request secure communications, and configure all of the PCs on campus to communicate normally.

C. You should configure all of your administrative PCs and servers to request secure communications for all transmissions.

D. You should configure all of your administrative PCs and servers to communicate normally.

5. Your remote users need to connect to your network for email access. You have two options for providing this access—you can configure your Windows 2000 server to provide Remote Access Services and have a pool of modems, or you can use virtual private networking. If you choose to use Layer 2 Tunneling Protocol VPN connections for your remote users, what would be the goal of using IPSec?

A. You want to make sure that packets that arrive from a specific remote user are, in fact, from that user.

B. You want IPSec to ensure that no one is able to read the contents of the packets coming from your remote users.

C. You want IPSec to ensure that the packets that are transmitted from the remote users are not altered on their way to the server.

D. All of the above.

6. **Situation:** You have a network infrastructure that resembles the following
    illustration:

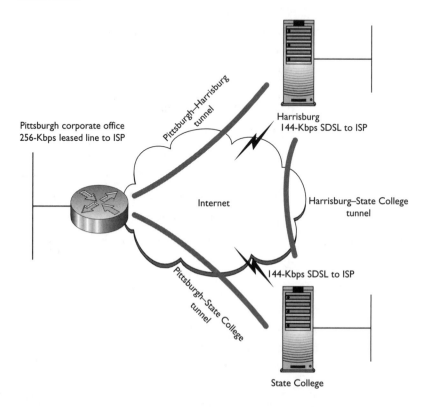

Your network consists of a diverse mix of clients: You have a Windows 2000
Active Directory infrastructure (both clients and servers), Macintosh clients, and
quite a few Windows 98 and Windows NT 4.0 clients. Your Windows 2000
servers at each office are configured to use Proxy Server to provide firewall services.
Your goal is to ensure that all data transmissions are secure as they travel through
the VPN connections to each of the offices.

Required Result: Implement IPSec so that it protects the data packets as they
travel between the offices.

Optional Desired Result: You would like to allow for end-to-end IPSec
encryption of data between all of your clients.

Proposed Solution: You use the Group Policy console to deploy an IPSec
policy to all of the PCs on the network. The IPSec policy tells machines to

request security for data transmissions. This way, you can utilize IPSec on all communications between endpoints on the network. You also configure Certificate Services to provide machine certificates so that encryption can take place on the packets going through the tunnels.

What results are provided from the proposed solution?

A.   The proposed solution produces the required result only.

B.   The proposed solution produces the required result and the optional desired result.

C.   The proposed solution does not produce the required result.

TEST YOURSELF OBJECTIVE 11.03

Installing and Configuring IPSec

IPSec is very easy to install in Windows 2000—it comes as part of the Windows 2000 operating system. To actually use IPSec to protect the communications on your network, you will need to implement an IPSec security policy on every computer that will be using IPSec.

You should know how to configure IPSec on both client and server machines throughout your network. You should be able to discuss the various means of implementing the IPSec security policies. Finally, you should know what dependencies exist for the methods in which you deploy IPSec.

- If you use Layer Two Tunneling Protocol (L2TP) to provide your VPN, you can use IPSec to provide your encryption. If you use Point-to-Point Tunneling Protocol (PPTP), however, you must use the Microsoft Point-to-Point Encryption (MPPE) protocol for this purpose.

- When using L2TP, the IPSec protection is optional; however, if you do not use any encryption on your VPN, your network resources will be vulnerable.

- Even after IPSec is operating on your network, there are still security risks—for example, the vulnerability of Data Encryption Standard (DES) and the improper transmission of keys.

exam
ⓦatch

The easiest way to deploy IPSec security policies is through the Group Policy console. Just remember that IPSec is configured on a per-machine basis, not per user. You cannot use security groups to filter which machines get the policy. If you only want a few machines to get the policy, you will need to place them in a new organizational unit (OU).

QUESTIONS

11.03: Installing and Configuring IPSec

7. You have a native Windows 2000 network infrastructure at your small company. You have 100 PCs and three servers. You would like to enable IPSec to provide authentication security for the packets traveling over the network. You are not especially concerned about encrypting the data at this point because the majority of the traffic is email based. How can you easily enable IPSec to provide security services on your PCs?

   A. You can go to each machine and enable the IPSec security policy from the Local Machine Policies console.

   B. You don't need to do anything to enable IPSec—it's included in the operating system.

   C. You can use the Group Policy console and define an IPSec security policy under the User Configuration settings. You can then apply this group policy to the site.

   D. You can use the Group Policy console and define an IPSec security policy under the Computer Configuration settings. You can then apply this policy at the domain or OU level.

8. You are the IS manager responsible for supporting the Special Investigation Unit (SIU) for your insurance company. The SIU shares the same network segment as the rest of the company. The company has a file server running Windows 2000, and the client PCs in the SIU are all running Windows 2000 Professional. You do not have a PKI. However, the remainder of the company

is still using a Windows NT 4.0 domain. You want to enable IPSec to provide encryption and authentication of data between the SIU client PCs and the SIU server. What needs to be enabled for this to work?

A. You need to set up an L2TP tunnel between your client PCs and the server.

B. You need to enable IPSec using a group policy for the SIU machines.

C. You need to provide a digital certificate for the machines that are using IPSec in the SIU.

D. None of the above.

9. **Situation:** You have a Windows 2000 Active Directory infrastructure. You have one domain, with nearly 1000 computers and ten file servers. All of your servers are running Windows 2000, as are 850 of your desktop PCs. You have 50 Windows 98 machines and 100 Windows 95 machines. Your human resources (HR) and accounting teams have their own file servers. Your legal department shares its file server with the executive team. The legal department would like their data to be encrypted. The HR team wants encryption as well. You do not want to encrypt the traffic going to the remaining file servers.

Required Result: Determine how to provide encryption to the legal and HR departments.

Optional Desired Results:

1. Determine the limitations your actions may have within the rest of the company.

2. Identify any technologies that may be required to support your decision.

Proposed Solution: You decide to place the Legal and HR file servers in their own OU (called High Security Zone). You create a group policy with an IPSec security policy and apply it to this new OU. The IPSec security policy is configured with a single rule, which states that all communications will be encrypted with 3DES and must be authenticated with Kerberos. You configure another group policy to enable IPSec security policies for the remaining Windows 2000 client PCs. You are aware that your Windows 95 and 98 PCs will not be able to communicate with the Legal and HR servers. You also identify that you will need to set up Certificate Services in your Active Directory domain to provide digital certificates to the machines that will be using IPSec.

What results are provided from the proposed solution?

A. The proposed solution produces the required result only.

B. The proposed solution produces the required result and one of the optional desired results.

C. The proposed solution produces the required result and both of the optional desired results.

D. The proposed solution does not produce the required result.

TEST YOURSELF OBJECTIVE 11.04

Implementing IPSec Security Policies

Once you have configured IPSec for basic operation on your network, you use IPSec security polices to define the methods by which you desire IPSec to protect your data transmissions. Windows 2000 comes with three policies already defined. You can define as many as you need to support your environment. Only one policy can be active per computer.

You will need to understand the various options that are available when modifying the built-in policies or creating new policies. These options are authentication methods, tunnel settings, connection types, IP filter lists, and filter actions.

■ The settings for IPSec are defined in security policies. Although you can create your own policies, Windows 2000 provides the following three templates: client (respond only), server (request only), and secure server (require security).

■ You can define the specific hashing algorithm (such as SHA1 or MD5) or encryption algorithm (such as DES or 3DES) to be used, depending on your security needs.

■ By defining filter rules and filter actions, you can determine which packets require IPSec processing and which packets can travel through unaltered.

exam

ⓦatch

All of the IPSec security policies that you configure will be available in every group policy that you implement. However, you can only apply one security policy to a machine at a time. To obtain the benefits of multiple security policies, just combine their settings into one big policy.

QUESTIONS

11.04: Implementing IPSec Security Policies

10. You are preparing to implement IPSec security policies in your network. You have a mix of Windows 2000 Professional and Linux workstations. You want to ensure that all of your client PCs can communicate with the file servers, no matter what security policy is in place. You also want to enforce 3DES encryption and SHA1 integrity checking. Which default IPSec policy for the servers provides these options?

    A. Client (respond only)

    B. Server (request security)

    C. Secure server (require security)

    D. Secure client (require security)

    Questions 11–13 This scenario should be used to answer questions 11, 12, and 13.

    You are the network manager for the R&D division of a major pharmaceutical corporation. A member of one of the product teams has asked for your help in protecting an idea. She is working on a new product idea that may revolutionize the way your company does business. She stores the majority of her research data on a Web server that is co-located in the server room. The competition is very fierce in your company, because this product could generate millions of dollars in revenue, and the engineer could receive thousands of dollars in incentive bonuses. Your job is to secure the data using encryption and authentication security as it travels between her Windows 2000 PC and the Windows 2000 server in the server room.

    The Windows 2000 server is named joker.w2k.smithdrugs.com; its IP address is 10.45.65.132. The user's workstation uses Dynamic Host Configuration Protocol (DHCP); the computer name is JONEC.rd.smithdrugs.com.

330 Chapter 11: Designing an IPSec Implementation Strategy

11. Which one of the following IPSec security policies should you set on the desktop to ensure that the data is protected by the full spectrum of Windows 2000 IP Security?

   A. You should set the client (respond only) default policy on the desktop PC.

   B. You should create a custom policy that only permits IP traffic between the engineer's PC and the server (10.45.65.132), uses high security, and does not allow unsecured communication.

   C. You should create a custom policy that has two rules. Rule 1 only permits IP traffic between the engineer's PC and the server (10.45.65.132), uses high security, and does not allow unsecured communication. Rule 2 allows unsecured transmissions, and will use security if asked to do so, for all IP traffic.

   D. None of the above.

12. How should you configure the IPSec security policy on the server? Assume that it only needs to share information with the client mentioned in the introductory text.

   A. Use the default secure server policy (require security).

   B. Use the default server policy (request security).

   C. Create a custom policy that requires that security be used for all traffic from all ports on all interfaces, and that unsecured traffic not be accepted.

   D. None of the above.

13. Which of the following encryption protocols used by Windows 2000 IP Security will give you the best protection against a brute-force attack on the data packet?

   A. 3DES

   B. DES

   C. MD5

   D. SHA1

14. **Situation:** You are the network specialist for a library in Atlanta. You have a very small Windows 2000 network and an Active Directory infrastructure. You use your domain controller as a router (via RRAS) and as a file server for the guest computers. There are 15 PCs in the library: two are in the office, three

are at the librarian stations, and the remaining ten are in an Internet lab. This lab is open to the public, as long as they are library members. The lab is on its own subnet. You want to protect the server against connections from FTP and Telnet sessions. You don't have Proxy Server, so you would like to use some of the built-in protection offered by IPSec.

Required Result: Protect the server from Telnet and FTP connections using IPSec.

Optional Desired Result: Allow access to the server from Telnet and FTP from your PC.

Proposed Solution: You use a group policy to push a custom IPSec security policy to the ten workstations in the lab. The policy contains a rule that blocks Telnet or FTP traffic originating from the lab computers with a destination of the library server. The following illustration shows the IP filter list for this rule.

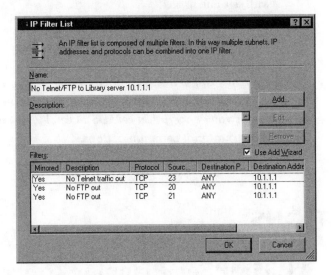

You don't need to configure anything to allow your PC to connect to the server. You will have access by default.

What results are provided from the proposed solution?

A. The proposed solution produces the required result only.

B. The proposed solution produces the required result and the optional desired result.

C. The proposed solution does not produce the required result.

IPSec Planning Considerations

Once you have a firm understanding of how IPSec operates and how to configure it for operation on your network, there are some planning considerations that you need to examine. You should look into how IPSec will authenticate the data and encrypt the data, as well as what circumstances might preclude you from deploying IPSec.

- When selecting an integrity algorithm, consider that SHA1 will provide more security but that MD5 will provide faster performance.

- DES is an industry-standard encryption algorithm, but it has been compromised by hackers. 3DES is a stronger algorithm that applies DES three times in a row with separate hashes.

- Some scenarios in which it is inappropriate to use IPSec are international communications and streaming media.

exam
ⓦatch

When implementing IPSec, you need to be very aware of where your encrypted packets are going. You cannot use strong encryption across the U.S. border (an example of strong encryption is MD5). Usually, 40- to 56-bit encryption is the limit for international communications.

QUESTIONS

II.05: IPSec Planning Considerations

15. You are planning to implement IPSec security policies on your file servers, which are accessible to a large number of corporate clients. Many of your clients run Windows 2000, but they are not in a trusted domain. How can you allow these Windows 2000 clients to authenticate against your IPSec-protected servers? (Choose all that apply.)

   A. You can configure your servers to use a third-party digital certificate, such as from VeriSign.

    B.   You can configure your servers to accept a preshared key.

    C.   You can just use the default Kerberos authentication.

    D.   All of the above.

16.   You are designing the Windows 2000 network infrastructure for an international financial consulting firm. They want to use IPSec to encrypt the financial information that they routinely send between their offices in New York, Munich, and Paris. What problems might this firm have with using IPSec encryption? (Choose all that apply.)

    A.   They cannot encrypt data that is sent over WAN links.

    B.   They cannot encrypt any data that is sent outside the United States.

    C.   They cannot use strong encryption on data that is sent outside the United States.

    D.   There are restrictions on using data encryption products when encrypting the data to go outside of any of the countries listed above.

17.   **Situation:** You are the senior engineer at a national systems integrator. You are preparing to configure your Windows 2000 server for incoming VPN connections. Your company has a Windows 2000 Active Directory infrastructure and is using a private Class A IP address on the internal network. A hardware-based router is providing network address translation (NAT) services. Your engineers would like to use their DSL and cable modem Internet connections at home to connect to the office via a VPN connection. They are pressuring you to allow L2TP VPN connections. They also want to use IPSec authentication and encryption on the communications between their laptops and the corporate RRAS (Routing and Remote Access Service) server to protect their data as it passes through the Internet.

    Required Result: Describe how you can configure Windows 2000 to allow L2TP/IPSec communications to the corporate network.

    Optional Desired Result: Describe how you can deploy an IPSec security policy to the engineers' computers.

    Proposed Solution: Since you cannot tunnel IPSec-encrypted packets through a firewall into a network using NAT, you decide to bend the rules. Your engineers' laptops will have valid public IP addresses from their ISPs. You decide to place a Windows 2000 server in your corporate network's demilitarized zone (DMZ). On the client, you configure the IPSec security policy to use IPSec tunnel mode, and provide the IP address of the server in the DMZ. You also configure the client to use ESP headers for encryption and authentication. You configure the Windows 2000 server in the DMZ to route the L2TP packets through the internal firewall to their ultimate destination. To deploy this policy to the engineers' laptops, you use the Group Policy console to push the policy to their machines when the engineers are in the office during the workday.

What results are provided from the proposed solution?

A. The proposed solution produces the required result only.

B. The proposed solution produces the required result and the optional desired result.

C. The proposed solution does not produce the required result.

TEST YOURSELF OBJECTIVE 11.06

Monitoring and Optimizing IPSec

After you have implemented IPSec in your organization, you need to continue to monitor its operation. As the volume of IPSec traffic in your organization starts to increase, you may observe performance degradation or possibly total failure. It's important to become familiar with the tools that can help you diagnose problems with IPSec and its operation.

You must also use monitoring to determine if you need to optimize your IPSec implementation. IPSec places a huge processing load on computers, especially when performing encryption.

- The tool that provides the most specific IPSec diagnostics is the IP Security Monitor (IPSECMON). This tool displays security associations, IPSec statistics, and ISAKMP/Oakley statistics, but it offers very little configuration flexibility.

- Using Network Monitor, you can observe whether ESP or AH packets are transmitted over the network, but you will not be able to read the contents of packets protected via ESP.

■ IPSec events can be found in all three sections of the Event Viewer (the system log, security log, and application log).

exam
⚠ atch

The best tool for monitoring IPSec operation is the IP Security Monitor. This tool is installed by default, but there is no shortcut for it on the Administrative Tools menu. You need to run IPSECMON from the Start menu or from the command prompt. This will bring up the IP Security Monitor.

QUESTIONS

11.06: Monitoring and Optimizing IPSec

18. You have configured your network computers to use IPSec authentication and encryption when sending or receiving any data. What tool or utility on the desktop PC will allow you to verify that IPSec is working properly?

   A. Network Monitor

   B. Event Viewer

   C. IP Security Monitor

   D. MMC with IPSec snap-in

19. You have just deployed an IPSec security policy to all of your servers and user computers. It's not very complicated—you just want to use IPSec to provide data integrity services on all packets exchanged between the clients and your servers. However, you begin to get a lot of calls to the help desk complaining that the servers are extremely sluggish. When you look at Windows Task Manager, you find that the servers are all running at nearly 99 percent processor utilization. What could be the problem?

   A. You have a number of users who are downloading large files from the servers.

   B. The processing of packets by IPSec is overwhelming the servers.

   C. The decrypting of packets by the network card is causing the server's processor utilization to go through the roof.

   D. All of the above.

20. You have secured your Windows 2000 file servers with an IPSec security policy that requires that all communications be secure between client PCs and the server. Everything is working properly with your domain-based computers, but you have a Windows 2000 Professional PC that is outside the domain and cannot connect to one of the file shares on the server. You manually configured this PC to use the preshared key for authentication. How can you check on the PC to see what the problem might be?

    A. Check the Event Viewer on the client that cannot connect to see if the IPSec policy agent left any messages.

    B. Use the IP Security Monitor to see if IPSec is working properly.

    C. Use Network Monitor to see if the packets are encrypted.

    D. None of the above.

LAB QUESTION

Objectives 11.01–11.06

Your company has just migrated to Windows 2000 from Windows NT 4.0. All of the file servers have been migrated, and 85 percent of the desktop and laptop computers have been migrated to Windows 2000. The remaining machines are running Windows NT 4.0.

You are running a Mixed-mode Active Directory infrastructure, even though all of your domain controllers have been migrated—just in case! You have configured Windows 2000 Certificate Services to be a certificate authority (CA) for your network.

Your Windows NT 4.0 RAS server was upgraded to Windows 2000. The server has ten connections available for PPTP and L2TP connections. You have 30 users who work primarily from the road; they connect using a dial-up connection to the local ISP, and then use a VPN connection to access the network.

You are using a private Class A address on your network and are using NAT behind your firewall. Your network has a demilitarized zone that holds the public Web server and the email server. You have three remote offices that connect to the corporate network via 128-Kbps Frame Relay circuits.

You would like to implement IPSec in your network. Please answer the following questions regarding planning for this implementation.

1. Can you use IPSec to secure the communications between all of your client PCs and servers? If not, which ones will be unsupported? Can you implement IPSec with these computers on your network?

2. How will your CA play into your IPSec implementation? Is it required for you to implement IPSec?

3. If you choose to configure end-to-end IPSec from a user in a remote office to the file servers in the corporate office, will NAT present a problem?

4. Can you use L2TP/IPSec for your remote users with your network infrastructure?

5. If you desire to use IPSec for providing data integrity and authentication between your clients and servers, is there any need to create elaborate custom IPSec security policies?

QUICK ANSWER KEY

Objective 11.01

1. B
2. C
3. A, C, and D

Objective 11.02

4. C
5. D
6. C

Objective 11.03

7. D
8. C
9. C

Objective 11.04

10. B
11. C
12. C
13. A
14. C

Objective 11.05

15. A and B
16. C and D
17. B

Objective 11.06

18. C
19. B
20. A

IN-DEPTH ANSWERS

11.01: Understanding IPSec

1. ☑ **B.** The Authentication Header (AH) is the component of IPSec that is responsible for providing integrity and authentication for packets as they travel between two hosts. The AH is placed between the IP header and the Transport layer header in the packet, as shown in the following illustration:

Original IP Header	IPSec (AH) Header	Layer 4 Header (UDP)	Application Data

☒ **A** is incorrect because MD5 (Message Digest 5) is a cryptographic algorithm used to encrypt data. **C** is incorrect because Encapsulating Security Payload (ESP) provides for the confidentiality (or encryption) of the data in the packet, using DES. **D** is incorrect because 3DES (a secret-key encryption algorithm) is also used for encryption, not authentication.

2. ☑ **C.** The simplest way to dramatically improve the performance of servers that are configured to encrypt data using IPSec/3DES is to replace the network interface card (NIC) with one that can offload the processing of IPSec to itself. Studies show that when a server performs software encryption of data, especially via 3DES, it slows the throughput to nearly 20 Mbps. However, if you offload that processing to a NIC, your throughput will increase to almost 70 Mbps, a 250 percent increase in performance. At the same time, processor utilization will drop from over 90 percent to 65 percent.

☒ **A** is incorrect because although more memory may slightly improve the performance, it will not have as much effect as a new network card. **B** is also incorrect, because a second processor will not give the performance benefits of a new NIC.

3. ☑ **A, C,** and **D** are correct. IPSec can be configured to use Kerberos authentication, certificate-based authentication, or preshared keys. When you establish an IPSec security policy, Windows 2000 will choose Kerberos

authentication by default. However, if you have installed and configured Windows 2000 Certificate Services, you can choose to use certificate-based authentication. You can also choose this option if you have a digital certificate from a third-party certificate authority (for example, VeriSign). Finally, you can choose to use a preshared key for authentication. This method is not recommended for production use, because it has the weakest security of the three methods.

☒   **B** is incorrect because MPPE is an encryption method that is used for Point-to-Point Tunneling Protocol VPNs.

11.02: Defining the Goals of IPSec on Your Network

4.   ☑   **C.** In this situation, your goal is protecting your administrative traffic from the prying eyes of a campus full of technical students. The easiest way to do this would be to configure all of your administrative computers (desktops and servers) to request secure communications for all transmissions. Since all of your assets will be configured to communicate in this manner, you will be assured that your communications will be covered under IPSec. You will also need to modify the security policy to provide encryption if desired (and your goal should be to encrypt sensitive data). You will need to configure Certificate Services to provide a computer certificate for this to work.

☒   **A** is incorrect because if you have *any* non–Windows 2000 PCs, they will not be able to communicate with the administrative servers. IPSec is not integrated into any of the legacy Microsoft operating systems. **B** is incorrect— since the clients will be initiating the communications, they will never request to use IPSec security. **D** is incorrect because you wouldn't be protecting any of your data transmissions with this option.

5.   ☑   **D.** All of the above. When you have users who are transmitting potentially sensitive data, such as email messages, across a VPN connection, you want the packets to arrive intact, secure, and unaltered. IPSec will provide all of these benefits.

☒   There are no incorrect answers.

6.   ☑   **C.** The proposed solution does not produce the required result. The required result is to protect the data packets as they travel between the offices

through the VPN tunnels. Since your environment is very well mixed in terms of client operating systems, you will not be able to do full end-to-end IPSec encryption—only the Windows 2000 clients have IPSec natively as part of the OS. You will need to configure your network so that the traffic between the clients and the VPN endpoint (the server) is unprotected and the traffic over the VPN connection is encrypted using IPSec. Your Windows 2000 clients will be able to do end-to-end encryption, and you can use the Group Policy console to enable this security policy. You cannot use Group Policy to manage your non–Windows 2000 clients.

☒ **A** and **B** are incorrect because the proposed solution does not produce the required result.

11.03: Installing and Configuring IPSec

7. ☑ **D.** The easiest way to enable IPSec on your workstations is to use the Group Policy console to configure an IPSec security policy. You can apply this group policy to either your domain or an OU.

☒ **A** is incorrect. Although you can enable IPSec security this way, you will be causing an administrative nightmare for yourself. A group policy is the easiest way to deploy this configuration. **B** is incorrect because IPSec is not enabled by default. You need to configure a security policy to allow IPSec to protect data packets. **C** is incorrect because IPSec security policy is not configured under the User Configuration settings in the Group Policy console. It is configured under the Computer Configuration settings.

8. ☑ **C.** In order to enable IPSec on the machines in the Special Investigation Unit, you need to make sure that the machines have a valid digital certificate for the machine account. IPSec works at the machine (rather than user) level, and thus each machine needs a certificate.

☒ **A** is incorrect because you do not need to create a tunnel between the client PCs and the server for IPSec to work properly. **B** is incorrect because you cannot use a group policy unless you have an Active Directory domain.

9. ☑ **C.** The proposed solution produces the required result and both of the optional desired results. In order to use IPSec to encrypt the traffic from the Legal and HR servers, you need to enable an IPSec security policy on each

server that instructs it to use ESP for encryption and integrity checking (see the following illustration).

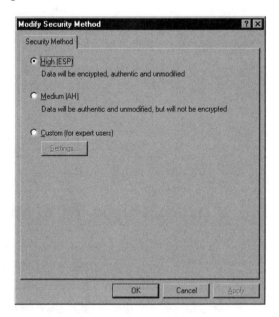

It's your choice as to the method of encryption—3DES is pretty secure. By configuring the policy to require encryption for all traffic on all interfaces, you have properly configured the server. To implement this policy, you should use the Group Policy console. By putting these servers in their own OU, you can apply the policy to them and only them. Next, by again using a group policy, you can configure the client PCs to use IPSec.

You correctly identified that a limitation of this solution is that your non–Windows 2000 PCs will not be able to communicate with the two secured servers. You also correctly identified that you will need digital certificates from a CA to allow your machines to use IPSec.

☒ **A, B,** and **D** are incorrect because the proposed solution produces the required result and both of the optional desired results.

11.04: Implementing IPSec Security Policies

10. ☑ **B.** The default security policy named server (request security) will provide the actions that are required in this question. This policy will accept unsecured

requests, but will then request that the sender use IPSec. It uses 3DES for ESP encryption, and Secure Hash Algorithm 1 (SHA1) for authentication.

☒ **A** is incorrect because the client (respond only) policy will communicate unsecured until asked to use security by another computer. This rule also uses Kerberos as the default authentication method. **C** is incorrect because the secure server (require security) policy requires that all communication be done securely—no unsecured transmissions will be accepted. **D** is incorrect because this is not a default policy in IPSec security.

11. ☑ **C.** To ensure that all of the traffic between the client PC and the server is sent with high security, you should create a custom policy for the client PC. This policy should have two rules: one to define how traffic to the specific server should be handled, and a second to define how everything else should be handled. For the first rule, you should create a filter list that specifies IP traffic from the PC's address to the server's address. The filter action will be to require security, the authentication method will be Kerberos, and the connection type will be LAN. The second rule will be for all IP traffic, the filter action will be to request security, and the authentication method will also be Kerberos. The following illustration shows these rules.

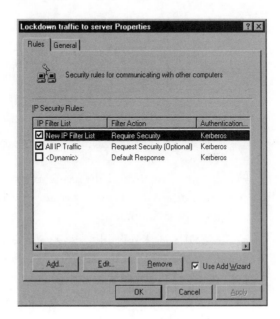

☒ **A** is incorrect because this will not configure the engineer's PC to send secure traffic to the R&D server. **B** is incorrect because it will not allow the engineer's PC to communicate with hosts other than the R&D server.

12. ☑ **C.** The policy for the server is a little easier. Since it only communicates with the R&D client, you don't need to worry about supporting nonsecure client traffic. You should create a custom policy that has a single rule: it will have an IP filter list that specifies All IP Traffic, a filter policy that specifies require security (set to negotiate security using High settings and/or ESP, and with all of the check boxes cleared, as shown in the following illustration), Kerberos as the authentication method, and All Network Connections for a connection type.

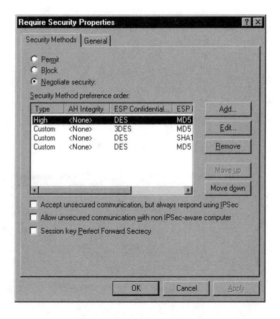

☒ **A** is incorrect because the secure server policy allows unsecured communications. **B** is incorrect because it will allow unsecured communications with non-IPSec computers.

13. ☑ **A.** 3DES, or Triple DES, gives you the strongest encryption allowed by Windows 2000 IP Security. DES is a 56-bit encryption technology, and 3DES performs the DES algorithm three times with three different keys.

☒ **B** is incorrect because 3DES provides stronger encryption than plain DES. **C** is incorrect because MD5 is not used for encrypting the packet data, but rather for ensuring the integrity of packet data—that is, for certifying that the data did not change once it left the sender's computer. **D** is incorrect because SHA1 is also used for data integrity, not encryption.

14. ☑ **C.** The proposed solution does not produce the required result. This solution does a great job of preventing the lab computers from initiating FTP or Telnet connections to the library server (10.1.1.1.). However, the requirement was to protect the server from any connection via FTP or Telnet. You should have created a rule that blocked FTP and Telnet from any host, and implemented that policy on the server rather than on the lab computers. To allow incoming connections from your own PC, you could create another rule that explicitly allows port 20, 21, and 23 traffic from your IP address.

     ☒ **A** and **B** are incorrect because the proposed solution does not produce the required result.

11.05: IPSec Planning Considerations

15. ☑ **A** and **B** are correct. When you have clients that do not use Kerberos, version 5, or are not in a trusted domain, you can use either a digital certificate from a certificate authority or use a preshared key. To use the digital certificate, you will need to either purchase one from a third-party CA or use an installation of Windows 2000 Certificate Services that is accessible to all parties. To use the preshared key, you need to provide all of the computers that are going to communicate with your servers a key to enter into the dialog box for IPSec security policy. This method is the least desirable because of the vulnerability of the key information.

     ☒ **C** is incorrect because you cannot use Kerberos authentication if the client PC is not in a trusted domain.

16. ☑ **C** and **D** are correct. This firm might have problems using IPSec because the United States has laws regulating what types of encryption can be exported outside the country, and many foreign countries (including France and Germany) have regulations about using encryption as well.

     ☒ When designing a network infrastructure that uses encryption to secure data as it travels over the network, be sure you understand the relevant laws of both the United States and the countries who will be receiving the data. The United States has specific regulations that do not permit the export of data using encryption technology stronger than 56-bit encryption. Many foreign countries have similar laws that govern both the import and export of information using strong encryption.

☒ **A** is incorrect because you can encrypt data that is sent over WAN links. **B** is incorrect because you can encrypt data sent outside the United States, but only using relatively weak encryption technology—that is, 40- and 56-bit encryption.

17. ☑ **B.** The proposed solution produces both the required result and the optional desired result. It's tricky using L2TP and IPSec when you are also using NAT on your internal network. For the most part, the recommendation is to avoid this configuration and use PPTP/MPPE instead. In this case, the engineers were just interested in using IPSec to protect the data as it traversed the Internet. Once it got to the corporate network, it could travel as unsecured packets. The solution is rudimentary, but it works. The solution for configuring the IPSec security policy on the laptops is also correct. The Group Policy console is the best tool for managing these policies.

☒ **A** and **C** are incorrect because the proposed solution produces both the required result and the optional desired result.

11.06: Monitoring and Optimizing IPSec

18. ☑ **C.** The IP Security Monitor will quickly allow you to see if IPSec is working properly on your desktop PC. The following illustration shows IPSec policies enabled:

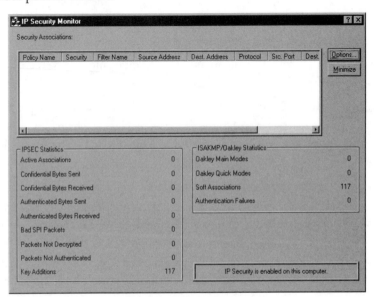

If this computer had been connected to another IPSec-protected system, you would see the statistics about the connection in this program. You can run this program by choosing Start, Run, IPSECMON.

☒ **A** is incorrect because Network Monitor is not available in Windows 2000 Professional. It is available in a limited format in Windows 2000 Server. **B** is incorrect because Event Viewer only shows limited information about certain IPSec-related events. **D** is incorrect because this is a fictional snap-in.

19. ☑ **B.** The best explanation for this problem, given the information presented, is that the new IPSec policy is causing the server to work overtime to examine the IPSec-protected packets.

☒ **A** is incorrect because normal file and print services don't usually tax the processor that much. **C** is incorrect because you aren't using IPSec to encrypt packets on your network.

20. ☑ **A.** A quick way to see the status of IPSec on a computer that is not functioning correctly is to examine the event logs. The IPSec policy agent will leave detailed messages regarding the status of the service. You can use this information to troubleshoot IPSec problems.

☒ **B** is incorrect because you won't see any data in IP Security Monitor if IPSec is not working properly. **C** is incorrect because you aren't using encryption.

LAB ANSWER

Objectives 11.01–11.06

1. No, you cannot use IPSec to secure the communications between all of your clients and servers. The Windows NT 4.0 machines do not support IPSec. You can implement IPSec on your network with these machines still in use; however, you will not be able to use the secure server policy until all of your PCs can communicate securely with IPSec.

2. You can use your CA to provide computer certificates to your PCs and servers. You can use the Group Policy console to deploy these via an automatic policy. The CA is not required in order for you to use IPSec.

3. In this example, NAT will not present a problem. You are using NAT on your internal network. The connections coming in from the remote office are on permanent circuits through the frame relay cloud. They all share the same private address scheme. If you use IPSec, there will be no translating of IPSec packets, so there will be no problems.

4. You cannot use L2TP/IPSec with this network configuration. Remember, NAT cannot be used in conjunction with IPSec. You will need to use PPTP for your VPN connections.

5. No, there is no need to create elaborate policies if you are simply using IPSec for data integrity and authentication. The default policies are more than adequate for such an implementation.

MCSE
MICROSOFT CERTIFIED SYSTEMS ENGINEER

12

Management and Implementation Strategies for Windows 2000

TEST YOURSELF OBJECTIVES

12.01　Designing a Strategy for Monitoring and Managing Windows 2000 Network Services

12.02　Designing Network Services That Support Application Architecture

12.03　Designing a Plan for the Interaction of Windows 2000 Network Services such as WINS, DHCP, and DNS

12.04　Designing a Resource Strategy

O nce you have your Windows 2000 network up and running, you will need to devise a strategy for managing your infrastructure as well as for implementing new services into your network design. A Windows 2000 network is a dynamic structure that needs continuous attention to keep it running in top form.

Your management and implementation strategy should cover a number of items, including an approach for monitoring and managing network services, a design for network services that support application architecture, a plan for the interaction of Windows 2000 network services, and a resource strategy.

Designing a Strategy for Monitoring and Managing Windows 2000 Network Services

All networks, including Windows 2000 networks, require a well-thought-out design for the management of their networking services. You should also create a strategy for the proactive monitoring of your network so that you can enable it to run at peak efficiency.

You should be very familiar with the built-in tools in Windows 2000 that allow you to manage your network infrastructure. You should also understand how to use services such as Network Monitor to monitor your network.

- Effective management of your network includes the proactive measurement of statistics in order to create baselines that can be used for comparison with network performance in the future.

- Using a Simple Network Management Protocol (SNMP) management console, you can view (and in some cases, modify) statistics and settings on SNMP-enabled servers and equipment.

- A network management design document must include methods used to respond to variances from acceptable performance as defined in the design document.

exam
ⓦatch

Although Windows 2000 does not come with an SNMP management console, it does come with an extensive set of Management Information Bases (MIBs) that can be used to manage many of the services in Windows 2000. You should be familiar with the general types of MIBs that ship with Windows 2000, and what you can do with them. For example, the MIB for the Windows Internet Naming Service (WINS) allows you to view the WINS database, as well as to change some of the parameters of the service from the MIB management console.

QUESTIONS

12.01: Designing a Strategy for Monitoring and Managing Windows 2000 Network Services

1. You have just completed implementing your new Windows 2000 network infrastructure. You have 40 offices, 17,000 users, 45 servers, and a very happy CIO. Although the project finished on time and on budget, there are still a few housekeeping steps that need to be done. The largest of these is to take a "snapshot" of the network today so that you can have something to look back on if trouble should arise later. How can you gather this baseline information for your enterprise?

    A. You can use Network Monitor to capture a week's worth of traffic so that you get a good idea of the traffic patterns on your network.

    B. You can use System Monitor to gather processor and network statistics from each of your servers and workstations and then combine these statistics into one large database of information.

    C. You can use the Windows 2000 SNMP agents in conjunction with an enterprise SNMP management console, such as one from Tivoli, to gather the data into a central database.

    D. All of the above.

2. As part of your network management strategy, you have decided to use an SNMP-based management product. One of the steps in setting up SNMP is to establish community names for use in your network. How should you define community names for your SNMP network devices?

    A. You should make sure that all of your devices are in the public community.

    B. You should assign a single hard-to-guess community name to your network devices that will be managed by SNMP.

    C. You should assign community names based on the locations of the devices, and use hard-to-guess community names.

    D. You should use multiple hard-to-guess community names, based on the amount of access each community will allow. Then, assign the appropriate level of security to each community name.

3. You are the network manager for a large company. You have 9,000 desktop PCs running Windows 2000 spread across 17 major offices and three small offices. You have 250 remote users who connect into the network through a VPN connection. You would like to implement a management strategy for your desktops that would allow you to gather statistics about bandwidth usage and memory usage so that you can proactively plan for upgrades. You do not want to purchase another system, such as System Management Server or Tivoli, to do this—you'd like to use the resources that you have at hand. Which one of the following strategies will allow you to gather this data without placing a burden on your network infrastructure?

    A. Configure a counter log on each desktop PC in the enterprise, and have it store the log file on a server in the corporate data center. You can then collect all of the log files from the server and manipulate them in a database, such as SQL Server.

    B. Configure a counter log on each desktop PC in the enterprise, and have it store the log file on a server in the same site or office location. You can use a copy process to pull all of the log files from the 20 offices to a central server in the data center. Once you have the log files, you can manipulate them in a database, such as SQL Server.

C. Configure an alert on each desktop PC in the enterprise, and have it send a message to an account on an Exchange server in the corporate data center. You can then collect all of the alert messages from the Exchange server and manipulate them in a database, such as SQL Server.

D. None of the above.

4. **Situation:** You are consulting for a medium-sized organization that has recently finished designing their Windows 2000 network infrastructure. You have been asked to design a management and monitoring strategy for this network.

Once completed, they will have nearly 3,000 desktop PCs running Windows 2000 Professional, 500 desktop PCs running Windows 98, and 200 laptops running Windows 2000 Professional. They have seven offices in the United States, plus one office outside London. Their infrastructure will have eight sites (corresponding to each location), each with a domain controller (DC). Dynamic Host Configuration Protocol (DHCP), Domain Name System (DNS), and WINS will also be running on servers at each site. Each office in the United States will be connected by a 1.544-Mbps circuit into a Frame Relay cloud, while the United Kingdom location will be connected to both the New York and Charlotte locations with a T1 circuit (for redundancy).

Required Result: Provide a solution so that the client company can connect to any of the domain controllers or member servers that are running services, such as DHCP, DNS, WINS, Internet Information Server, and so forth, regardless of the state of the network links to the site.

Optional Desired Results:

1. The client will be using an SNMP network management application to monitor the servers on the network. Describe how the servers should be configured so that they will work with this application.

2. Describe how the client can use the Microsoft Management Console (MMC) to perform low-level status updates of all their critical services.

Proposed Solution: You propose to connect an analog modem to each of the domain controllers. You will then configure Routing and Remote Access Service (RRAS) on these servers to accept a single RAS connection. This will give you an out-of-band management interface into the server and into the network segment to which the server is connected. To allow the use of SNMP, you will configure the TCP/IP Properties on each server to accept SNMP connections, and provide the IP address of the SNMP management application's console. You will also configure the Public community with Read and Create rights. Finally, you will create a custom MMC that has the snap-ins for DNS, DHCP, WINS, and RRAS installed. You will then instruct the client on how to use the MMC to monitor these critical services.

What results are provided from the proposed solution?

A. The proposed solution produces the required result only.

B. The proposed solution produces the required result and one of the optional desired results.

C. The proposed solution produces the required result and both of the optional desired results.

D. The proposed solution does not produce the required result.

TEST YOURSELF OBJECTIVE 12.02

Designing Network Services That Support Application Architecture

Windows 2000 provides a great platform for supporting medium- to large-scale application architectures. These architectures can include e-commerce solutions, joint project development solutions, Internet service providers (ISPs), and virtual offices.

You need to be able to identify how Windows 2000 network services can benefit each of these types of application architectures, and know how to implement Windows 2000 in support of these activities. Windows 2000 services that will be of immediate benefit are Clustering, Network Load Balancing (NLB), Internet Authentication Service (IAS), and Internet Information Server (IIS).

■ Features such as Network Load Balancing provide support for Web applications by allowing multiple Web servers to appear as one to the outside world.

The Internet Authentication Service is a great feature for ISPs who want
scalability in their dial-in solutions. By using IAS to authenticate users against
the Active Directory, rather than managing a database on every network access
server, ISPs can save significant management time and money.

QUESTIONS

12.02: Designing Network Services That Support Application Architecture

5. Which of the following features of Windows 2000 would provide the most
   benefit to an Internet service provider that has 35,000 customers? This ISP's
   primary business activity is providing 56 Kbps and ISDN dial-up access to the
   Internet. They have 40 points of presence (POPs) in a metropolitan area, all of
   which are connected via an OC-3 Synchronous Optical Network (SONET)
   ring. The ISP has two T3 circuits going to different Tier 1 providers.

   A. Network load balancing

   B. Internet Authentication Services

   C. Four-way Clustering

   D. Large memory support

6. You are designing a network architecture to support your new e-commerce
   Web site. Your initial traffic projections are that you will receive 500 hits per
   minute for the first week or so, and then the traffic will gradually increase
   to 1,000 hits per minute. Your e-commerce application will be running on
   Internet Information Server 5.0, using Active Server Pages, DCOM, and a
   little Java. The application will use a SQL Server 7.0 database on the back
   end. All of these services will run on Windows 2000 Advanced Server. Which

of the following services provide high availability and redundancy to your e-commerce application? (Choose all that apply.)

A. Using Network Load Balancing to distribute the incoming HTTP requests across multiple servers.

B. Using Windows Clustering to provide failover for the servers running SQL Server 7.0.

C. Using Windows Clustering to provide failover for the servers running IIS.

D. Using RRAS to provide OSPF routing into your network.

7. You are the network manager for a small insurance company. Your network is a combination of Windows 2000 and Windows NT 4.0. You have 125 claim representatives who work from their homes. They work primarily with a client/server database that holds the claims data; they also use Microsoft Office for custom forms and word processing documents. Your company uses Exchange 5.5 and Outlook 2000 for messaging and public folders. Which of these Windows 2000 technologies provide support for this virtual office scenario? (Choose all that apply.)

A. RRAS

B. SQL Server 7.0

C. Proxy Server 2.0

D. IPSec

8. Which of the following Internet Authentication Service features are of most interest to large network providers such as ISPs?

A. Centralized auditing of network access

B. Centralized administration of access servers

C. Centralized authentication of user accounts

D. Worldwide remote access for clients

E. All of the above

TEST YOURSELF OBJECTIVE 12.03

Designing a Plan for the Interaction of Windows 2000 Network Services such as WINS, DHCP, and DNS

Network services such as WINS, DNS, and DHCP often must communicate important information with one another over the network. For example, when a WINS client receives new IP addressing information from a DHCP server, that WINS client must register its new IP addressing information with a WINS server. A DNS server may need to communicate with the WINS server to obtain IP addressing information about that same client.

By combining services within your infrastructure, you can free up valuable hardware for other purposes. There are drawbacks to combining services, however, such as having two services contending for the same disk channel.

- One way to improve network performance is to combine network services. This can reduce both the amount of time it takes for networking services to communicate with each other and the amount of network bandwidth required for services intercommunication.

- Be careful when combining network services. Avoid combining services that compete for the same hardware resources.

exam
ⓦatch

For this exam, it is important to understand the ramifications of combining services such as Exchange and Active Directory on a single server. Be careful not to choose answers that pair services that rely heavily on writing to transaction logs or databases, because these are not good services to team up on a server.

QUESTIONS

12.03: Designing a Plan for the Interaction of Windows 2000 Network Services such as WINS, DHCP, and DNS

9. You are redesigning the network infrastructure for a large financial services corporation. They are migrating to Windows 2000 and have an existing Windows NT 4.0 network. They have a mix of Windows 2000, Windows NT 4.0, and Windows 98 clients. This company has 37 offices across the United States, and each office has nearly 800 employees. The locations are connected with 128-Kbps Frame Relay circuits. Every office has a minimum of five servers to provide network services (not counting the file/print and application servers). One server is configured as the primary domain controller (PDC), the second and third are backup domain controllers (BDCs), the fourth is the DHCP server, and the fifth provides WINS. What benefit (if any) would this company realize if they were to combine some of these services onto one server?

   A. They would not realize a benefit. DHCP and WINS are not compatible on the same server.

   B. They could free up bandwidth, because DHCP and WINS communicate extensively with each other during normal operation.

   C. They could free up hardware, because WINS and DHCP could easily be placed on one of the BDCs.

   D. None of the above.

10. A small company has contacted your firm to help with a problem. They have a Windows 2000 network at their single location. They have 350 clients running Windows 2000 and Windows 98. They have three servers: two domain controllers and one server running Microsoft Exchange. One DC also runs DNS, WINS, and DHCP. They recently needed to rebuild one of their servers to place it into service as an intranet server. They chose the second DC to fulfill this role. Before they rebuilt it, they moved WINS and DNS over to the

Exchange server, and moved DHCP to the domain controller. Now, a week after that move, their Exchange server is experiencing an extended period of extremely high processor and disk utilization. What could be the problem?

A. The WINS database became corrupted in the migration to the new server.

B. The server is receiving an abnormally high number of domain name resolution requests.

C. The Exchange server and WINS are competing for control over the disk hardware.

D. All of the above.

11. You are responsible for a large Mixed-mode Windows 2000 network. You have 10 DHCP scopes that are being served by 22 DHCP servers, and you have 12 WINS servers throughout the network. As time has gone by, you have upgraded your network links between offices from 128-Kbps circuits to T1s. You are finding that maintaining WINS and DHCP has become an administrative headache. You are also preparing to upgrade the server hardware in your offices, and you are looking for ways to reduce costs. You are considering consolidating your WINS and DHCP services into eight two-way clusters strategically placed throughout the network as a means of controlling management and hardware costs. What will Clustering do to help solve your problem? (Choose all that apply.)

A. It will allow you to consolidate multiple services into a single cluster that provides fault tolerance.

B. Clustering will allow you to maintain a single copy of a DHCP scope on the cluster, instead of multiple copies on multiple servers that only have 50 to 80 percent of the total addresses.

C. You will be able to load-balance incoming requests to the WINS servers across the cluster server addresses.

D. You will have a net decrease in the number of servers that you must support for DHCP and WINS.

12. **Situation:** You are a Windows 2000 consultant who has been called in to help a client reduce some of their network management costs. They are not a large company—they have 800 employees in a three-building campus. They have a

substantial online presence, with a Web site that records nearly 200,000 hits per day. They recently began their migration to Windows 2000, but still have a large number of Windows 98 and Windows NT 4.0 desktop machines. All of their servers have been converted to Windows 2000. The following illustration shows their network infrastructure:

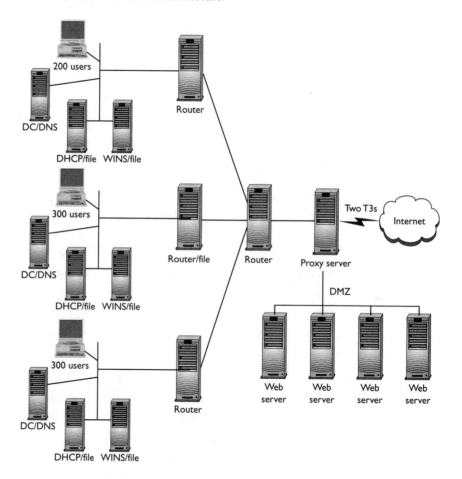

The company wants to reduce costs in one major area: hardware maintenance. They also want to improve the fault tolerance and availability of network services, and lower the bandwidth utilized by nonclient traffic.

Required Result: Propose a solution to help reduce hardware maintenance costs by eliminating extra hardware.

Optional Desired Results:

1. Propose a solution to make this network infrastructure more efficient.

2. Combine services or add services where necessary.

Proposed Solution: After reviewing their architecture, you find a couple of areas where hardware can be consolidated. First, you recommend that the client replace all the software-based routers in each of the campus buildings, and the software-based router between the proxy server and the campus, with a hardware-based router and switches. This arrangement will reduce the total cost of ownership for the routing solution dramatically over time. Next, you recommend that the client add a high-speed network segment that is central to the entire organization (that is, a core). The following illustration depicts the new design:

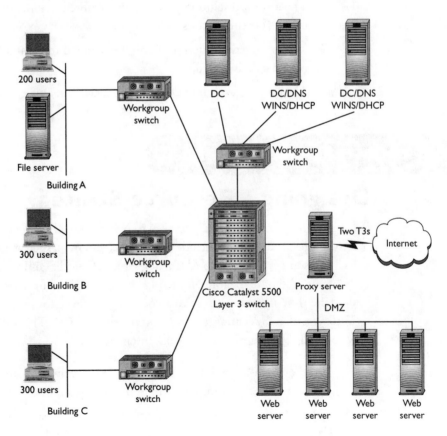

You suggest that they consolidate the three WINS servers into two, and move them to a segment that is central to the entire organization. One WINS will be the primary server, and the other will be a backup. Next, you recommend that the same consolidation be applied to the DHCP and DNS servers. With 800 users, they do not need to have three dedicated servers for WINS, DHCP, and DNS. A primary and backup for each will suffice. For even more consolidation, you can place the DNS, DHCP, and WINS services on the same server (and have the same configuration for the backup server). Finally, leave the file servers on the segments closest to the users who will be accessing them. If everyone accesses all of the servers, place them on the core segment for easy access by all.

What results are provided from the proposed solution?

A. The proposed solution produces the required result only.

B. The proposed solution produces the required result and one of the optional desired results.

C. The proposed solution produces the required result and both of the optional desired results.

D. The proposed solution does not produce the required result.

TEST YOURSELF OBJECTIVE 12.04

Designing a Resource Strategy

When designing your network, you need to plan for the placement and management of network resources. These include the obvious resources, such as DHCP and DNS, as well as resources such as Global Catalog servers, firewalls, and so forth.

You must also have the foresight to plan for growth in your network. You must understand the corporate goals so that you can plan ahead for projected growth.

You must plan for centralized or decentralized resources. This will have an effect on how you design the supporting network infrastructure.

- You should always build extra capacity in your network plan so that you will not be surprised by future growth of the corporation.

- Pay careful attention to where you place enterprise resources, such as Global Catalog servers, so that they can service the users in the most efficient way.

When you are designing a network, it is usually cheaper to add extra capacity at the start than to shoehorn it in when you run out. Keep this in mind during the design phase. Some technologies, such as Frame Relay, allow for burst transmissions that exceed the committed capacity. If you find through testing that you are regularly exceeding your Committed Information Rate (CIR), build in more room now, rather than wait until you need it but don't have it.

QUESTIONS

12.04: Designing a Resource Strategy

13. **Situation:** You are designing a Windows 2000 network infrastructure for your client, an international banking institution with offices in the United Kingdom, France, Germany, Italy, South Africa, and Australia. They have a total of 17 large international offices. Your client also has four major locations in the United States, plus a data center. There are a fair number of branch offices in all the countries for handling small customer transactions. They have acquired two large banks in the past year, and their plan includes the acquisition of two more competitors in the next 12 months. All of their major locations are connected into a Frame Relay cloud. The small branch offices are connected into the cloud using 56-Kbps circuits, whereas the large offices use 256-Kbps circuits. The client is currently using Lotus cc:Mail for messaging, but is planning to migrate to Exchange 2000 very shortly. They will also be introducing Internet access to small groups of employees over the next 6 to 12 months. You are concerned with the planning for short- and long-term growth of the company and the network. The client is worried that the WAN will not support the traffic demands of the near future. They are also concerned that the Windows 2000 routing protocols are not up to the demand of so many locations.

    Required Result: Determine if the WAN circuit speeds will provide enough bandwidth for short- and long-term use.

    Optional Desired Result: Choose a routing protocol that is supported by both software- and hardware-based routers and that scales well.

Proposed Solution: After reviewing the network information, you feel that the network is not going to be able to support the future needs of the company. The 56-Kbps links will not withstand the introduction of Internet access at the end of the fiscal year. Active Directory replication and Exchange replication will also severely tax the bandwidth. Because of the complexity of the network, you choose to use Open Shortest Path First (OSPF) as the routing protocol. By using OSPF, you can aggregate the routes in each area and shorten the time required for the OSPF route table to propagate throughout the network.

What results are provided from the proposed solution?

A. The proposed solution produces the required result only.

B. The proposed solution produces the required result and the optional desired result.

C. The proposed solution does not produce the required result.

14. You are preparing to design the migration from Windows 95 to Windows 2000. You currently have 4,000 desktop PCs in 12 offices. The administrator in each office is responsible for maintaining that office's own file and print resources. The corporate IT department provides direction for IP addressing, hardware recommendations, and software licensing. You report directly to the CIO of the corporation. He wants to know which would be a better organizational model for your Windows 2000 network infrastructure—centralized or decentralized. What will you tell him? (Choose all that apply.)

A. A centralized model will work best because you can have all of your administrative staff in one location.

B. A decentralized model will work best because you will be able to have local administrators available to maintain the local systems.

C. A centralized model is the better choice because you can combine some of the enterprise services on larger systems at a central location.

D. A decentralized model is better because you can delegate the administrative responsibility down to the office level, thereby freeing your high-end technical staff to concentrate on architectural issues.

15. You have a multisite network architecture. When designing a WINS infrastructure for your network, what are the benefits of a decentralized design for deploying the WINS servers?

   A. Less administration is required for the decentralized design.

   B. With a decentralized design, there will be less NetBIOS traffic going across the WAN links.

   C. You will have less WINS servers with a decentralized design.

   D. None of the above.

16. When looking at the placement of network services, you should try to reduce the amount of network traffic that is generated accessing the services. However, some services are better off left in a central location. Which of the following services should be placed in close proximity to the users who will be accessing them? (Choose all that apply.)

   A. Global catalog

   B. DNS

   C. WINS

   D. DHCP

LAB QUESTION

Objectives 12.01–12.04

You have just been hired as the network architect for a large Philadelphia-based marketing company. Your predecessor left you in charge of migrating the organization from a mixed network consisting of practically all of Microsoft's operating systems to Windows 2000. The departing architect had been in the middle of the network design when he was lured away by a consulting firm.

Your new company has six offices: Philadelphia, New York, Los Angeles, Sacramento, London, and Munich. There are nearly 1,400 employees in the United States, and another 400 in Europe. The offices in the United States are connected by 56-Kbps and 128-Kbps circuits via a Frame Relay network. The European locations are connected to each other by a 128-Kbps fractional E1 circuit, and then connected to the Philadelphia office by a T1 circuit.

The company has numerous legacy Windows NT 4.0 servers scattered throughout the enterprise providing WINS, DHCP, DNS, and other services. From the looks of things, there doesn't seem to be a plan for the placement of these services. You count 12 WINS servers, 14 DHCP servers, and four DNS servers. Some of the services are combined on one server, whereas other offices have dedicated WINS servers and dedicated DHCP servers.

You find from your research that each office has a network administrator, but that person spends the majority of his or her day fighting help desk fires. There is a corporate help desk, but its staff doesn't understand the network. Your predecessor did most of the level 3 troubleshooting for the network. You count at least 120 open tickets in the help desk database related to network problems (from the client to inaccessible shares).

The company's CIO wants to be assured that when the new Windows 2000 network is implemented there will be a process in place to allow for proactive management. She also wants to know how you can clean up the mess regarding the abundant servers on the network. Basically, she wants to know if you can build an efficient, functional Windows 2000 network infrastructure.

Please answer the following questions related to your network design:

1. What services could you combine to reduce the number of redundant servers on the network?

2. Is there a network management solution built into Windows 2000? If so, how do you implement it?

3. Are there any services that might benefit from a cluster server implementation?

4. How does SNMP fit into your planning?

5. Do you see any issues with the current WAN environment with regard to network growth?

QUICK ANSWER KEY

Objective 12.01
1. D
2. D
3. B
4. B

Objective 12.02
5. B
6. A and B
7. A and D
8. E

Objective 12.03
9. C
10. C
11. A, B, and D
12. C

Objective 12.04
13. B
14. B and D
15. B
16. A and C

IN-DEPTH ANSWERS

1. ☑ **D.** All of the above. When attempting to retrieve data regarding the performance of your network, you can use any of these methods to gather the data into a format that is easy for you to understand. It's important to understand that each of these methods has its pros and cons, and that you will need to work around these to accomplish the task. Network Monitor is a great tool for capturing network traffic for analysis. The version that is included in Windows 2000 Server can only see the traffic inbound and outbound from a single server, however. If you use the version from System Management Server, you can see all of the packets on the network. System Monitor is another good utility for viewing the performance of specific resources on a system. For instance, you can configure System Monitor to capture data regarding processor utilization. Finally, SNMP as a whole is a good tool for viewing and manipulating data and settings on remote systems. Again, Windows 2000 only ships with an SNMP agent, not a management console; the latter is required to see the data collected via the SNMP agent.

   ☒ There are no incorrect answers; they are all correct.

2. ☑ **D.** When designing your SNMP communities, you need to have a good understanding of what an SNMP community is. It is simply a collection of hosts grouped together for administrative purposes. A device can be a member of multiple communities. However, an SNMP agent will only accept requests from management systems that are in the same community. A good solution is to assign multiple community names to a device, and give varying levels of security to each community. For example, you may decide to keep the default community name of Public, and only give that community read access. This means that if a management system is also in the Public community, it will be able to get information from the SNMP agent. You then may decide to create a

community with a hard-to-guess name, such as "219XOholdSouthSNmp," as shown in the following illustration:

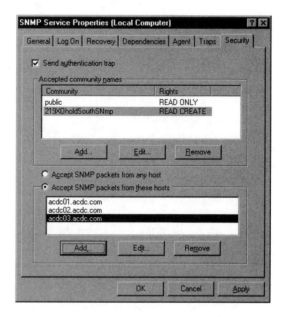

You can then assign this community the rights to read and create objects on the device. By using multiple communities, you can segment who can and cannot modify the device's settings via SNMP.

☒   **A** is incorrect because if you place all your devices in the Public community, you are leaving yourself exposed to a security risk. You should not use the Public community for anything but simple read access, if at all. **B** is incorrect because you cannot have varying levels of security for your SNMP management systems. **C** is also incorrect. Although it is common to group SNMP communities around locations, you cannot give yourself the flexibility to have multiple levels of access to your SNMP agents if you have only one community per location.

3.   ☑   **B.** The strategy outlined in this answer provides the best method for collecting the data from the PCs and moving all of that data to a central location for manipulation and analysis. By saving the log files on a server in the same location as the PC, you are reducing the amount of bandwidth that you would have consumed if every PC sent its log files directly to the data center.

☒ **A** is incorrect because you would quickly saturate your WAN connection from all of the PCs that are attempting to save their counter logs to a share located in the corporate data center. **C** is incorrect because you would definitely overwhelm the bandwidth of the WAN links if every machine began sending alert messages to an Exchange server. Also, by using an Exchange server, you are not using the built-in processes available in Windows 2000.

4. ☑ **B.** The proposed solution produces the required result and one of the optional desired results. The client wants to be able to have access to any of its DCs or member servers that host services, such as DHCP or DNS, regardless of the state of the WAN links. Your proposal to place an analog modem on each of the DCs is a good idea. If the WAN link to the site goes down, you can connect to the server via Remote Access Services (RAS) to manage it. By virtue of having RAS installed and configured, you will also have access to the network to which the server is attached. This is called an *out-of-band connection*.

Your solution for using SNMP is incorrect. You will need to install the SNMP agent on each of the servers that is to be managed by SNMP. Once this has been done, you will need to configure the SNMP agent on each server and add Community Names, Trap Destination(s), and Accepted Community Names. This will allow your server to interoperate with the SNMP management system.

Your solution for using the MMC is correct. By configuring a custom MMC with all of the snap-ins for the critical services, the client can open one utility and see the status of all of the services.

☒ **A, C,** and **D** are incorrect because the proposed solution produces the required result and one of the optional desired results

12.02: Designing Network Services That Support Application Architecture

5. ☑ **B.** Internet Authentication Services (IAS) will provide the most benefit to this ISP. With 40 POPs and 35,000 customers, they have a huge task in maintaining the user accounts for their network. Without IAS, they would have to maintain the user accounts on every one of their network access servers. With IAS, they can maintain all of their users in Active Directory, and use Remote Authentication Dial-In User Service (RADIUS) to authenticate the

dial-in customers against the database. This solution could conceivably scale to hundreds of thousands of customers.

☒ **A** is incorrect because Network Load Balancing is a great technology for spreading the load of connections coming into a service, such as a Web server, over multiple servers that use a single virtual IP address. However, this customer's primary activity is providing network access, not Web hosting. **C** is incorrect, again because the customer is not primarily in the business of application serving. They could benefit from Clustering on their critical servers, such as the DNS servers, but IAS still provides much more benefit to their organization. **D** is also incorrect, because the benefit provided by IAS is much more valuable than Large Memory Support.

6. ☑ **A** and **B** are correct. Windows 2000 offers two services that provide high availability and redundancy to your e-commerce Web site. The first is Network Load Balancing. By spreading your Web site across multiple physical servers and implementing NLB to provide a virtual IP address, you can allow your Web site to handle many more incoming requests than a single server could handle.

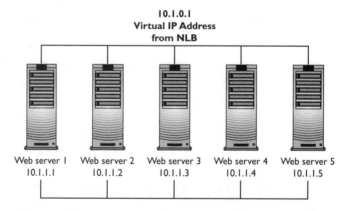

Next, by using Windows Clustering, you can have either two servers (with Windows 2000 Advanced Server) or four servers (with Windows 2000 Datacenter Server) provide failover protection to the SQL Server database that is stored on a shared disk array. If the primary server fails, the next server will come online and begin handling requests.

☒ **C** is incorrect because although you are providing redundancy for a single Web site, you will have one to three additional servers sitting practically idle while the primary server gets overwhelmed by HTTP requests. **D** is also incorrect, because with the amount of traffic expected to hit this site, you will want to depend on hardware-based routing for this network.

7. ☑ **A** and **D** are correct. Routing and Remote Access Service and IPSec provide the best virtual office support. By configuring RRAS to allow dial-in access to your network, you can extend the corporate network out to the home office users. By configuring IPSec, you can secure the data that travels over these links, whether via a VPN connection or an RAS connection.

   ☒ **B** and **C** are both incorrect because they are not native Windows 2000 technologies. Proxy Server 2.0 is another Microsoft product that provides firewall and caching technology to your Windows 2000 network, and SQL Server 7.0 is a relational database management system that provides enterprise database support to your network.

8. ☑ **E.** The IAS feature of Microsoft Windows 2000 provides all of these benefits to Internet service providers. By using IAS, they can have detailed auditing of most network access events. IAS also allows ISPs to have centralized administration and management of their access servers. By pulling the user account database in to the core of the network, the ISP can maintain a single database of user accounts (Active Directory) rather than a database on every access server. Furthermore, IAS allows for the centralized authentication of users as they attempt to access the network. These users are authenticated via RADIUS against Active Directory before being allowed onto the network. Finally, using IAS will allow the ISP to offer worldwide remote access for client computers. The ISP can place a RADIUS proxy at all of their points of presence to forward the authentication requests to the IAS server at the core of the network.

   ☒ There are no incorrect answers.

12.03: Designing a Plan for the Interaction of Windows 2000 Network Services such as WINS, DHCP, and DNS

9. ☑ **C.** Whoever sold this company on having a dedicated server for both WINS and DHCP did them a disservice. They could easily put these services on one server to conserve hardware. One of the BDCs would be a valid choice. Once this is done, they can use the extra servers for Windows 2000 projects.

☒ **A** is incorrect because you can place both of the services on a single server. **B** is incorrect because WINS and DHCP do not communicate to each other during normal operation. DNS and DHCP in Windows 2000 *do* communicate a lot during dynamic registration of client records.

10. ☑ **C.** The most likely problem is that the configuration of WINS and Exchange is causing the hard disks to be unable to keep up with the read/write requests being made by the two databases. This is a case in which combining services is not a good idea. Exchange (and Active Directory, for that matter) has very specific guidelines regarding the location of its database and transaction files. These guidelines are designed to minimize the problems associated with having large amounts of disk access attempts being made to the same physical disk. By introducing WINS to this server, this company has added another resource-intensive database that is also trying to use the disk for reads and writes.

☒ **A** is incorrect because this would cause WINS to malfunction specifically, rather than causing the server's disk and processor utilization to shoot up. **B** is incorrect because DNS requests wouldn't cause the disk utilization to spike for extended periods.

11. ☑ **A, B**, and **D** are correct. Clustering can bring significant improvements in availability to services such as DHCP and WINS. By having two or more servers clustered together, you can have a single copy of a database that is shared between the two servers; if one server should fail, the next can pick up with the same database information without having to go through elaborate measures to synchronize the databases. A good example of this is with DHCP, where you can keep a single scope on the cluster rather than on multiple servers. Finally, you will ultimately have fewer servers to manage or maintain.

☒ **C** is incorrect because Clustering is not the same as Network Load Balancing. Although both use the term *cluster,* NLB is the service that assigns a virtual IP address that can be used to reference multiple servers on the back end.

12. ☑ **C.** The proposed solution produces the required result and both of the optional desired results. The original design for this network had too many servers deployed for too little work. A network with 800 users simply does not need to have three of everything. By properly designing the underlying network infrastructure, you can consolidate many of these services into one or two

boxes, and still have room to grow in the future. The addition of the hardware-based router/switch allows for very fast packet transfer from one building segment to another, and also to the network services core (to which the WINS, DHCP, DNS, and DC services were relocated). This will allow for a more efficient use of the available bandwidth. By consolidating all of these services into three boxes, you have now freed up 75 percent of the file servers for other uses, such as file and print services.

☒   **A, B**, and **D** are incorrect because the proposed solution produces the required result and both of the optional desired results.

12.04: Designing a Resource Strategy

13.   ☑   **B.** The proposed solution produces the required result and the optional desired result. You correctly identified that the current WAN architecture will not support the new technologies that are going to be introduced, such as Active Directory, Exchange, and the Internet. You might suggest that the large sites upgrade to T1 circuits, and that the small sites upgrade to either 128-Kbps or 256-Kbps circuits, or maybe even switch to a broadband technology such as DSL. OSPF is a great choice for a routing protocol on this network. OSPF is very stable, and scales nicely for medium to large networks.

☒   **A** and **C** are incorrect because the proposed solution produces the required result and the optional desired result.

14.   ☑   **B** and **D** are correct. A decentralized model will work best for this company. You already have a trained group of technicians located in the branch offices. It would not be hard to bring these people up to speed on Windows 2000 administration.

☒   **A** and **C** are both incorrect. Although a centralized model is good in some scenarios, this company would be better suited with a decentralized model, for the reasons outlined previously. You already have technical staff located in the branches, and Windows 2000 adapts very well to this model.

15.   ☑   **B.** By utilizing a decentralized design for your WINS infrastructure, you will have less NetBIOS traffic going across your WAN circuits. In a decentralized WINS design, you place your WINS servers in a hub-and-spoke arrangement (as opposed to having all of them at the core of your network). Client PCs send

their NetBIOS requests to a WINS server close to their location, which then replicates its database to a core WINS database.

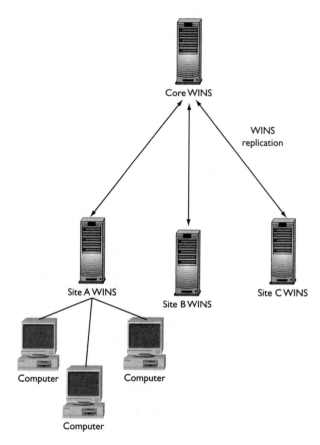

You have more administration due to the increased number of WINS servers, but less traffic is generated from clients on the WAN links.

☒ **A** is incorrect because in any decentralized approach, you are pushing the administration further out into the network, rather than having it all at one location. This will require more administration to manage. **C** is incorrect because you will have more WINS servers—you could get away with two or three if they were centralized, but in this design you will have two or three at the edge of your network, with one or two at the core for redundancy.

16. ☑ **A** and **C** are correct. There should be a Global Catalog server located at every site. The global catalog processes queries concerning the location of Windows 2000 services. If an Active Directory client cannot access a Global Catalog, it will not be able to resolve universal groups.

WINS is used to keep NetBIOS broadcasts on the network to a minimum. If you place all of your WINS servers in a central location, you will be negating the effect of having them, since there will still be a lot of traffic on the links.

☒ **B** is incorrect—since DNS uses IP unicasts for name resolution, there is no limitation on broadcasts, such as there is with NetBIOS and WINS. It's usually better to keep your DNS servers in a central location. **D** is incorrect because you can use IP helper addresses to help client PCs get IP addresses across routed connections.

LAB ANSWER

Objectives 12.01–12.04

1. A good solution to the problem of the numerous servers would be to combine the DHCP and WINS services onto a single server, rather than having a dedicated server for each process. Some of the offices already have this. Ensure that each office has a WINS/DHCP server, and that all WINS databases replicate with a master WINS server in the corporate headquarters. Place two DNS servers in the United States and two in Europe for redundancy on opposite sides of the transatlantic WAN circuit.

2. There is no network management solution built into Windows 2000. Although Windows 2000 does ship with the SNMP agent, you still need a third-party management console to gather data from the agent. Given the need to monitor the network, it might be prudent to purchase an SNMP management station and implement SNMP monitoring on the critical services in the infrastructure.

3. Given the scenario, the only services that would benefit from Clustering would be DHCP and WINS.

4. As mentioned in the answer to question 2, SNMP would be a good choice for network monitoring and management. By using an SNMP management station, you can continuously capture statistics from your network devices and can run detailed reports based on the data.

5. The current WAN links are too small to adequately support the future growth of this company. They should increase the intersite links to 256 Kbps or higher to make Active Directory replication more dependable. Also, if they were to open up Internet access to the company, this could cause some problems unless a product such as Proxy Server were introduced.

MICROSOFT CERTIFIED SYSTEMS ENGINEER

Practice Exam

T his practice exam is made up of two testlets. These testlets are scenarios that provide background on a specific company and that pose a unique set of circumstances. Please read and review each carefully. A series of multiple-choice questions, based on the information provided, will follow each testlet.

TESTLET 1: AEN SOLUTIONS INC. CASE STUDY

Company Profile and History

AEN Solutions Inc. is a networking consultancy company based in Atlanta, Georgia. It started five years ago as a small group of technical people, all with Microsoft and Novell networking experience, offering general networking consultancy and bespoke project work. Since then, it has grown in success and size, specializing predominantly in Microsoft networking services rather than Novell. They have 250 full-time employees spread over the following departments:

- Finance and Administration
- Sales and Marketing
- Human Resources
- Legal
- IT

Because of expansion, the Finance and Administration Department, together with the Legal Department, had to be moved to a different building a few miles away. They outsource their publishing requirements (manuals, marketing literature, etc.) to one single publishing company that is based in Denver.

Because this is a technically orientated company, the IT Department holds the largest proportion of employees and is split between those who work on specific projects, those who support the inhouse systems, and those who offer first-line support for existing customers. Being still a relatively small and young company whose business relies on a dynamic market, this department remains fluid enough for the majority of people to move around within the IT Department. However, it is coordinated by the IT Manager, and under him is the Help Desk Manager, the Network Administration Manager, and the Chief Project Manager. A lot of the development work is conducted onsite, so it's not unusual for over half of this department to be out of the office at any one time. Additionally, this department frequently takes on short-term contractors when required for specific projects and when they need to supplement their own resources.

Most of their customer base is in America, but they do have a few European customers. In particular, they won a six-month contract for a financial institution based in London, England, so they decided to set up a temporary office there where the developers are currently based.

Because the company is very technically orientated, they are aware of some of the benefits that Windows 2000 could offer their own company and wish to take advantage of some of the new features and increased reliability it has to offer. It is also important for their own business knowledge to invest in Windows 2000 so they can offer up-to-date technologies for their customers. Many of the IT staff have been to introductory courses on Windows 2000 to help to supplement their existing Microsoft knowledge and experience. However, they decided to ask for an outside, objective analysis of their company requirements to help them in their migration plans.

While the overall mood is positive toward embracing Windows 2000, management is understandably nervous about the impact on the day-to-day business. Their business is to look after other companies' businesses, so it is doubly important to ensure a smooth transition with minimal disruption. In particular, they host customer Web sites on Windows NT 4.0 servers on their extranet, and while they see the benefits of upgrading these, they are contradictorily bound to guarantee their availability or face financial penalties.

Systems Infrastructure

The company's technical infrastructure is actually quite fluid, because it must accommodate the changing demands and needs of the technical work they do—and it provides the flexibility for an expanding company. For example, if a contract includes hosting a Web site for a customer, AEN must incorporate this into its existing IT resources, which may require purchasing a new server or upgrading an existing one. Similarly, if a project includes a certain specification server or application, this must also be incorporated into the infrastructure.

Despite their networking specialization, they have found that their internal network infrastructure has grown more piecemeal than planned, but essentially the IT department houses all Windows NT 4.0 user accounts and the majority of the internal company resources (which includes application servers and a mail server running Exchange 5.5). There are additional domains for Finance and Administration, Legal, Sales and Marketing, and Human Resources.

The company uses the network address 169.254.0.0/20 with two permanent hardware routers between one subnet at the branch office (which houses the Finance and Administration Department, and the Legal Department) and the other at headquarters. However, new subnets occasionally arrive and disappear at headquarters if it's desirable for project work, and Windows NT 4.0 servers are used for these temporary routers.

They have a pool of public addresses, which are assigned to the group of extranet machines. These include clustered Web servers (running IIS4), Exchange Server 5.5 with SMTP and X400 connectors, a VPN server, and two proxy servers. These are all multihomed Windows NT 4.0 servers that reside on a one-way trusting domain with a T3 carrier to the Internet. However, for historic reasons, their Internet DNS server continues to be hosted externally on the Internet by their provider and their registered Internet domain name is AEN-solutions.com. They currently have just one internal DNS server on Windows NT 4.0 Server for internal use, and with their predominantly Microsoft platform, they rely heavily on WINS servers (they have four split between the two locations). They have three Unix servers that host a mixture of applications and a few Unix workstations.

AEN also has a large number of workstations and servers simply for testing in the Projects division. These include Novell servers and Windows NT 4.0 member servers with a mixture of test machines that can multiboot between various operating systems (for example, Windows for Workgroups, Windows 9x, and Windows NT 4.0 workstations and servers) running a mixture of protocols.

The illustration on the following page provides an overview of AEN's current networking infrastructure.

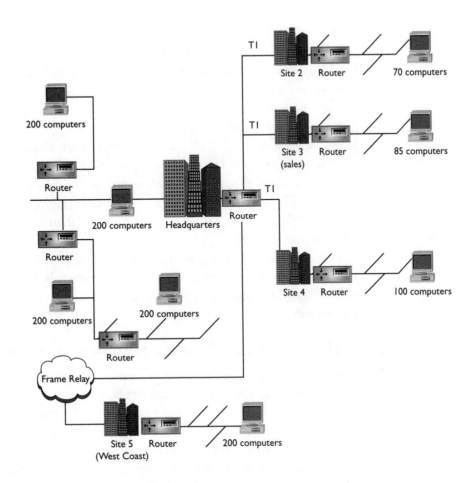

Interview with the Network Administrator Manager

We have a nightmare of systems to support—they seem to just keep multiplying, which I suppose is understandable considering the company has expanded and is taking on more projects. Not only must we support the internal systems to keep all the departments working, but also we have to supply the resources for our business in the form of servers and workstations. I'm sure it could be much better organized, and I'm keen on the concept of consolidation—both for servers and for collapsing our mixture of Windows NT 4.0 domains into something central and more manageable. Thankfully, bandwidth isn't an issue on our network, but I see no point in needlessly cluttering the network. We need a spring-cleaning!

Initial expense is not as important as the overall ROI, so if you can put in a good business case for implementing changes with the best technical solution for our requirements, then I may be able to clear new hardware and upgrades etc., with the CEO.

You must take into account that our Internet services we offer customers are vital—they are one of our first concerns with as much built-in fault tolerance as we can get and 24/7 support. But second to that is probably remote access for IT staff when they're onsite, and also for sales and marketing people when they're on the road.

One of the things that isn't directly my responsibility is the London office—thank goodness that takes care of itself, or I'll have something else to add to my workload! This is because it came about as a separate and distinct project, so it's rather alienated from the rest of the company. I don't think anybody has thought about properly integrating it with HQ—communication so far has been very ad hoc. You'll have to talk to the London Project Manager who is responsible for this site about what the networking infrastructure is there, and how they currently liaise back with us. Certainly, nobody's told me there are any problems with the current setup, but the future is anybody's guess in this fast-moving industry.

Interview with the Project Manager in London

We're doing project work to help a financial institution implement e-commerce solutions integrating their Web site with backend legacy hosts. Most of the development work we do in the office, test it as rigorously as we can on our test network, install it onto their test network, and then gradually incorporate it into their existing systems.

We test with a scaled-down version of their infrastructure, which means a Web server (IIS4) cluster running various components talking to a simulated AS400 system (actually running on another Windows NT 4.0 machine). All the developers here have fairly highly specified Windows NT 4.0 workstations and servers with a pool of laptops (also running Windows NT 4.0) for when we go onsite. Otherwise, we use our customers' existing infrastructure, so they are happy that our applications work on their systems.

There are only 15 of us in this temporary office, so our network is just peer to peer with static addresses assigned from 10.0.0.0/8. One machine has a V56 modem that we use mainly for a dial-up Internet connection to connect to the company's VPN. That allows us to connect to HQ to access remote resources if necessary, although our mail is currently redirected to personal accounts on our ISP. To be honest, we don't need to communicate with HQ very often because we're rather a self-contained unit; however, it's possible that might change if we grow in size and take on more business.

Technical Challenges and Considerations

As instructed, you've talked to the various departments and managers about their priorities and requirements to help identify where Windows 2000 could benefit them the most, as well as identify limitations and potential problem areas.

Interview with the External Publishing Company Representative

We predominately use Apple Macintoshes, but we have a few Windows 98 machines here as well. We've been in business for over ten years and consider ourselves a fairly stable company with a comfortably established customer base and no immediate plans for expansion. We've been doing all the publishing work for AEN Solutions since they first started so we've built up a good working relationship.

Communication is usually by email and fax, and when we need to transfer large documents, we use their FTP site. Unlike AEN, we're not a highly technically oriented company, but we seem to get by okay.

Interview with the Sales and Marketing Manager

We all have laptops, and my staff are frequently on the road. Our customer database is held on an SQL Server in this department, and any entries must be synchronized and updated frequently so all salespeople can access this data. All related paperwork, though, is held on a separate server also in this building—we really must find a way to better integrate the two someday. Apart from ensuring availability of this data, I guess our main priority is to have stable and reliable laptops—I want my people busy doing impressive demonstrations and presentations to bring in the sales. They don't have the time or inclination to fiddle with technology when things go wrong or don't work the first time.

Personally, I would have liked them to have Windows 98 for the Plug-and-Play features and the power management, but we were advised to have Windows NT 4.0 Workstation for better reliability and security. However, Windows NT 4.0 doesn't stop salespeople from coming back without their laptop, either having it stolen or simply leaving it on customer sites! I'm not sure which is worse—wondering if other people have been able to access our customer details and quotations, or wondering how long it's going to take to get my salesperson functional again with the various applications we need.

Interview with the Finance and Administration Manager

My staff are all office based with Windows NT 4.0 workstations. We have our own printer pool and server here to process invoices, delivery notes, etc. The Legal Department impresses on us that our data storage for customer financial information must be very secure—and we also run the inhouse payroll. Only I have permissions to some directories, and I'm keen to keep it that way rather than having to trust various administrators over at HQ.

Interview with the Legal Manager

My staff handles the legal side of customer contracts and those for short-term contractors. We can work quite closely with Finance and Administration, and we're similarly office based with Windows NT 4.0 workstations. We store the majority of our data on our own application server at HQ, which makes it easier for them to backup, I believe.

Interview with the Human Resources Manager

We're office based, running Windows NT 4.0 workstations and necessarily interacting with all the other departments. However, we have the most integration with the IT department simply because they have the greatest number of staff. The majority of our data is stored on our own applications server that resides in the IT Department, and they look after this server—which is fine by us!

Interview with the Help Desk Manager

People frequently come and go on the help desk—it depends on what is happening in the Projects division. We're mostly office based to take first-line support for existing customers, and we have a centralized customer help system that sits on one of our application servers. However, it's sometimes necessary to go onsite to resolve a problem, and then employees take a laptop from a pool. All employees must be able to have remote access to company resources when they need it—sometimes when onsite, this means using customers' machines rather than our own because of their security policies.

Growth and Expansion Plans

The most likely area of expansion identified is the London project.

Interview with the Chief Project Manager

The London project was originally seen as a six-month contract that required frequent onsite work, so we decided it would be easier to set up this temporary office in London. Now it looks like it could be a much longer-term project with possibly indefinite work coming from it. The work has gone so well that not only is the customer talking about extending the contract from six months to two years and widening the scope of the project, but they're also recommending us to other businesses with similar requirements. Therefore, I can see this having great potential, although it's difficult to estimate and justify until the people at the top have made their decisions and signed the papers.

Interview with the London Project Manager

Our customer has no immediate plans to migrate to Windows 2000—sees it as too risky until the new technologies have matured more. Here in the UK we see a much more conservative reaction when it comes to change, upgrades, and migrations—and this seems particularly so when dealing with host legacy solutions. So, while I personally wouldn't be opposed to migrating our office's network, I can't honestly justify it at the moment because we don't have the time or funding resources and there's no immediate requirement. I hope you won't take away our VPN connection, though! Because of the time difference between the two countries, there's been a couple of occasions when I've needed something from one of the servers back in HQ and couldn't ask them to email it because they weren't at work yet—and the VPN let me dial in and track it down myself, which saved a delay that would have been best part of the working day.

TESTLET 1: QUESTIONS

1. How aggressively/cautiously would you recommend this company migrate to Windows 2000 now so they can benefit from features only realized when the network is running in native mode and all Windows NT 4.0 workstations and servers have been upgraded?

   A. This company's aim should be to upgrade all workstations and servers to Windows 2000.

   B. This company's aim should be to upgrade all PDCs/BDCs to Windows 2000, and then switch to native mode to get the best options from Active Directory.

   C. This company's aim should be to upgrade all Windows NT 4.0 servers to Windows 2000 to benefit from better resilience and the flexibility that dynamic disks offer, but remain in mixed mode.

   D. This company's aim should be to selectively upgrade servers and workstations.

2. You need to decide upon the AD naming structure, and you recommend having a separate namespace from your public Internet DNS name. You decide on AEN-internal.com. Which AD structure would be better for this company?

   A. One root domain with child domains for all departments.

   B. One root domain with child domains for all geographical departments.

   C. One domain with OUs for all departments.

   D. One domain with OUs for all geographical departments.

3. What would you recommend immediately for the London office, given that this temporary office has been marked as a potential permanent office and may have to accommodate more employees?

   A. Put in place a Point-to-Point WAN link between this office and HQ, so that they can be incorporated into the main network and more easily benefit from company resources.

B. Put in place a RIS server. so that any new projects here can get up and going quickly.

C. Put in place a Windows NT 4.0 server BDC, so they can authenticate with the main network, which is then ready to be upgraded to a Windows 2000 DC later.

D. All of the above.

E. None of the above.

4. What aspects of the publishing company would you recommend changing? (Choose all that apply.)

A. Give them a local account on a VPN server that is a member server so they can use their Windows 98 machines to transfer data securely over the Internet when needed.

B. Implement a demand-dial routed connection to HQ for when they have data to transfer.

C. Set up an SMTP site for them on one of your Web servers.

D. Verify the security of the FTP server.

5. Remote access is obviously very important for this company since many of its users are mobile. It's very important that they can get access to the company resources they require—but securely. Which of the following do you recommend? (Choose all that apply.)

A. The RAS server with modem bank should be decommissioned on security grounds, and remote access should instead be via one of two VPN servers (two for resilience and load sharing).

B. You should enforce L2TP with IPSec for all connections.

C. Enforce L2TP with IPSec for some users.

D. Select the Access by Policy in the Dial-in tab of each user to ensure remote access policies are enforced.

E. Select Dial-in permission in the Dial-in tab of all users, and then remove any remote access policies.

F. Set the lowest authentication protocol to be MSCHAPv2.

6. Given that this company's main name server was WINS and there's only one internal DNS server, one of your main considerations before migrating to a Windows 2000 infrastructure should be to concentrate on this. What would you recommend short term? (Choose all that apply.)

    A. Introduce a Secondary DNS server on a Windows NT 4.0 server now to get IT personnel up to speed on implementing and managing DNS servers within their existing Windows NT 4.0 infrastructure.

    B. Build a new Primary DNS server when you upgrade the PDC to Windows 2000 and start from scratch.

    C. Implement a Secondary DNS server on a Windows 2000 server to the existing DNS on the Windows NT 4.0 server.

    D. A caching-only DNS server on a Windows 2000 server in the London office.

7. When configuring DHCP scope options, which machines would benefit from short leases? (Choose all that apply.)

    A. Staff in Sales and Marketing

    B. Project workers

    C. People in the London office

    D. Just the IT contractors

    E. None of the above

8. You decide to centralize all IP assignments by using DHCP, which includes configuring the RAS servers to use DHCP rather than a static address pool. When a Windows 2000 Professional dials in, however, it receives the IP address of 169.254.53.18 with the subnet mask of 255.255.0.0. There are no errors in the event logs on these machines, but you know the IP address should be 169.254.x.x with subnet mask of 255.255.240.0. What's the cause of the wrong subnet mask?

    A. The client must have overridden the IP address assignment.

    B. The RAS server must have the wrong default subnet mask.

    C. The RAS server should use DHCP Relay to obtain the DHCP scope options.

    D. The RAS server cannot communicate with a DHCP server.

    E. None of the above.

9. Bearing in mind that security is important in the Finance and Administration Department, which of the following would offer the best recommendation? (Choose all that apply.)

   A. Upgrade all machines that handle this secure data to Windows 2000 and enforce the use of IPSec.

   B. Implement smart cards in the Finance Department for a more secure login, and implement EFS on the servers storing the data.

   C. Implement a VPN within the company for transferring sensitive data from workstations to servers, and make use of PPTP with MPPE encryption rather than upgrading all machines to Windows 2000 for IPSec encryption.

   D. Implement an internal firewall on the WAN link between HQ and the branch office.

   E. Use the new AD structure to achieve the security required.

10. The Network Manager is keen to use Dfs. What would be its best benefit to this company in the short term? (Choose all that apply.)

    A. Provides fault tolerance and ensures data services to users.

    B. Shares data access over distributed servers.

    C. Simpler and unified view of resources.

    D. None; Dfs would not benefit this company.

11. With a view to a more integrated network, what would you recommend with respect to the Novell servers and accounts? (Choose all that apply.)

    A. Implement GSNW.

    B. Implement FPSN.

    C. Migrate the accounts into the Windows 2000 AD.

    D. Migrate all file volumes to Windows 2000 file shares.

    E. Migrate all printers into Windows 2000 Active Directory.

    F. Do nothing.

12. Routers should be checked to ensure they are performing as efficiently as possible and eliminate any unnecessary "chatter." Which of the following should be configured on the company's routers? (Choose all that apply.)

    A. RIP for IP

    B. RIP for IPX

    C. SAP

    D. AppleTalk

    E. OSPF

13. On the IIS servers that are being used to host customers' Web sites, which one of the following Windows 2000 supported options could benefit the company most?

    A. DNS round robin to spread the network load between servers

    B. A distributed cluster to allow upgrades without service interruption

    C. Upgraded network cards to include onboard memory to offload some of the networking processing to ensure a faster response time

    D. Implementing IPSec for better security

    E. Network load balancing between servers for a faster response

14. The London office could make more frequent use of an Internet connection if it were shared among all staff rather than just available on one machine. For example, there have been times when they've needed to access vendor Web sites; in particular, the Microsoft Web site for developer information. They've also occasionally needed to download new drivers and hot fixes. While the London Project Manager is happy to allow everybody in that office access to Web sites and download files, he would like to keep an eye on which sites are being accessed and what is being downloaded. This is partly to see if he should ban certain non-work-related sites but also to monitor their Internet use to see if the link should be upgraded in the future. If they had one Windows 2000 server in their network, would ICS or NAT be useful in the London branch for Internet access?

    A. Definitely; either one of these offer one of the immediate benefits that Windows 2000 could provide for this small network.

    B. NAT could be used, but not ICS.

    C. Configuring the RRAS service for a routed connection would be better.

    D. Proxy Server would be better.

15. Both the Sales and Marketing Manager and the IT Manager were keen on the concept of using RIS for a fast and efficient method of automatically deploying Windows 2000. Assuming you have the necessary Windows 2000 infrastructure to support RIS (AD, DNS, DHCP), where could the company benefit from RIS? (Choose all that apply.)

    A. For upgrading existing Windows NT 4.0 workstations such as the laptops belonging to Sales and Marketing

    B. For all new machines that come into the network that need to install Windows Professional

    C. Salespeople for when they lose their laptops and need to get a new one up and running again quickly

    D. New project work and test machines

16. Given that this company has (and will likely to have for some time) many downlevel clients, and you have identified the priority requirement for a smooth-running network, which of the following would you recommend with regard to a WINS strategy that would minimize broadcast traffic? (Choose all that apply.)

    A. Consolidate WINS servers so there's just one Primary and one Secondary at HQ.

    B. Keep the existing four WINS servers, two at HQ and two at the branch office.

    C. Ensure the routers can support IGMP, and then use multicasts to automate replication between WINS servers.

    D. Manually configure standard push/pull replication between WINS servers.

17. If the London office were happy to use DHCP instead of static addresses and decided to use ICS on a Windows 2000 Server for a shared connection to the Internet, could they use this to connect directly to HQ when they needed to log on the HQ network? (Choose all that apply.)

    A. Yes, this offers a cheap and viable way for them to log on the HQ network.

    B. Yes, if they could use IPSec for security reasons.

    C. No, they should connect over a VPN connection.

    D. No, firewalls and routers will block NetBIOS.

18. If desktops throughout the departments were upgraded to Windows Professional, which of the following would you recommend to help protect their data? (Choose all that apply.)

    A. Using software RAID where multiple disks were available

    B. Using group policies to assign applications

    C. Using offline folders

    D. Using group policies to redirect folders

    E. Installing CDMCONS

    F. Creating and regularly updating a recovery disk

    G. Scheduling regular backups

19. Which of the following would be viable options for immediately using Terminal Services on a Windows 2000 server?

    A. It could be useful for the salespeople for when they were in the office for a more central control of their resources for a lower TCO.

    B. It could be useful for developers on Windows NT 4.0 workstations while waiting for their machines to be upgraded so they can migrate to Windows 2000.

    C. It could be useful for administering remote DCs over slow WAN links.

    D. It could be useful for the branch office users because their sessions could be monitored and controlled by IT staff if they were having technical problems.

20. When looking to upgrade the Web server clusters to Windows 2000, which of the following conditions must be met? (Choose all that apply.)

    A. Windows 2000 Advanced Server must be configured as a member server and not a DC.

    B. Systems must share a SCSI bus for disk storage.

    C. Minimum memory for each system is 256MB RAM.

    D. Network cards must be PCI.

    E. Software RAID 5 must be configured for the required fault tolerance.

TESTLET 2: NEW SILICON VENTURES LIMITED CASE STUDY

Company Profile and History

New Silicon Ventures Limited is a European electronics design company with offices in England, France, Italy, and Belgium. The company has just relocated its headquarters to a new five-floor building in London. There are regional offices in Paris, Rome, and Brussels. There are also five branch offices in England.

Interview with the Chief Executive Officer

New Silicon Ventures Limited has grown very rapidly over the last five years from a very small team to being an important player in the electronics industry. Most of our growth has been from within, but we are always on the lookout for potential acquisitions. I expect that the number of staff will double over the next three years and that we will establish a presence in more countries.

Interview with the Human Resources Manager

We currently employ over 1,000 staff, located as follows:

London Headquarters:	500
Paris Regional Office:	50
Rome Regional Office:	150
Brussels Regional Office:	250
Branch Offices:	15 at each of the 5 branch offices

The turnover of staff is reasonably high. In this industry, people are often headhunted by other companies. We are taking steps to improve our retention rates. For example, we are allowing people to work from home in cases where it can be justified.

Interview with the IT Manager

As you might expect, in an electronics company, most of the staff is highly IT literate. Providing IT facilities to knowledgeable staff is no easy feat, and their very high demands are keeping my team busy. Sometimes I think it would be easier if the employees didn't know as much and were less inclined to change computer settings and solve problems themselves.

The growth rate of the company has been so fast that it has been difficult to keep up, and some of our IT facilities have been "flung together." I would like my staff to spend much less time on routine administration and more time on proactive work to improve our service.

Systems Infrastructure

Interview with the IT Manager

A single team that reports to me provides all IT support. Most of the staff is located in the London office. Each of the regional offices has a network administrator. A central help desk handles all user queries and problems.

Interview with the Network Manager

Each of the regional offices is connected to London using 2.048-Mbps leased lines. The branch offices are connected to London using dial-up 64-Kbps ISDN lines.

At present, each regional office has its own domain, as does the headquarters in London. The five branch offices in England are part of the LONDON domain.

Unix-based DNS servers (that do not support SRV records) are located at the headquarters and regional offices. One domain name is used, newsilicon.com. The DNS server at London hosts a primary zone for the domain, and the regional offices host secondary zones.

The headquarters building has one subnet per floor, and each of the regional offices has three subnets. The branch offices each consist of a single subnet. Each member of staff has a PC, and these are distributed evenly over the subnets. Our subnets are connected using routers that do not relay any broadcast packets.

We use a private IP network address of 172.18.0.0 and have a direct connection to the Internet at headquarters.

Technical Challenges and Considerations

Interview with the Chief Information Officer

Some of the company's executives are concerned that their data might be compromised. To this end, we have provided them with their own server, EXECUTIVE, and ensured that file permissions are secured very tightly. However, we would like to strengthen this further by securing the data that travels between the server and PCs. The executives usually use their own PCs, but because they are often at other offices, they are very likely to log on at other PCs. They only use the EXECUTIVE server.

Interview with the IT Manager

All our PCs and servers currently run Windows NT 4.0. We would like to upgrade to Windows 2000 as soon as possible. However, there are a number of issues that we need to solve now. We seem to have very high usage of all of our leased lines. I'm not totally sure why they should be so highly used, but I'm told it is mostly Internet traffic. The bills for our ISDN lines are also very high, and I'd like to get these down.

Some of our servers will have to stay at Windows NT 4.0 because they are running specialized applications, and our suppliers won't be ready to upgrade the applications for many months.

Many of our design teams use Unix workstations for their work, but they need access to the Windows NT 4.0 servers for shared documents.

Interview with the Network Manager

I've been tasked to provide access to our network to home users over the Internet. I need to make sure that all traffic is encrypted, and that only authorized users have access.

Interview with the Network Administrator

Users often complain of slow Internet access at the European offices. This isn't surprising, given that all Internet access is through the London office.

We allocate IP addresses manually. Sometimes users change the IP settings, and we have problems with duplicate IP addresses.

Interview with the Help Desk Staff

There are a number of problems that we often get calls about from users. It would be great to solve these issues:

- Users often can't browse to a server using Explorer, even though they know that the server exists.
- Users regularly call to ask what server a particular document is kept on. We have a list of server names and shares that we use as reference.

Growth and Expansion Plans

Interview with the IT Manager

The number of subnets is expected to double over the next three years, in line with the growth plans for the business.

Over the next few months, we plan to add a Web server to our network to allow our customers and partners to review our work. However, it is absolutely critical that we only allow selected users to use the Web server, and that any incoming traffic to the Web server does not impact our own network. We want our Web server to use our domain name and to be known as newsilicon.com.

Interview with the Network Manager

We are thinking about extra leased lines between Paris and Rome, and Rome and Brussels to improve the resilience of our network.

We've just installed a Proxy Server at the London office to give us some protection on our Internet connection.

TESTLET 2: QUESTIONS

1. Which of the following protocols are required for the New Silicon Ventures network? (Choose all that apply.)

    A. AppleTalk

    B. NetBEUI

    C. NWLink

    D. TCP/IP

2. You would like to improve the speed of Internet access for users at the regional offices, reduce the utilization of the leased lines, and have the ability to manage who has Internet access. How would you achieve this?

    A. Use the Proxy Server at the headquarters office only.

    B. Install a direct connection to the Internet at each of the regional offices.

    C. Use Network Address Translation (NAT) at each of the regional offices.

    D. Use the Proxy Server at the headquarters, and install a Proxy Server at each of the regional offices.

3. Which subnet mask will meet the company's current requirements, accommodate the company's growth plans, and provide for the maximum number of hosts?

    A. 255.255.248.0

    B. 255.255.252.0

    C. 255.255.254.0

    D. 255.255.255.0

4. How would you make network shares easier to find, and provide fault tolerance so that they would still be available if any one server failed?

    A. Create a stand-alone Dfs root on a member server, add each network share as a Dfs link, and configure additional replicas for the root and each link.

B. Create a stand-alone Dfs root on each workstation, and add each network share as a Dfs link.

C. Create a domain Dfs root on a member server, add each network share as a Dfs link, and configure additional replicas for the root and each link.

D. Copy the contents of all of the network shares to a server. Advise users to use that server to locate shares. If the server fails, users can access the shares in their original locations.

5. How many domains should you plan for the company to have after the completion of the upgrade to Windows 2000?

A. 1

B. 4

C. 5

D. 9

6. You are installing one DHCP server at headquarters. What else will you need to do to allow PCs on the other subnets at headquarters to use the DHCP server? (Choose all that apply.)

A. Install a DHCP Relay Agent on each of the other subnets.

B. Nothing, the PCs on other subnets can use the DHCP server via the router.

C. Configure each PC with the address of the DHCP server.

D. Configure the DHCP server with a scope for each subnet.

7. Which of the following methods would be the most appropriate for configuring the TCP/IP addresses of PCs at the branch offices?

A. Use a DHCP Relay Agent.

B. Use Automatic Private IP Addressing.

C. Use a DHCP server at the branch office.

D. Use Routing and Remote Access to allocate an IP address to each PC from the static address pool.

8. You have decided to use DHCP to automate the allocation of IP addresses for the company. What is the minimum number of DHCP servers you should install to minimize the amount of DHCP traffic over the WANs (assuming that DHCP Relay Agents are available as needed)?

   A. 1

   B. 6

   C. 9

   D. 19

9. To resolve the problem of users not being able to browse for servers, you have decided to implement WINS servers.

   Proposed Solution: Install a WINS server at each office (nine in total). Configure the WINS servers as a hub-and-spoke model for replication, with the WINS server at London as the hub. Configure push/pull replication between the hub WINS server and each of the other WINS servers in both directions. Configure all clients with the address of the WINS server on their site. Install a WINS Proxy Agent on each subnet.

   Required Result: Provide local WINS resolution for all network resources.

   Optional Desired Results:

   1. Minimize traffic over the WAN lines.

   2. Ensure that WINS queries can still be resolved in the event of any one WINS server failing.

   Which of the following results will your proposed solution produce?

   A. The proposed solution produces the required result and both of the optional results.

   B. The proposed solution produces the required result and only one of the optional results.

   C. The proposed solution produces the required result and none of the optional results.

   D. The proposed solution doesn't produce the required result.

10. You have decided to provide access to the corporate LAN over the Internet for staff from home. You want home-workers to use smart cards for authentication. Which authentication protocol should you choose?

    A. EAP-TLS

    B. PAP

    C. MS-CHAP

    D. IPSec

11. You have decided to use a virtual private network (VPN) server at headquarters to provide access to the corporate LAN over the Internet for staff working from home, for customers, and partners. You also want the VPN server to be exposed to the Internet. Which of the following would be the most appropriate solution?

    A. Install a VPN server on subnet A using PPTP tunneling with MPPE encryption.

    B. Install a VPN server on subnet C using PPTP tunneling with MPPE encryption.

    C. Install a VPN server on subnet A using L2TP tunneling and ESP encryption.

    D. Install a VPN server on subnet C using L2TP tunneling and ESP encryption.

12. What would be the best way to protect the traffic between the EXECUTIVE server and the PCs used by executives?

    A. Configure an IPSec policy on all servers and PCs that require security.

    B. Configure an IPSec policy on the EXECUTIVE server and all PCs that require security.

    C. Configure an IPSec policy on the EXECUTIVE server that requires security. Configure an IPSec policy on Executive PCs to use IPSec if requested.

    D. Configure an IPSec policy on the EXECUTIVE server that requires security. Configure an IPSec policy on all PCs to use IPSec if requested.

13. In considering the migration to Active Directory, you need to review the capabilities of the existing Unix DNS servers. Which of the following features of Windows 2000 DNS is essential for the operation of Active Directory?

    A. SRV records

    B. Incremental zone transfers

    C. Dynamic updates

    D. Integrated zones

14. You have decided to consider adding DNS servers at the branch offices to reduce DNS traffic over the ISDN lines. What type of DNS service should you install at the branch offices?

    A. Primary zone

    B. Secondary zone

    C. Caching-only server

    D. Active Directory integrated zone

15. Which of the following methods for updating routing tables would be appropriate for New Silicon Ventures Limited? (Choose all that apply.)

    A. RIP

    B. OSPF

    C. BAP

    D. SAP

16. On which subnet at headquarters would you place the Web server for the company, bearing in mind the company's security requirements?

    A. Subnet A

    B. Subnet B

    C. Subnet C

    D. On any one of subnets D, E, F, or G

17. How would you ensure that any incoming Web requests are directed to the company's Web server? (Choose two.)

    A. Use packet filters on the Proxy Server to redirect all incoming connections to port 80 to the Web server.

    B. Add an A record to the DNS server managed by the company's ISP that contains the name of the Web server and the external IP address of the Proxy Server.

    C. Add an A record to the DNS server managed by the company's ISP that contains the name of the Web server and its IP address.

    D. Use the Web publishing mapping feature of Proxy Server to forward all requests to the Web server.

18. How would you address the concerns of the IT manager that users spend too much time browsing Web sites that are not relevant to their work?

    A. Create a list of allowable sites for browsing, and implement a domain group policy that installs the list in Internet Explorer on each user's PC.

    B. Use domain filters on the Proxy Server to deny access to all sites except for the list of allowable sites.

    C. Use domain filters on the Proxy Server to allow access to all sites except for the list of disallowed sites.

    D. Create a list of disallowed sites for browsing, and implement a domain group policy that installs the list in Internet Explorer on each user's PC.

TESTLET 1: ANSWERS

1. ☑ **D.** This company's aim should be to selectively upgrade servers and workstations. For example, the salespeople's laptops could immediately benefit from Plug-and-Play, better power management, and EFS. Even VPN servers could benefit from bandwidth control, higher security, and a more granular control over authentication. Application servers could benefit from the more flexible dynamic disks, mount points, remote storage etc. However, a good plan for migration would be to migrate the master PDC at HQ once the AD structure has been decided upon (and in particular, the DNS and DHCP infrastructure to support it). When this is in place, the company can immediately benefit from RIS and group policies for deploying software and security policies, etc., on user machines that are running Windows 2000.

    ☒ **A** is not an option; they have some Unix servers and must continue to have Novell servers for testing purposes. **B** is not the best recommendation, because they may want to add a Windows NT 4.0 DC into the network (remember, they must have a flexible and fluid networking infrastructure)—backward compatibility with downlevel clients and servers is important for this company despite their being actively pro-Windows 2000 and having the technical expertise and will to migrate. Another good reason to advocate caution is because there's little for this company to gain from the benefits of a native network in comparison with larger companies (for example, the ability to scale better with reduced network traffic, universal groups, nested groups, etc.) as **B** would suggest. **C**, upgrading all Windows NT 4.0 servers to Windows 2000, would include their Web servers that currently host customer sites—much testing should be conducted on these machines before even considering upgrading them to ensure full compatibility and equivalent (or better) performance after the upgrade. It goes without saying, however, that all upgrades or replacements should be thoroughly planned, tested, piloted, and then carefully introduced and monitored.

2. ☑ **C.** This is the best answer given the size, history, and potential fluidity of this company. It also ties in with the requirement to simplify the logical network structure.

☒   **A** and **B**, which suggest child domains, are not the best options for this company because although in larger companies it is often desirable to have a single root domain with child domains to minimize replication traffic, this would not seem applicable here. Another reason for multiple domains is to ensure administration boundaries, which are often required for political (legal or business) reasons, and this would not seem to be the case with this company. Instead, OUs offer maximum flexibility: for example, you can delegate authority of the Finance and Administration OU to the Finance and Administration Manager. IT could be split into three OUs, or perhaps better still to nest Project and Help Desk OUs inside IT. You could then assign group policies to each OU. **D** is not the best option for this company because although the company is quite fluid and needs to remain flexible, their departments seem fairly stable—in contrast with their geographical locations.

3.   ☑   **E.** None of the above is the best answer for this office with the information you've been given. Until things are more certain, this section of the company should be left until they are more certain about the future of the existing project and new projects.

☒   **A**, **B**, **C**, and **D** are incorrect. Their appropriateness would depend on the WAN bandwidth between them and HQ. There's no sense in upgrading machines and their network if they are all going to be dismantled. Even if the project does succeed, they may find it more advantageous to move to a new office, which may already have an existing network infrastructure they could use. However, there's nothing to stop you from planning for possibilities; for example, assigning this network one of the spare subnets would ensure a new site in AD when joining this network to the company network. You could then consider which servers should be located in London (for example, if the machines participate in Active Directory, there should be a Windows 2000 DC hosting the global catalog at each site) to minimize the traffic over the WAN and provide fault tolerance if the link goes down. However, you don't know yet what link would be used; obviously, if this office were to be incorporated into the company network, it would be prudent to start thinking about the network link between the two sites so that they can share the same central resources. Otherwise, this office will not benefit from centralized administration and they will spend their time managing their own network rather than concentrating on their customer project work.

4. ☑   **D.** Taking it for granted that they will continue to transfer large amounts of data by FTP when needed (because this seems a satisfactory solution for everybody), the FTP server should be checked to ensure that anonymous access is disabled so that only the publishing company can connect with an agreed username/password. Ensure your FTP server is thoroughly protected by NTFS (always good to check the basics!) and that it's not running any services/protocols that aren't needed. If the publishing company had fixed IP addresses and always used the same machines, you could tie down access on IP addresses—but it's unlikely if they don't have a permanent Internet connection. For additional security, you could consider changing the default FTP ports to thwart attempts to detect FTP access to Internet users. However, it's always dangerous to change the way something has been working, and you'll need to change not just the server and the client (remember the client side isn't under your control because this belongs to a separate company), but potentially firewalls and routers. Don't go overboard on security where it's not necessary!

☒   **A** is incorrect. Giving them a local account on a VPN server that is a member server so they can use their Windows 98 machines to transfer data securely over the Internet when needed would technically work fine, but is it necessary? They haven't asked for an alternative method of transferring data. The data in question is either large files for publishing content, or emails for quick "keeping in touch" and instructions. Although not integrated (email for one and FTP for the other), these methods do fit their purposes, and although neither technology is best suited in reverse (attaching large files by email or sending short text files by FTP), they do act as a backup means of communication for each other. Additionally, transferring all data via a VPN connection will undoubtedly be much slower than using FTP. Nobody has said that security is an issue with the transfer of data from the publishing company; therefore, providing the FTP site isn't anonymous, the VPN solution seems to present more problems than benefits. Similarly, **B** would work, but again there seems to be no evidence that this is required at this stage. Because this is an outsourced, independent company, it is rather dangerous to suggest they change their infrastructure—who is going to fund and support these changes, for example? **C** is not a good recommendation; the existing arrangement is better, appears to work without technical problems, and nobody is dissatisfied with it!

5. ☑ **C.** You could enforce L2TP with IPSec for users you know will be using Windows 2000 and are configured to use IPSec (for example, your salespeople who probably pose the highest security risk).

   ☒ **A** is not a good option because you must ensure a remote access solution. Some users may not have Internet access and/or have Internet connectivity problems (for example, ISP router down). A dial-up point-to-point link is not necessarily unsecure and always offers a good backup to Internet access—even if it is more expensive and potentially slower. **B** would strongly jeopardize users being able to connect when needed; for example, if they were connecting from a Windows NT 4.0 workstation. **D** is not a correct answer because this option is only available when running in native mode (which is unlikely to be a short-term objective for this company), and remote access policies can be used without this option. **E** would stop anybody from connecting; although you should use the dial-in permission on user accounts when in mixed mode, there must be at least one matching policy (for example, Default Remote Access Policy, which is any day, any time) before a connection can be accepted. **F** is also not a good option for this company because although MSCHAP, version 2, is a more secure authentication protocol than MSCHAP, SPAP, or CHAP (it offers mutual authentication for example),there is no evidence that all remote users will be able to use it. If all Sales and Marketing staff had Windows 2000 Professional on their laptops, you could guarantee they would support MSCHAP, version 2, but you might leave high and dry some technicians if dialing in from customer sites using customer machines. Although security is important, compatibility and the need to ensure a service are more important in this company.

6. ☑ **B.** This is the most sensible option. This company is unusual in that they do not already have a mature DNS solution—their Internet DNS is outsourced, and their main name server to date has been WINS (because they are predominantly a Microsoft-only network). Unlike most companies you will probably come across when migrating to Windows 2000, there seems to be little evidence here that they were actually using their existing single DNS server (any serious dependency on DNS would assume least a secondary DNS server). Starting from scratch seems to offer minimal disruption and will allow you to tightly integrate DNS with the new AD structure. But don't forget to check if any applications or machines were using the previous DNS server (particularly the Unix machines). Workstation reconfiguration will be easy enough with the

new DNS server defined as one of the DHCP scope options. You will have to decide on your internal DNS and AD namespace, and it is recommended that you register this even if you fully intend to keep it private within your company. This is another reason to start from scratch at this point—it may not be possible or desirable to register the existing Windows NT 4.0 DNS namespace. Additionally, the company may prefer to change the namespace that was originally being used because of the greater importance this will now have in the new network infrastructure.

☒ **A** is not the best option, although it's viable if they specifically preferred to do this. Although it's always advisable to have at least one other DNS server for fault tolerance and load balancing, there seems little point in building on the minimal DNS solution they have, and going this route will delay implementing a DDNS solution in a Windows 2000 network. **C** is not the best answer because a Windows 2000 DNS server that is secondary to a Windows NT 4.0 Primary DNS server will be unable to take advantage of DDNS and SVR records, for example, and again, you will not be able to use DDNS and Active Directory. It would be much better to scrap the existing DNS server and look to implement two DDNS servers in the new Windows 2000 network. **D** is a very bad choice as this company currently stands. Once a WAN link is in place between the London office and HQ, this may be a viable option to minimize network traffic between clients and DNS servers. Bearing in mind the London office has no immediate plans for upgrading to Windows 2000, it may be more prudent in the short term to recommend a Windows NT 4.0 DNS server for this purpose to minimize additional network administration on an otherwise unfamiliar new platform. However, at the moment, there is no WAN link in place to link the London network with HQ, and the choice of DNS server for this site should not be decided upon until the future of this office is clearer.

7. ☑ **E.** With their current addressing scheme that provides over 4,000 addresses per subnet, they are not going to be short of IP addresses; hence, no need to define short leases to pool a limited resource. Short leases mean more network traffic as workstations seek to release their license when only 50 percent has expired (by default, this is every four days). If IP addresses were in short supply, then salespeople and the test machines would be good contenders for short leases. At the moment, the London office users do not use a DHCP server, either locally or at HQ. If they had in place a WAN link between their London

office and HQ, and they made use of DHCP Relay to a DHCP server at HQ, then they would benefit most from long leases to minimize renewal traffic over the WAN. In contrast to using short leases, this company would benefit from defining long leases—and you should also change the registry on the RAS and VPN servers (when migrated to Windows 2000) so that more than the default of 10 addresses is allocated on startup.

8. ☑ **E.** The default Class B subnet mask is used because it is the expected behavior of a Windows 2000 dial-up client to assume the default subnet mask for the IP address it receives.

☒ **B** and **C** are incorrect because although some IP options are obtained from the RAS server if not using DHCP Relay (for example, the DNS and WINS servers), the subnet mask is not one of these options. **D** is incorrect because although 169.124.x.x with the subnet mask of 255.255.0.0 will be used if the RAS server was not able to communicate with a DHCP server and so resorted to using APIPA (which uses this reserved address), an error would be logged on the RAS server's event log to indicate that this was the problem.

9. ☑ **E.** This is the best option here because you can put the Finance Department into an OU and delegate authority to the Finance and Administration Manager, who may then decide to secure data with EFS (if not shared) or assign NTFS permissions to protect shared data, and later possibly employ IPSec policies and security policies to users/computers in that OU.

☒ **A, B, C,** and **D** are less appropriate because the security issue expressed was with storing the data rather than transferring it across the network or securing the WAN link. It is not secure to transfer this data unencrypted (using a VPN or IPSec would counteract this), but there is no evidence that they fear an internal breach of security when it comes to transferring the data (after all, it is not crossing a public network). Also, there was no evidence to suggest that the data transfer occurs at regular intervals, which if it did would make it easier to capture the data across the network. Instead, the best answer here is to pay special attention to the AD structure so the network administrator can fully delegate responsibility of a Finance OU to the Finance and Administration Manager, who then may decide how to assign appropriate NTFS permissions to secure data and later possibly IPSec policies and security templates. Note also that you cannot use EFS to secure data (as option B suggests) if multiple people need to access it.

10. ☑ **A.** Although the benefits of Dfs would normally be B and C, in this particular company, A is probably more relevant because it sounds as if their data is already shared among too many servers, and the IT manager has shown an interest in consolidation in the network reappraisal. Consolidating servers will help them rationalize their data storage into a more coherent and central data storage that can be better protected. In addition, if being stored on Windows 2000 dynamic disks, it will allow them to more easily reconfigure volumes when necessary without having to bring down the server and interrupt service. Consolidating servers is often a multistaged operation, and migrating staff onto Dfs initially will actually help minimize disruption to users if the actual physical location of the data storage is kept hidden from them as it is changed. Obviously, somebody has to update the Dfs with the new changes, but these need only be made once and centrally—users will be unaware when/if the physical location of their server has changed during the server consolidation process. Dfs would offer fault tolerance in that users would not be expected to change their mappings when/if their storage location changed. If you are changing server locations frequently, you should also consider configuring a low TTL on your Dfs links until the data locations are finalized.

    ☒ **B** and **C** are not the correct answers for short-term benefit in this company. Although once the server consolidation is complete, in the long run, this company will indeed reap these benefits. **D** is not correct because this company could benefit immediately from using Dfs.

11. ☑ **F.** The Novell servers were clearly for Novell testing and do not house production resources. Consequently, they should not be upgraded or integrated into the new Windows 2000 network. If they exist for testing existing applications, they should be tested on a native NetWare environment. This is one example of when not to think Windows 2000, which is why all the other options are incorrect.

12. ☑ **A.** RIP for IP is the only protocol listed that should be configured on this company's routers. There are currently few routers, and they only need to pass TCP/IP traffic—any NetBIOS and/or IPX traffic is for testing purposes and we have no evidence that this traffic should leave their own segment. In the existing network with just two internal routers, there is a good case for static routing rather than a "chatty" protocol such as RIP. However, bear in mind the company's mission that network administration should be minimal with the need for a fluid infrastructure (for example, software routers are sometimes added

ad hoc). Also, bear in mind potential company growth. For these reasons, RIP for IP is a safer choice. However, it would be prudent to ensure that RIP, version 2, rather than RIP, version 1, was being used on all routers if possible to use multicasts rather than broadcasts.

   ☒   **B** and **C** are incorrect because, as stated, there is no evidence to suggest that NetWare routing is required. **D** is incorrect because although the publishing company uses Apple Macintoshes, there is currently no need to have a routed network with theirs and no perceived possibility of change. **E** is incorrect because although it is a less chatty dynamic routing protocol than RIP, it is certainly overkill for such a small number of routers and will require a higher administrative overhead.

13. ☑ **B.** Fault tolerance and maximum uptime are the priorities on these servers above load balancing, response times, and security. This is why the other options, although they could offer Web server improvements, are less beneficial to this company. Note also that you cannot implement network load balancing on a server also running Clustering Service, and that IPSec would only offer better security if the connecting client also supported IPSec (which is a dangerous assumption to make on a public Web server!).

   ☒   **A, C, D**, and **E** are incorrect.

14. ☑ **D.** Although it's true that both NAT and ICS can be used on a Windows 2000 server, both are suitable for small networks, and both Web access and FTP are translatable. Also, there would seem little need to restrict access to users or employ the caching facilities of Proxy Server.

   ☒   **A, B**, and **C** are incorrect. There is a requirement for monitoring usage and potentially banning access to certain sites, and these solutions do not offer this. Additionally, to employ the routing service, you would need to have public Internet addresses on all PCs rather than just one public Internet address, which is an expensive option. In addition, all machines would have to change their current IP addressing scheme because they are currently using a private address range that will not route (and similarly they would have to use DHCP if using ICS).

15. ☑ **D.** New project work and test machines are most likely to benefit from RIS, providing they are installing from scratch Windows 2000 Professional (Windows 2000 Server is not supported), and these machines either support PXE or have PCI network cards that are supported with RIS.

☒   **A** is incorrect because you cannot use RIS for upgrading—only installing a new version of Windows 2000 Professional. **B** is incorrect because all new machines may not support PXE or one of the RIS-supported network cards. **C** is similarly incorrect because laptops invariably use PCMCIA cards, which are not supported on the RIS bootup disk. If the laptops had docking systems with PCI cards, and these PCI cards were supported on the RIS bootup disk, then they could take advantage of RIS. However, there is no supporting evidence of such docking systems in this company.

16.   ☑   **B** and **D** are the best options for this company and their requirements—have a total of four WINS servers and manually configure standard push/pull replication between WINS servers.

☒   **A** would usually be a good idea for a company of this size—more WINS servers are not better in many respects because there is a higher risk of corrupting the WINS database. However, Microsoft advises having a WINS server at each geographical site, and also having a secondary for fault tolerance. This would be less of a problem for this company because each site has its own subnet, so if the WAN link were to fail, machines could still communicate with each other on their own subnet by broadcasts. However, the requirement was to keep broadcasts to a minimum, which would require additional WINS servers for the additional fault tolerance. Multiple WINS servers require a replication configuration, so you should decide on a replication scheme that best supports your network. **C** is not a good option for the company for one reason: They often add software routers ad hoc to the network when needed, and it is risky to assume that they will remember to configure these for IGMP even if they can support it.

17.   ☑   **C.** The London office needs to connect over a VPN connection.

☒   **A** is incorrect because ICS includes a DHCP allocator that would conflict with the company's DHCP servers (once connected) and stop functioning. **B** is incorrect because IPSec is not translatable (and neither is Kerberos). **D** is incorrect because although firewalls and routers often block NetBIOS, it is possible to configure them such that they will pass NetBIOS traffic—but it's not desirable.

18.   ☑   **B, C, D, F**, and **G** are correct. All of these things can help to protect users' data on their Windows Professional. **B** will automatically ensure that the correct applications—and files within those applications—are always available

to identified computers or users. **C** will allow important files to be stored both centrally and locally; in effect, offering an automatic backup and ensuring a copy of the data is available even if the network connection or server is unavailable. **D** will result in important data being transparently stored on a secure server, which is more likely to be better protected than a workstation. **F** is an easy task for a user to complete, and should help to ensure a quick disaster recovery for missing system files, corrupted boot.ini, bad MBR, etc. **G** is now much easier with Windows 2000 because not only can you use the native backup program with jaz drives and disks, but the Scheduler is a vast improvement from asking users to run scripts with AT commands.

☒　**A** is incorrect. Using software RAID where multiple disks were available is never an option with workstations in either Windows 2000 or Windows NT 4.0—you can only implement software fault tolerance on servers. **E** is not usually recommended for desktop machines where you can easily access the Windows 2000 CD and install the Recovery console from there if needed. It requires an additional 7MB hard disk space to preinstall it, which is a big price to pay on "noncritical" machines. You would usually preinstall CDMCONS on DCs to save time in emergencies, or on laptops for when they are offsite. Most of the laptops in this company are used by salespeople, who are not the target audience for this command-line utility.

19.　☑　**D.** This is the only viable option for suggesting that this company use Windows 2000 Terminal Services—this alone seems a rather weak reason to suggest they start using this client/server solution. Technical problems have not been highlighted as a problem by staff in the branch office, but if they were to have problems, it would obviously be easier and quicker for somebody in IT to take control of their session than it would be to physically go to their site.

☒　**A** is incorrect because although terminal services usually bring the benefit of a lower TCO, this would not be the case for this company in this department. They must also have laptops and they are offsite regularly, so they would end up with two systems rather than one integrated one. Better to use group policies and offline folders with these users to achieve that lower TCO. **B** is often a good reason to use Terminal Services, but not in this case where the users are developers who are likely to run memory-hungry and processor-intensive applications (for example, compilers and developer tools), which are not highly compatible with Terminal Services. **C** is often a good reason to use

Terminal Services in administration mode; however, in this company's case, there are no slow WAN links yet!

20. ☑ **B, C**, and **D** are correct for server clusters in Windows 2000.

☒ **A** is incorrect because you can configure a Windows 2000 Advance Server as either a member server or a DC, although they must belong to the same domain. Remember that the cluster service is dependent on authentication, so ensure that a DC will remain available. **E** is incorrect because you cannot use software RAID with cluster services; it must be hardware RAID.

TESTLET 2: ANSWERS

1. ☑ **D.** TCP/IP is essential for a Windows 2000 network.

   ☒ **A** is incorrect because AppleTalk is required for computers such as Apple Macs that use the AppleTalk protocol and there are none in the network. **B** is incorrect because NetBEUI is not strictly required in a Windows NT 4.0 or Windows 2000 network. In a Windows 2000 network, NetBIOS is not needed at all. However, New Silicon Ventures has some servers that will remain at Windows NT 4.0; therefore, NetBIOS will still be in use. However, NetBEUI is not required to support NetBIOS, because NetBIOS can work over TCP/IP. **C** is incorrect because NWLink is only required for computers that use IPX/SPX, such as NetWare Clients and Servers. There are none of these in the network.

2. ☑ **D.** A Proxy Server is designed to connect networks to the Internet, and provides Web caching. Whenever a Web page is accessed, Proxy Server stores the page in a local cache. When a Web page is requested, Proxy Server will check the local cache first to see if the page is stored there. If it is, then Proxy Server returns the page without having to get it from the Internet, thereby improving performance. By installing a Proxy Server at all of the regional offices, the amount of Internet traffic over the leased lines will reduce over a period of time. Proxy Server can also be used to restrict Internet access to specific users.

   ☒ **A** is incorrect because it will not help reduce the amount of Internet traffic over the leased lines. It may improve the speed of Internet access, but this will depend on how busy the leased lines are. **B** is incorrect because it will not provide the ability to manage who has Internet access. It will improve performance and reduce the utilization of the leased lines. **C** is incorrect because NAT does not help with the performance of Internet access; it provides a way of translating public IP addresses to private IP addresses.

3. ☑ **B.** The number of subnets currently is 19, one for each floor of the headquarters (five), three for each of the three regional offices (nine), and five for the branch offices. It is expected that the number of subnets will double; therefore, the subnet mask needs to allow for 38 subnets. To achieve this, six

bits from the third byte of the IP address need to be used for subnets (giving $2^6 - 2 = 62$ subnets). The number of available subnets is reduced by two, because a subnet number of all 0s or all 1s is not allowed. To use six bits for a subnet means that the mask value is $128 + 64 + 32 + 16 + 8 + 4 = 252$; therefore, the subnet mask is 255.255.252.0.

☒ **A** is incorrect because it would only allow for 30 subnets ($2^5 - 2 = 30$); enough for the present, but not enough for future growth. **C** and **D** are incorrect because more bits are used for subnets than are necessary. Although they provide for more than 38 subnets, they do not maximize the number of hosts available.

4. ☑ **C.** A domain Dfs root is used to provide access to network shares from a single location. Each network share is added as a link, enabling users to browse available shares from this single location. A domain Dfs root allows the network share topology to be replicated to other servers using Active Directory as well as the contents of the shares of themselves, thus providing fault tolerance.

☒ **A** is incorrect because a stand-alone Dfs root cannot be used to replicate the topology of a Dfs root. **B** is incorrect because a Dfs root can only be installed on servers. **D** is incorrect because it does not allow for replication of the contents of the shares, and if the main server fails, users will still have to know where each share was located.

5. ☑ **A.** Only one domain is needed for the company under Windows 2000. Each office can be implemented as an Active Directory site for management purposes.

☒ **B**, **C**, and **D** are incorrect because more than one domain is not needed. Several domains are only needed under Windows 2000 if different parts of a company have to have different domain names, or if there is a highly decentralized IT management structure.

6. ☑ **A** and **D** are correct. The routers do not forward broadcast packets. DHCP uses broadcast packets, so a DHCP Relay Agent will be needed on the other subnets. A scope for each subnet that a DHCP server will service must also be configured with valid addresses for the subnet.

☒ **B** is incorrect because DHCP will not work via the router as it stands. **C** is incorrect because each PC does not need to know the address of a DHCP server; having to add the DHCP server address would defeat the purpose of DHCP.

7. ☑ **C.** A DHCP server with an appropriately configured scope would provide automatic configuration of IP addresses in line with the company's requirements for minimum administration. No ongoing configuration would be required on each PC other than to initially set Obtain an IP Address Automatically in TCP/IP Properties. By using an appropriate IP address range, each branch office can communicate with the rest of the network.

   ☒ **A** is incorrect because the DHCP Relay Agent would need to contact a DHCP server elsewhere on the network whenever a DHCP packet is sent by a PC at the branch office. This would cause the ISDN line to be brought up, thereby incurring dial-up charges. **B** is incorrect because it would make communication with other sites impossible. Automatic Private IP Addresses (APIPA) are in the range 169.254.0.1 to 169.254.255.254. Each branch office would have the same network ID and potentially duplicate addresses. Although PCs at any particular branch office would be able to communicate within the subnet, they would not be able to communicate with other sites. Allocating addresses from the same network ID at several offices would mean that there is no way to properly configure the routing tables. APIPA is useful for small companies with a small network that consists of a single subnet. **D** is incorrect because Routing and Remote Access is not used to allocate IP addresses to clients on a network, but to clients that connect directly to a remote access server. If each PC had its own modem and dialed a remote access server directly, then this would be a way to allocate IP addresses.

8. ☑ **C.** Installing a DHCP server at each site will mean that PCs can obtain TCP/IP configuration information from a local DHCP server, thereby minimizing DHCP traffic over the WANs. There are nine sites, so nine DHCP servers are needed.

   ☒ **A** and **B** are incorrect because there aren't enough DHCP servers to have one at each site; therefore, some DHCP traffic would go over the WANs. **D** is incorrect because 19 DHCP servers (one per subnet) are not necessary.

9. ☑ **C.** Each office has its own local WINS server; therefore, local WINS resolution is provided. Replication has been configured between the WINS servers; therefore, each WINS server will have information about all network resources. This meets the required result. Configuring push/pull replication means that WINS replication traffic will occur throughout the day and when a sufficient number of changes have been made to the WINS databases. To

minimize WINS traffic, only pull replication should be used. This allows the frequency of updates to be specified, perhaps confining replication traffic to overnight. Clients have been configured with only one WINS server address. If this server fails, they will not use another WINS server. To do this, the clients should be configured with two or more WINS server addresses. Windows 2000 allows up to 12 WINS servers to be specified. The WINS Proxy Agent is not relevant, because it is used to forward NetBIOS queries from non-WINS clients to a WINS server. Thus, neither of the optional results is met.

☒ **A, B**, and **D** are incorrect because the proposed solution produces the required result, but neither of the optional results.

10. ☑ **A.** EAP-TLS stands for Extensible Authentication Protocol–Transport Level Security. The EAP protocol allows authentication mechanisms such as smart cards to be used.

☒ **B** and **C** are incorrect because they do not support smart cards. PAP provides unencrypted authentication. MS-CHAP provides encrypted authentication for Microsoft operating systems. **D** is incorrect because IPSec is not an authentication protocol; it is a network protocol that is used to secure communications between networks and computers.

11. ☑ **B.** PPTP tunneling will work through the Proxy Server, and MPPE encryption will ensure that all traffic between home users and the corporate network is secured. The Proxy Server protects subnet C from the Internet.

☒ **A** is incorrect because it exposes the VPN server to the Internet. **C** and **D** are incorrect because encapsulating security payload (ESP) encryption does not work with Network Address Translation (NAT), as provided by the Proxy Server. L2TP tunneling uses the ESP feature of IPSec to encrypt data that also encrypts the IP header, thereby preventing NAT from working.

12. ☑ **D.** IPSec is used to encrypt traffic over the network. IPSec can be implemented using group policy or setting TCP/IP properties directly. There are three predefined policies: respond only, request security, and require security. The require-security policy means that a server will not use unsecured communication and will always encrypt traffic. The respond-only policy means that a client will use IPSec if requested, but otherwise will not. If the client cannot or is not set to use IPSec, it will not be able to communicate with a server that requires security.

☒   **C** is incorrect because the Executives sometimes use other PCs; therefore, all PCs need to be enabled to use IPSec if requested. **A** is incorrect because this would cause all traffic on the network to be encrypted. This is not needed and will reduce performance, since there is a performance hit for using IPSec. **B** is incorrect because it means that PCs will not be able to communicate with other servers that do not need the protection of IPSec.

13.   ☑   **A.** SRV records are used to locate network resources such as domain controllers. This is the only feature that is essential for Active Directory to work. Other DNS (that is, not Windows 2000) implementations can be used with Active Directory, as long as the use of SRV records is supported.

☒   **B, C**, and **D** are incorrect because they are not essential for Active Directory to work. Incremental zone transfers will reduce the amount of zone replication traffic required; this is useful over WAN links. Dynamic updates are used to allow Windows 2000 clients and DHCP to automatically register host names and IP addresses with DNS. Integrated zones are zone database files that are stored in Active Directory rather than in the traditional text-based zone database files. Storing the files in Active Directory offers advantages such as automatic replication.

14.   ☑   **C.** A caching-only server has no zones stored on it. The server will forward all queries to the DNS server at the regional office and cache the results for future use. Over time, this can reduce WAN traffic as a local cache (at the branch office) of frequently queried names is built up. Additionally, because there are no zones on the DNS server at the branch office, there is no zone replication traffic.

☒   **A** is incorrect because there is only one domain name for the company, and the primary zone for the domain name is located in London at headquarters. It is not possible to have another primary zone for the same domain name. **B** is incorrect because a secondary zone would need to receive zone updates from another DNS server. This would create DNS traffic over the ISDN lines. **D** is incorrect for the same reason as B is.

15.   ☑   **A** and **B** are correct. RIP and OSPF are routing protocols that automatically update routing tables. New Silicon Ventures will soon be installing additional leased lines that will create multiple routes between some of its offices. A protocol such as RIP or OSPF will be able to detect when a route fails, and adjust the routing tables accordingly. RIP is much easier to set up than OSPF, though OSPF scales to very large networks much better than RIP does.

☒ **C** is incorrect because it is not a routing protocol. Bandwidth Allocation Protocol (BAP) is used to manage multiple-link connections by adding or dropping links depending on bandwidth usage. **D** is incorrect because Service Advertising Protocol (SAP) is used on IPX networks. There are no IPX devices in the New Silicon Ventures network.

16. ☑ **B.** The Web server needs to be protected from general access by people on the Internet; therefore, it needs to be located "behind" the Proxy Server. It is a requirement that incoming traffic to the Web server does not impact the office subnets. These requirements mean that subnet B is the best place for the Web server.

☒ **A** is incorrect because it exposes the Web server to the Internet. **C** and **D** are incorrect because they place the Web server on the office subnets.

17. ☑ **B** and **D** are correct. Web publishing mapping is used on Proxy Server to direct incoming Web server requests. The internal address of the Web server would have to be added to Web publishing mapping. In addition, an entry for the DNS name of the Web server needs to be present in the DNS zone for newsilicon.com managed by the company's ISP. This entry would contain the IP address of the Proxy Server, because this is the only machine accessible by Internet users.

☒ **A** is incorrect because packet filters are used to specify which IP traffic is allowed to pass through the Proxy Server based on source and destination IP addresses and ports. They cannot be used to redirect traffic to other machines. **C** is incorrect because the IP address of the Web server is a private address, and is therefore not reachable by Internet users. Any incoming traffic to the company's network must specify the IP address of the Proxy Server.

18. ☑ **B.** Proxy Server uses domain filters to restrict outbound traffic. Using domain filters, access can be restricted to a single computer based on its IP address, a group of computers based on an IP address and subnet mask or a domain name. In this case, the company's requirements would be met by denying access to all sites and then explicitly adding allowed sites.

☒ **A** and **B** are incorrect because this facility is not available. **C** is incorrect because it would require a never-ending list of disallowed sites. It would be much simpler to list the allowed sites.